Quantitative
Models in
Psychology

Quantitative Models in Psychology

Robert E. McGrath

American Psychological Association

Washington, DC

Published by
American Psychological Association
750 First Street, NE
Washington, DC 20002
www.apa.org

To order
APA Order Department
P.O. Box 92984
Washington, DC 20090-2984
Tel: (800) 374-2721; Direct: (202) 336-5510
Fax: (202) 336-5502; TDD/TTY: (202) 336-6123
Online: www.apa.org/pubs/books
E-mail: order@apa.org

In the U.K., Europe, Africa, and the Middle East, copies may be ordered from
American Psychological Association
3 Henrietta Street
Covent Garden, London
WC2E 8LU England

Typeset in Meridien by Circle Graphics, Inc., Columbia, MD

Printer: The Maple-Vail Book Manufacturing Group, York, PA
Cover Designer: Minker Design, Sarasota, FL

The opinions and statements published are the responsibility of the authors, and such opinions and statements do not necessarily represent the policies of the American Psychological Association.

Library of Congress Cataloging-in-Publication Data

McGrath, Robert E., 1956-
 Quantitative models in psychology / Robert E. McGrath.
    p. cm.
 Includes bibliographical references and index.
 ISBN-13: 978-1-4338-0959-0 (alk. paper)
 ISBN-10: 1-4338-0959-1 (alk. paper)
 1. Psychology—Statistical methods. 2. Psychology—Mathematical models. I. Title.

 BF39.M393 2011
 150.1'5195—dc22
                                              2010042431

British Library Cataloguing-in-Publication Data
A CIP record is available from the British Library.

Printed in the United States of America
First Edition

doi:10.1037/12316-000

To Deborah, my best friend:
"What a planet," I whisper. "To allow such a thing."
(*A Kind of Flying: Selected Stories*, Ron Carlson)

Contents

Preface

I can remember exactly the moment when the seed was planted that has grown into this book. I was reading an article by the brilliant Paul Meehl (1986) in which he considered why conclusions clearly supported by empirical evidence can have so little impact on psychologists' practices in applied settings. One of his musings about this paradox included the following:

> But what can you expect, when I find that the majority of clinical psychology trainees getting a PhD at the University of Minnesota do not know what Bayes' Theorem is, or why it bears upon clinical decision making, and never heard of the Spearman–Brown Prophecy Formula! (Meehl, 1986, p. 374)

The sense of astonishment he expressed in that final exclamation point only enhanced the feelings of inadequacy I experienced while reading that sentence. I was a few years out of a doctoral program where I had supposedly learned to be a psychological scientist. I was even teaching research methods and statistics to doctoral students in psychology. The truth was that, despite my training, I knew next to nothing about either Bayes' theorem or the Spearman–Brown prophecy formula. At that point I was not even sure why I should care about those things.

Out of that moment of self-doubt came a long-term commitment to developing a deeper understanding of quantitative methods. As a teacher, I was also led to think about whether it is possible to define a body of knowledge all psychologists should learn about quantitative methods. It has been suggested that quantitative methodology represents the single common denominator in all doctoral-level training for psychologists (Aiken, West, & Millsap, 2008). If that is true—and I believe it is—and quantitative concepts provide the common language all psychologists are supposed to share, what are the concepts we all need to know to make conversation possible?

My efforts eventually led me to conclude that psychologists often never develop a framework for understanding quantitative methods. To expand on this point, and to explain the gaps this book is intended to address, I like to draw a distinction between quantitative methods themselves, such as *t* tests and reliability coefficients, and what could be called *foundational theory* in quantitative methods. Many psychologists receive training in only the former: They learn when to use a select set of statistics, the assumptions underlying their use, and ideally what those statistics mean. There is no debating that is essential information for any person who wants to be an author or a consumer of psychological research. What I became increasingly interested in was the *why* of quantitative methods. As I read further, I came to realize, for example, that Bayes' theorem is not just a statistical method; it is the starting point for a completely different way of thinking about the process of inferring general conclusions from specific data sets. This discovery rocked my world (well, maybe not quite) because it suggested that the null hypothesis significance testing I had learned as if it were the authoritative approach is only one of a variety of methods available for this purpose, and a logically flawed one at that. This growing understanding prepared me for the critical analysis of null hypothesis significance testing that has had a tremendous influence on psychologists' thinking about statistics in subsequent years.

The process also allowed me to rethink long-standing traditions in the education of psychologists about foundational issues. To focus on one example that appears early in this book, proposals to use robust statistical methods really deserve discussion in the context of parametric assumptions. However, because robust methods are not part of the traditional entry-level training in statistics, many psychologists are unfamiliar with them and do not understand why they are important. In this book, which is intended to offer a broad survey of what psychologists should know, that omission is corrected.

There are several factors that I suspect contribute to psychologists' learning so little about the foundational aspects of quantitative methods in their field. The first is that there is only so much time. Social, clinical, and experimental psychologists have enough to learn without having to become experts in quantitative methods. Given the importance of the *how*, there is not much time left for *why*. The second factor is that psychology does not really attract people interested in the philosophical aspects of quantitative methods. Most psychologists see statistics and scales as tools to be used to achieve a goal, and the *why* is not a particularly captivating question.

Even so, I think *why* is important for several reasons. Asking *why* helps psychologists see the limitations in the methods they are using.

It prepares them to conduct or consume research in which a variety of statistical strategies are used. It also helps them think more deeply about their areas of study. In fact, in terms of preparation for lifelong learning in quantitative methods, *why* may well be far more important to learn than *how*. If you join me, I hope you find my journey into the land of *why* to be useful, informative, and perhaps even interesting.

In a project as ambitious as this, there are bound to be errors and oversimplifications. I would like to express my gratitude to two reviewers who spent many hours identifying some of those errors. They contributed tremendously to the final product you are reading, and I am deeply in their debt.

Quantitative
Models in
Psychology

Introduction

> However much we detail a transmitted description, it will always be unnecessarily precise for some and fragmentary for others. (Lem, 1968/1983, p. 84)

Because this is a book about how psychologists develop and use quantitative models, it seemed like a good idea to start by defining what I mean by a quantitative model. A **model** may be defined as *a representation of some phenomenon, created as a means of learning more or communicating information about that phenomenon.*[1] We come into contact with models constantly: road maps and recipes are just two examples of models that are used on a daily basis. **Quantitative models**, *models that use numerical representations,* have played a particularly important role in the progress of science since the time of Galileo. While this book was in progress, I was pleased to see an article published (Rodgers, 2010) asserting that the testing of models has become the focal issue in psychological research in recent years.

In fact, some scientists have equated scientific models with quantitative models. For example, Sir Francis Galton (1879), who introduced some of the quantitative approaches still popular in psychology, stated that "until the phenomena of any branch of knowledge have been subjected to measurement

---

[1]As this sentence demonstrates, I present terms of interest in **bold.** In general, the term is associated with a definition in *italics*, although sometimes I have opted for illustration by example rather than a formal definition.

and number, it cannot assume the status and dignity of a science" (p. 149). We can ignore controversies about whether scientific models are or should always be quantitative and simply note that such models have played an important role in the progress of many sciences. They do so for several reasons. They add a level of precision to predictions that make them both more useful and more easily tested. Also, quantifying something means being specific about what that something is, so it encourages explicit definition of terms. In psychology and most of the social sciences, quantitative modeling is largely (though not exclusively) accomplished using methods derived from the branch of mathematics known as *statistics*.

Quantitative Models in Psychology

Few would argue with the great contributions that quantification has made to physics, chemistry, and the physical sciences in general. In contrast, there is still a great deal of skepticism about the potential for quantifying the psychology of the human. At times, I have even heard this skepticism expressed by students of psychology. This skepticism takes several forms.

Opponents of psychology as a science sometimes suggest that the attempt to create quantitative models of human experience demeans that experience by disrespecting its essential humanness. This argument implies that psychologists are attempting to capture what is essential about people in their quantitative models. Philosophers love to argue about issues such as the essential character of things. I will avoid these arguments for the present, though I tend to enjoy them personally because the practice of science is usually driven by pragmatic considerations. If a model proves useful, then use it. At different times and in different contexts, different levels of abstraction may be useful, and what is essential may change. There may be times when it is worth perceiving each individual as a unique entity, a snowflake unlike all others. At other times, it is worth talking about the behavior of individuals of type X, and at still others about the behavior of all members of the species. At times, a more nuanced and detailed analysis of a phenomenon is warranted. This can be particularly true when attempting to understand the personal experience of individual humans. Various qualitative and case study methods have emerged that can be particularly relevant in such circumstances (e.g., Creswell, 2006). When the goal is to draw broad and general conclusions, though, quantitative methods are of great value.

A second concern has to do with the use of statistics. Given the degree to which we are inundated with statistics every day trying to "prove" one point or another, it is easy to forget that the use of statistics is intended primarily to introduce objectivity into model building. It says something about how our society views quantitative models that almost everyone seems to know the expression, attributed to Benjamin Disraeli, "There are three types of lies: lies, damned lies, and statistics." My best response is this: If you think it is easy to lie with statistics, you should see how easy it is to lie without them.

The final concern I address here is whether psychology will ever be able to achieve the level of numeric accuracy demonstrated in some other sciences. This is still an open question, and many doubt the possibility. I will only point out as a response that physics took 1,000 years or more to become a quantitative science. I suspect the potential for the quantification of psychology will remain uncertain until neuroscience has revealed much more about the convergence of mind and brain. In the meantime, the pragmatic response is again the best: If quantitative models provide what seems to be helpful information, then psychologists will use them. In fact, much has already been accomplished by the quantification of overt behavior and the self-report of mental experiences even though questions about their accuracy remain valid.

Are Models Always Realistic?

The definition I provided for a model, as a representation of some phenomenon, might be taken as implying that models are intended to map something that already exists. A road map or the model of the solar system you made in elementary school is clearly attempting to provide a representation of something that exists independently of the model. However, this is not always the case. For example, artificial life has become a popular topic of research. Using computers, it is possible to create artificial versions of species, or even to create new species, whose behavior is determined by a set of algorithms. Those algorithms may or may not accurately reflect the neural system of the actual species; in the case of a nonexistent species, there is not even a neural system that exists to model. Even without the assumption that the model reflects the functioning of some species accurately, though, many scientists find the capacity to generate behavior similar to that of a species using computer algorithms a useful source of information (for a recent discussion of how useful this is as a scientific method, see Webb, 2009); that is, a model may be developed using invented, rather than reality-based or discovered, elements because it is thought to be useful or interesting, not because it is thought to be realistic. As you will see in the coming pages, the term *theory* is sometimes used interchangeably with the term *model,* but technically the former term has a stronger implication of an accurate representation of real-world events than the word *model.*

When a model is intended to be realistic, the great challenge is achieving an optimal balance between the competing goals of accuracy and simplification.[2] What defines that optimal balance can depend on the purposes of the model. A road map that included pictures of every building and every sign would become useless as a simple means of figuring out how to get from one point to another. When looking for a particular store, there are maps available online that provide a photographic panorama of each street. These offer a useful adjunct to the traditional road map; that is, even realistic models are influenced by considerations of what is useful.

I mention this issue of the degree to which a model is a discovery of reality or an invention of something new because you will come across both types of models in this book. The inferential method known as *null hypothesis significance testing* is a good example of an invented model. Cobbling together pieces from logic and probability theory, Sir Ronald Fisher and his descendants established something that previously did not exist. The same could be said of psychometric theory (see Chapter 6, this volume). In contrast, latent-variable modeling (see Chapter 7, this volume) and the types of models described in Part III of this book are intended to provide an accurate representation of some phenomenon that exists independently of its measurement. In some cases, the dividing line between realistic and invented models is not completely clear. The point is that models are not always intended to tell you more about what exists; models can also be useful for providing you with a new way of thinking about something.

This Book

This book is distinct from other books on quantitative methods in several ways. First, it focuses on the conceptual underpinnings of quantitative methods. The intent is to ensure that psychologists share a common understanding of how their quantitative methods function. The goal is to improve the level of discourse on whether our current quantitative practices are optimal or whether we should consider other options. Second,

---

[2]This issue of the purpose and problems of mapping or modeling has inspired several very enjoyable short stories I would recommend to the reader, including Borges's (1999) *On Exactitude in Science* and Lopez's (2000) *The Mappist.*

it encompasses the full spectrum of activities in psychology that involve quantitative modeling. These include the statistical process of generalizing from samples to populations, the use of measurement instruments to generate quantitative scales, and the modeling of real-world patterns and relationships. Other books tend to focus on one only one of these components; in fact, whole books have been written about some of the topics that here comprise only a single chapter, or even a portion of a chapter. So consider this a survey of the various ways in which psychologists are using quantitative models, and the controversies surrounding those uses.

I wrote this book with three groups in mind. For the person who wants to become a competent consumer of research, this book will help you to understand the studies you read. It should also help you understand references in the literature to controversies in inference and help you prepare for a future in which other inferential strategies become more popular. There are complex statistical strategies that are only starting to become commonplace in psychology, and a strong foundation in the rationale of quantitative methods will make it easier to understand what those methods are doing even if the mechanics escape you. I think this book will be particularly helpful to the graduate student who completes a single course in statistics but will be useful to all people who want to be able to read research and understand what they read.

For the person who wants to collaborate on research with statistical consultants, this book will provide you with the basic information you need to discuss your options with your consultant. It will not provide you with enough information to conduct those analyses by yourself, but it should give you the basic tools you need to understand what is being recommended to you.

For the person who wants to conduct his or her own statistical analyses, this book is *not* going to be enough to prepare you for the role; however, it will provide you with the conceptual foundations to help organize your subsequent learning about statistics. In particular, many of the tables in this book have been designed as references for answering common questions about statistical methods and terms. If you read this book once and never look at it again, I will have failed in my goals. I hope when you have to deal with quantitative concepts in the future you will come back to this book as a ready source regarding most of the key concepts.

I do offer one warning: This book should not be your introduction to statistical methods in psychology. It is intended for behavioral and social scientists—current or budding—at the graduate level and beyond, and there is an expectation of familiarity with basic concepts in statistics. My goal is not to introduce you to quantitative methods but to help you think about them.

This book attempts to achieve these lofty goals through a conceptual introduction to quantitative methods that addresses three topics:

1. models for drawing inferences about populations from samples;
2. models of quantitative measurement; and
3. the process of modeling psychological phenomena quantitatively.

The book is divided into three parts reflecting these themes. Part I has to do with the topic of *inference*, of drawing conclusions about populations from samples. The focus is on various methods that have been suggested for controlling errors due to sampling. The controversies surrounding the use of significance tests are reviewed, as are other models of inference. Although it is widely recognized that significance testing is a deeply flawed inferential strategy, as should become evident to the reader, a good deal of Part I focuses on significance testing because such tests ubiquitous in psychological research reports (Cumming et al., 2007). A strong understanding of these methods *and their weaknesses* remains essential for psychologists.

Much more detail is provided about inference than is typical in statistics textbooks. To repeat, the goal of this book is to help the reader understand the current state of inferential methods in the behavioral sciences, to prepare for changes in the foreseeable future. This includes discussions of such topics as Bayesian methods, meta-analysis, interpreting the literature in light of poor statistical power, and others that are rarely covered in basic texts.

After a great deal of thought, I decided to organize Part I chronologically. This organization seems to me to be the best for helping the reader understand the current controversies and the alternative options. It begins with a summary of basic concepts in inferential methods that will probably sound familiar even to students in their first graduate statistics course, but I tend to find most students appreciate a review of those concepts.

The term *quantitative models* refers not only to statistical methods of inference but also to the use of instruments to convert observations of the real world into quantitative data. Part II has to do with the nature of measurement, in particular the creation of quantitative variables as an approach to studying psychological phenomena and the quantitative methods used to learn about those variables.

Because all statistics rely on the measurement devices we use to generate numeric variables, I consider the models underlying those measurement devices an essential component of understanding quantitative methodology. Even so, if you are reading this textbook for a course on statistics you may find you are instructed to skip Part II completely. Omitting it should not affect your understanding of the rest of the book much. Even so, I hope you will choose to read it at some point because it addresses issues in measurement a little differently than other textbooks.

Part III is more applied in focus. Where Parts I and II have to do with understanding the use of numbers in psychology, Part III provides an introduction to the actual quantitative modeling of psychological phenomena. Part III is unique to the current text and brings together a great deal of material that I find is unfortunately missing from most psychologists' training. It is my intention in Part III to provide some basic information about how statistical methods can be used to design a model of psychological phenomena, how you can think intelligently about which statistics to use when, and what those statistics tell you.

I should also note that this book has both descriptive and prescriptive elements. As you will see, I spend a good deal of time describing common statistical practices in psychology even when I disagree with them. I want to provide you with the basic foundations you need to understand statistical practice as it exists in current psychology, but I also want you to understand what is wrong with them so it will make sense as those practices change over time.

This book is intended as a basic resource for any individual who will conduct behavioral research or who will interpret behavioral research. It is for those people who skip the Results sections in the articles they read but feel guilty about it. It is for those people who must be able to understand quantitative methods regardless of whether they ever intend to engage in research. It is for those people who want one source that will give them the conceptual models that underlie the practice of quantitative analysis in psychology. It is, in short, intended for any student of behavior who wants to know what he or she is doing at a deeper level.

MODELS OF INFERENCE

Preliminary Concepts in Inference

1

P art I of this book focuses on *models of inference*, that is, models psychologists use to draw quantitative conclusions about a population from a sample. In this first chapter, I briefly review basic concepts that are needed to understand the inferential methods discussed later. You have probably learned about most of these concepts before; some of them are even covered in undergraduate statistics courses. If you feel comfortable with basic concepts in statistics, such as sampling distributions, you might decide to skim this chapter or move on to Chapter 2. I usually find that even students who did very well in previous statistics courses appreciate a review of the basics, though. Because the material in the next four chapters builds on an understanding of the concepts covered here, I recommend reading all the way through them and making sure you feel comfortable with the information. You may find some of it too basic, but it is often best to make as few assumptions about background knowledge as possible.

This chapter focuses primarily on the nature of sampling distributions. I take up the discussion of how sampling distributions are used specifically for inferential purposes in Chapter 2. As a result, this chapter may strike you as a little abstract. The practical connection will emerge later, I promise.

The Problem of Error

I begin with a question that has troubled just about every student of psychology I have ever known: Why do quantitative methods have to be so ridiculously complicated? The answer is that the statistical methods popular in psychology were designed to address one of the most important obstacles facing modern science, the issue of **error**, which can be defined informally as *the degree to which what the scientist observes is incorrect.* It may seem obvious that scientists need to be concerned about the possibility of error in their observations, but the formal analysis of error did not really rev up until the late 18th century. Before that time, physical scientists tended to focus on phenomena in which the effects were so large compared with the amount of error involved that the error could be ignored for practical purposes. The speed at which an object falls, or what happens when two substances are mixed and burned, are matters in which the results are usually obvious to the naked eye. In those cases in which error was not trivial scientists usually looked to improvements in the technology as the solution. For example, Sobel (1995) wrote an entertaining book about the 400-year quest to find a method for accurately measuring longitude. The solution ultimately involved building a better clock. Once a clock was developed that could accurately track time, a ship's navigator could use the difference between local time and English time to determine position precisely. Finally, it is often a simple matter to repeat a physical measurement many times in order to minimize error further.

By the late 18th century, astronomers were dealing with situations in which error was a serious problem. Chemistry and physics were experimental sciences in which the researcher could easily replicate the study, but astronomy relied on observation of events that were often unusual or unique. Also, small differences in measurements could translate into huge differences at the celestial level. As the number of observatories increased and the same event was being measured from multiple locations, astronomers became troubled by the degree of variation they found in their measurements and began to consider how to deal with those variations.

The solution involved accepting the inevitability of error and looking for methods that would minimize its impact. Perhaps the single most important strategy to emerge from this early work had to do with combining observations from multiple observers—for example, by computing their mean—as a way to produce more reliable estimates. More generally, mathematicians saw in this problem a potential application for a relatively new branch of mathematics that has since come to be known as statistics.

The problem astronomers faced had to do with errors in the act of measurement, and that topic is the focus of Chapter 6. Errors can also occur when drawing conclusions about populations from samples. For example, suppose the variable height is measured in each member of a sample drawn from the population of U.S. citizens, and the mean height is computed. The mean of a sample is an example of a **statistic**, which can be defined as *a mathematical method for summarizing information about some variable or variables.* More specifically, it is an example of a **descriptive statistic**, *a mathematical method for summarizing information about some variable or variables in a sample.* There is also presumably a mean height for the population of U.S. citizens. This mean is an example of a **parameter**, *a mathematical method for summarizing information about some variable or variables in a population.* It is an unfortunate fact that descriptive statistics computed in a sample do not always perfectly match the parameter in the population from which the sample was drawn. It has been estimated that the mean height of adult American males is 69.4 inches (176.3 cm; McDowell, Fryar, Ogden, & Flegal, 2008), and this is our best guess of the parametric mean. One sample might have a mean of 65.8 inches (167.1 cm), another sample a mean of 72.9 inches (185.2 cm), and so forth. Those differences from the true value result from **sampling error**, *error introduced by the act of sampling from a population.*

Inferential statistics are distinct from descriptive statistics and parameters in that they are *mathematical methods for summarizing information to draw inferences about a population based on a sample.* Whereas descriptive statistics refer to samples, and parameters refer to populations, inferential statistics attempt to draw a conclusion about a population from a sample. An important feature of inferential statistics is the attempt in some way to control for or minimize the impact of sampling error on the conclusions drawn.

The inferential methods now used in psychology are rooted in the core statistical concept of **probability**, *the expected frequency of some outcome across a series of events.* I expand on this definition later, but for now it will do quite well for understanding the early work on inference. For example, saying the probability that a coin flip will result in a head is .68 means that if it were possible to observe the entire population of coin flips with this coin, the proportion of heads would be .68. However, because it is impossible to observe the entire population this statement is purely hypothetical. Note that this definition suggests a probability is a parameter.

The formal study of probability began in the 17th century. At first, mathematicians focused primarily on probability as a tool for understanding games of chance. They were particularly interested in games such as roulette or card games that are based on random events. A **random event** can be defined as *an event for which outcomes are determined* *purely by a set of probabilities in the population.* For example, we know the probability of rolling a 7 with two dice is .17 (rounded off), whereas that of a 12 is only .03. This difference occurs because there are many possible combinations that can produce a 7—a 1 and a 6, a 2 and a 5, and so on—but only two 6s will produce a 12. Over many rolls of the dice, we can expect that the proportion of 7s will equal the probability of a 7 in the population; if it does not, the dice may be fixed.

Probability theory allowed mathematicians to make predictions about the probability of each possible outcome from a roll of the dice or the spin of the roulette wheel. Today anyone who watches a poker tournament on television can see the probability that each player will win the hand updated after every card is dealt, but 300 years ago the idea that random events could be predicted was revolutionary.

It was Pierre-Simon LaPlace, in his 1812 *Analytic Theory of Probabilities,* who first suggested that probability theory based on random events could be used to model error in the observation of naturally occurring events (Gillispie, Grattan-Guinness, & Fox, 2000). This was a profound insight, and it provides the foundation for most of the quantitative methods popular in psychology today. In particular, one concept in probability theory came to play a central role in understanding error in samples: the sampling distribution. I start with a relatively simple example of a sampling distribution, the binomial distribution.

Binomial Distributions

A **sampling distribution** can be formally defined as a *probability distribution for a sample statistic across an infinite series of samples of equal size.* This concept is not as complicated as it sounds, and it can be demonstrated with a simple example. Imagine I have 10 coins for which the probability of flipping a head equals the probability of flipping a tail, both being .50. I flip the 10 coins and count the number of heads. I flip them again and count the number of heads, flip them again, then again and again, millions of times. In a sense, I have replicated a "study" millions of times, each of which involved a sample of 10 coin flips. In each study I have gathered the same descriptive statistic, the number of heads in the sample. I could then chart the number of samples with 0 heads, 1 head, 2 heads, and so on, up to 10. Such a chart would have each possible value of the sample statistic "number of heads" on the *x*-axis. On the *y*-axis would appear the proportion of samples in which each value appears (see Figure 1.1).

Of course, no one is actually going to sit down and observe all those samples of 10 coin flips. The mathematician Blaise Pascal derived a formula (although the formula seems to have been known centuries

FIGURE 1.1

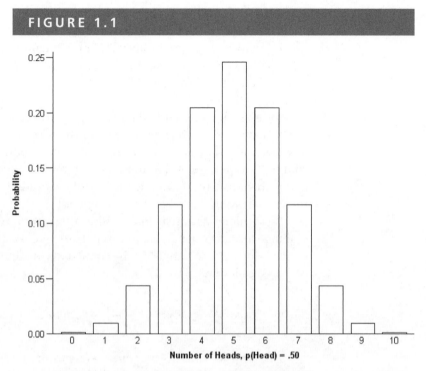

The binomial distribution for samples of 10 coin flips for
p(Head) = .50.

earlier) for computing the probability of getting 0 heads, 1 head, and so
forth, out of 10 coin flips without ever collecting any data. This formula,
called the *binomial formula,* requires three conditions. First, the variable
on which the statistic is based can take on only two values. *A variable that
can take on only two values* will be referred to as a **dichotomous variable**.
The statistic "number of heads in 10 coin flips" is based on the variable
"outcome of one coin flip." That variable is dichotomous because it has two
possible values, heads or tails. Because 10 coins are being flipped at a time,
the count of the number of heads across the 10 coins is a sample statistic.

The second condition is that the probability of each of the two values
in the population must be known, or at least there must be a reasonable
assumption about what those probabilities would be. For now we believe
the coins are fair, so that the probability of both a head and a tail equals .50.

Third, the result of each coin flip must be a random and independent
event. This is one of those simplifying conditions that are sometimes
necessary to make a model work. I have already provided a definition
for a random event: The proportion of heads and tails in the sample is
determined solely by the probability of a head or tail in the population.
Other than this general information about the population of coin flips

using this coin, the observer has no information to help predict the result of a particular coin toss. Notice that *random* as used in statistics is not a synonym for unpredictable. If I know the probability of a head for a particular coin is .80, I am more likely to be right if I predict a head rather than a tail. However, I have no further information about any particular coin toss.

Independence occurs when *the outcome of one observation has no effect on the outcome of any other observation.* In the present example, whether one coin flip is a head or tail has no effect on the outcome of any other coin flip. In the case of coin flips, if one flip were affected by the result of the previous flip—if heads tended to follow heads, for example—then the events would no longer be independent.

Pascal demonstrated that if these three conditions are met the binomial formula can be used to compute the probability of any number of heads for any size sample. In the context of coin flips, the formula can be stated as follows:

$$p\left(f \ Heads \middle| N \ coin \ flips\right) = \frac{N!}{f!(N-f)!} p\left(Head\right)^{f} p\left(Tail\right)^{(N-f)}. \qquad (1.1)$$

The term $p(f \ Heads | N \ coin \ flips)$ refers to the probability of getting exactly f heads given a sample of N coin flips. $p(Head)$ is the population probability of a head, $p(Tail)$ is the population probability of a tail, and $!$ is the factorial operator. The $N!$ means "multiply all integers from 1 to N." One characteristic of the factorial operator is that $0! = 1! = 1$.

Suppose the probability of a head for a certain coin is .60 and the probability of a tail is .40. If you flip that coin seven times, the probability of exactly three heads would be

$$p\left(3 \ Heads \middle| 7 \ coin \ flips\right) = \frac{7!}{3![7-3]!}\left(.60^{3}\right)\left(.40^{(7-3)}\right)$$

$$= \frac{7(6)(5)(4)(3)(2)(1)}{3(2)(1)[4(3)(2)(1)]}(.216)(.0256)$$

$$= .194, \qquad (1.2)$$

and the probability of exactly seven heads in seven flips would be

$$p\left(7 \ Heads \middle| 7 \ coin \ flips\right) = \frac{7!}{7![7-7]!}\left(.60^{7}\right)\left(.40^{(7-7)}\right)$$

$$= \frac{7(6)(5)(4)(3)(2)(1)}{7(6)(5)(4)(3)(2)(1)[1]}(.0279936)(1)$$

$$= .028. \qquad (1.3)$$

To put this in words, if the probability that any one coin flip will result in a head is .60, then the probability that three out of seven coin flips will result in heads is .194: This outcome should occur in 19.4% of samples of seven coin flips. The probability that all seven will be heads is .028, so 2.8% of samples of seven coin flips will result in exactly seven heads.

If you are already distressed by the mathematics involved, I want to assure you that these computations are presented here only to demonstrate how a sampling distribution can be generated. It is unlikely you will ever have to create a sampling distribution in practice, but it is important that you have some sense of the process.

The binomial formula was used to generate the *y*-axis values in Figure 1.1 by setting the probability of a head and a tail to .50. These probabilities are also listed in Table 1.1. Figure 1.1 and Table 1.1 offer alternative presentations of a **binomial distribution**, *a sampling distribution of a statistic derived from a dichotomous variable.* As noted previously, in this case the dichotomous variable is the outcome from a single flip of a coin, and the statistic is the number of heads in each sample of 10 coin flips.

Several points can be made about the information provided in Table 1.1 and Figure 1.1. First, binomial distributions are not exclusively useful for coin flips. Binomial distributions are relevant whenever the variable is dichotomous, whether that variable is improvement–no improvement, male–female, left–right, opposed to health care reform–supportive of health care reform, or whatever.

Second, it is important to understand the differences among a sampling distribution, a sample distribution, and a population distribution. The *sample distribution* is the distribution of some *variable* in a *single sample*. In the present example, this would be the frequency of heads and tails in a single sample of 10 coin flips. The *population distribution* is

TABLE 1.1

Binomial Distribution for 10 Coin Flips With $p(Head) = .50$

No. heads	Probability	No. heads	Probability
0	.00098	6	.20508
1	.00977	7	.11719
2	.04395	8	.04395
3	.11719	9	.00977
4	.20508	10	.00098
5	.24609		

Note. Notice that the 11 probabilities add up to 1.0 (ignoring rounding error), indicating they exhaust the options.

the (usually hypothetical) probability distribution of some *variable* in the *entire population*. In the example, this would be the probability of a head and the probability of a tail in the entire population of coin flips. The *sampling distribution* is the hypothetical distribution of some *statistic* across a *series of samples* of the same size drawn from some population. Whereas the sample and population distributions gauge the relative frequency of outcomes for a *variable* (in the present example, head vs. tail), the sampling distribution gauges the relative frequency of outcomes for a *statistic* (the number of heads). These differences are summarized in Table 1.2.

Finally, the sampling distribution in Figure 1.1 was generated *without ever collecting any data*. This is an important feature of many of the sampling distributions used in psychology, making it possible to generate expectations about sample statistics and their variations across samples even before the data are collected. Specifically, a sample outcome will be compared with expectations based on the sampling distribution to draw conclusions about a population.

Table 1.3 and Figure 1.2 provide a second example of a binomial distribution for 10 coin flips, this time with coins fixed to produce heads 80% of the time. This is an example of a **noncentral distribution**, *a sampling distribution that is based on some value for the parameter other than the neutral point*. What defines the neutral point varies across sampling distributions. In the case of dichotomous variables, the neutral point occurs when the probability of both outcomes is .50. Notice that when the population probability of a head is set to .80 the probabilities in the sampling distribution shift to the right so the distribution is no longer symmetrical. The distribution becomes noncentral. This shift should make sense. Now the most likely outcome is eight heads out of 10, and less than 4% of samples will contain five heads or fewer.

TABLE 1.2

Comparison of Sample Distributions, Sampling Distributions, and Population Distributions

Condition	Sample distribution	Sampling distribution	Population distribution
It is a(n):	Observed distribution	Hypothetical distribution	Hypothetical distribution
Of a:	Variable	Statistic	Variable
In a:	Sample	Series of samples of equal size drawn from a population	Population
Example:	No. of improved/ unimproved individuals in a sample of 500 patients	Improvement rates across many samples of 500 patients	Probability of a patient improving in the population

TABLE 1.3

Binomial Distribution for 10 Coin Flips With *p(Head)* = .80

No. heads	Probability	No. heads	Probability
0	<.00001	6	.08808
1	<.00001	7	.20133
2	.00007	8	.30199
3	.00079	9	.26844
4	.00551	10	.10734
5	.02642		

Note. Notice that the 11 probabilities add up to 1.0 (ignoring rounding error), indicating they exhaust the options.

Compare Figures 1.1 and 1.2 for a second. Suppose you are presented with a coin, and you are wondering whether it is fair (i.e., that heads and tails are equally likely) or whether it is fixed to produce too many heads. In statistical terms, the question you are asking is whether the probability of a head for this coin is .50 or some value greater than .50.

FIGURE 1.2

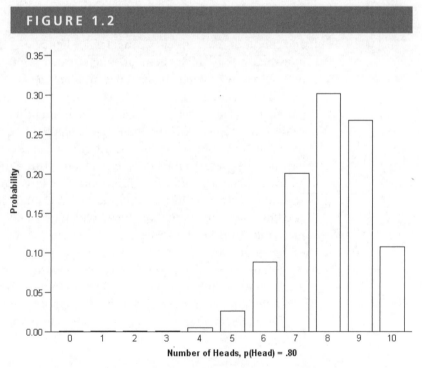

The binomial distribution for samples of 10 coin flips for *p(Head)* = .80.

If you flip the coin 10 times and get nine heads, you know this is a much more likely occurrence if the coin is fixed to give too many heads. I use this sort of comparison between sampling distributions in Chapter 3 to explain the concept of power. For now I hope you are starting to see how a sampling distribution is useful for understanding the correspondence between samples and populations.

The Sampling Distribution of the Mean

Not all variables allow only two values, of course. Most attributes of interest to psychologists are conceptualized as a dimension. For example, people are believed to fall along a dimension of academic achievement from very low to very high. The term **dimensional variable** refers to *variables that imply at least some ordering of cases and are typically associated with a relatively large range of scores.*[1] Dimensional variables can be contrasted with **categorical variables,** *variables in which there is a qualitative difference between two or more values,* of which dichotomous variables are the simplest form. Examples of dimensional variables would include rank ordering of the attractiveness of different products, scores on intelligence tests, and counts of the frequency of aggressive behaviors. Even responses on individual questionnaire items are often treated as dimensional so long as the choices are ordered, for example, from *strongly agree* to *strongly disagree.*

Because dimensional variables can take on more than two values, the binomial distribution is no longer relevant, and the probability of each value in the population is no longer particularly interesting. For example, the probability of each height in the American population is actually less informative than the population mean because the former involves an overwhelming amount of information whereas the latter captures an important aspect of that information in a single number. In many circumstances the population mean, which is usually represented using the symbol μ (the Greek lowercase letter mu), is the single most interesting parameter.

Suppose a study is conducted concerning the impact of a nutritional supplement on intellectual functioning. A sample of 300 members of the U.S. adult population is gathered, and for 6 months the sample members use the supplement daily. At the end of 6 months, an intelligence test is

---

[1]In the psychological literature, dimensional variables are often referred to using more specific mathematical terms, such as *continuous, ordinal, interval,* or *ratio variables.* I discuss why this practice is often technically incorrect in Chapter 8.

administered that is believed to have a mean score of 100 and a standard deviation of 15 in the U.S. adult population. Suppose that the mean score for the sample proves to be 102.5. Setting aside problems with the design of this study,[2] the basic question is this. The sample had a higher mean score on the intelligence test than is true of the general population. This may have occurred because the supplement improves intellectual functioning, so the mean score in the population of people who use the nutritional supplement is higher. However, it is also possible the difference is simply due to sampling error. How do you tell which is the case?

The sample statistic of interest here is the sample mean, which will be symbolized by $\bar{Y}$. Statisticians have developed several sampling distributions that are relevant when estimating the degree of sampling error associated with sample means. The most basic is the **sampling distribution of the mean**, which is *the probability distribution for sample means across an infinite series of samples of equal size.* For example, the sampling distribution of the mean could be used to compute the probability of a sample mean of 102.5 if in fact the population μ equals 100, that is, if the supplement has no effect.

One important feature of the sampling distribution of the mean is that if sample members are randomly and independently sampled from the population, the mean of the sampling distribution (i.e., the mean of the sample means) always equals the mean of the variable in the population. In statistics, this feature is stated more formally in terms of the **expected value** of the sample mean, *the value for a sample statistic that results when each possible value of the statistic is weighted by its probability of occurrence in the sampling distribution and summed.* For example, suppose a statistic, Z, can have only three values that occur with the following probabilities in a sampling distribution based on some population:

Value	Probability
1	.40
2	.25
3	.35

According to the definition provided, the expected value for this statistic would be

$$E(Z) = (1 \times .40) + (2 \times .25) + (3 \times .35) = 1.95. \tag{1.4}$$

If *the expected value of a sample statistic equals the value of the corresponding parameter,* then that statistic is considered an **unbiased statistic**. So if

---

[2]This is admittedly a lousy study. To cite just one particularly serious problem, there is no control group and everyone is getting the active treatment. As a result, it is possible that any effects could be due to expectations about the treatment.

Z is a sample statistic that corresponds with the parameter θ, and if Z is an unbiased statistic, then θ also equals 1.95 in the population from which the samples were drawn.

The expected value of the sampling distribution of the mean (i.e., the mean of the sample means) will equal the mean of the variable in the population, making the sample mean an unbiased estimator of the population mean. If this were not the case, if the mean of the sample means did not equal the population mean, then the mean would be a **biased statistic.**

To return to the nutritional supplement study, imagine a population of individuals given the nutritional supplement treatment. If the nutritional treatment has absolutely no effect on intellectual functioning, then the μ for this population should be exactly the same as that for the general population, 100 (assuming the members of this population are randomly and independently drawn from the general population). This also means the expected value for the sampling distribution of the mean will also equal 100: $E(\bar{Y}) = \mu = 100$.

Alternatively, what if the nutritional supplement treatment actually improves intellectual functioning? If so, we would expect the following: $E(\bar{Y}) = \mu > 100$.

Of course, there is also the possibility the nutritional supplement interferes with intellectual functioning, in which case $E(\bar{Y}) = \mu < 100$.

To simplify matters, I will ignore this last possibility for now, but I return to it in Chapter 2.

Consider what all this means for deciding whether the nutritional supplement improves intellectual functioning. The sample had a mean score of 102.5. If the treatment is ineffective, and $\mu = 100$, then the additional 2.5 points is just sampling error. If instead the treatment does improve intellectual functioning, then the additional 2.5 points is due at least in part (because there is still sampling error) to the treatment. The question is how to decide between these two possibilities.

Just as in the case of the binomial distribution, there is a formula available that allows you to compute the sampling distribution of the mean, though I will not trouble you with it. As in the case of the binomial formula, the formula for the sampling distribution of the mean requires certain conditions. One of these conditions is knowledge of the expected value for the sampling distribution. One way to deal with this in the present case is to assume the treatment is ineffective, which means assuming that $\mu = E(\bar{Y}) = 100$. Using this assumption it is possible to compute probabilities associated with various sample values if the treatment is ineffective. Here is where it gets interesting. Suppose it turns out that a sample mean of 102.5 or higher would be very rare if the treatment is ineffective; suppose, for example, a sample mean this high would occur only once in every 1 million samples if $\mu = 100$. That would seem to be

FIGURE 1.3

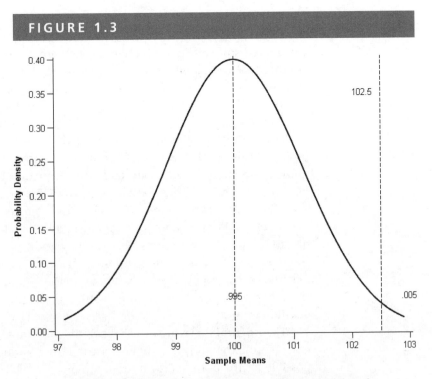

A sampling distribution for the mean where nutritional treatment had no effect. The expected value (the mean of the means is at 100). The probability that a sample mean will be 102.5 or greater is only .005; 99.5% of the sample means fall below 102.5.

pretty good evidence that in fact $\mu > 100$ and the treatment has increased mean intelligence test score.

For example, in Figure 1.3 I have provided a sampling distribution of the mean that would fit this situation. Notice that the *y*-axis for the binomial distributions in Figures 1.1 and 1.2 reads "Probability," but in Figure 1.3 it refers to the "Probability Density." This has to do with a feature of some of the sampling distributions I will discuss. The sampling distribution of the mean does not involve computing the probability of a specific sample mean, such as 102.5; instead, it is used to compute the probability that a range of values will occur. That is why in the previous paragraph I referred to sample means of 102.5 *or higher. Probability density* is simply a technical term resulting from that feature of the sampling distribution of the mean.

According to Figure 1.3, a sample mean of 102.5 or greater would occur only five times in 1,000 if the treatment is ineffective and the result is due to sampling error; the probability of a sample mean lower than

102.5 is .995. A sample mean that occurs only five times in 1,000 if the population mean is 100 (if the treatment is ineffective) could be considered sufficiently unlikely that we might feel comfortable concluding that this sample mean probably suggests the treatment was effective. This example brings us closer to understanding how sampling distributions can be used to answer questions about a population based on a sample.

Using the sampling distribution of the mean to determine the probability of sample means requires other important conditions besides knowing the population mean. First, the shape of the sampling distribution of the mean changes as the population distribution changes. For example, if the distribution of scores on this intelligence test is skewed negatively in the population (with many scores near the high end of the distribution and fewer scores near the low end), then it would make some sense that the sampling distribution of the mean will also be skewed negatively. To simplify matters when using the sampling distribution of the mean, statisticians frequently assume the population is normally distributed.

The **normal distribution** is one of the most important concepts to emerge from the study of sampling distributions. Various definitions are possible for the normal distribution, but one that will be useful for our purposes is *a symmetrical bell-shaped distribution characterized by a fixed proportion of cases falling at any particular distance from the distribution mean in standard deviation units.* For example, 34.134% of scores will fall between the distribution mean and 1 standard deviation above the mean, and because the normal distribution is symmetrical the same percentage of scores falls between the mean and 1 standard deviation below the mean. About 13.591% of the scores fall between 1 and 2 standard deviations above the mean. Strict relationships also exist for smaller increments in standard deviations: 19.146% of the scores will fall within 0.5 standard deviation above the mean, 14.988% of the scores will fall between 0.5 and 1 standard deviation above the mean, and so forth (see Figure 1.4).

Why did statisticians tend to assume populations are normally distributed? Early in the process of learning about error, it was discovered that sampling distributions based on samples derived from random and independent events have a remarkable tendency to approximate normal distributions as the size of the samples in the sampling distribution increase. For example, suppose we are interested in measuring family incomes in the American population. This variable tends to be positively skewed: Most families are clustered together at the lower end of the distribution, making less than $100,000 per year. However, there is a very small set of families that make millions, tens of millions, even hundreds of millions of dollars per year. Those families skew the distribution in the positive direction.

FIGURE 1.4

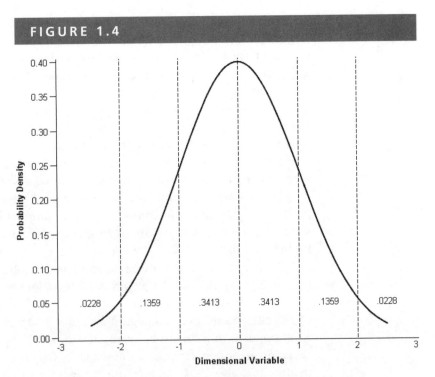

This is a normal distribution. Values on the *x*-axis reflect distances from the mean in standard deviations, e.g., 2 on the *x*-axis is two standard deviations above the mean, −.5 is one-half standard deviation below the mean, and so forth. The probability is .1359 that a sample statistic will fall between one and two standard deviations above the mean (13.59% of sample statistics will fall in that interval).

Now suppose we collect many, many samples from this population and compute the mean annual income for each sample, but each sample includes only 10 families. It should not be surprising to find the sampling distribution of the mean is also positively skewed, with most means clustered at the bottom end of the distribution and an occasional mean that is in the millions. Now suppose instead that the sampling distribution of the mean is based on samples of 10,000 families. In this case, something remarkable will happen: The resulting sampling distribution of the mean will closely approximate the symmetrical normal distribution. In the case of the sampling distribution of the mean this magical tendency to approach normality as sample sizes increase came to be referred to as the *central limit theorem,* although this tendency also proves to be true for the binomial distribution and many other sampling distributions. This tendency to approach a normal distribution with increasing sample size is referred to *asymptotic normality*. Why this happens need not trouble us; it is only important to know that it does happen.

Given the tendency for sampling distributions to look more normal as sample sizes increase, and given that many of these statistics were developed at a time when statisticians did not have access to information about entire populations, it seemed reasonable to assume that random events working in the population would also cause many population distributions to be normal. So when statisticians needed to assume a certain shape for a population distribution, the normal distribution seemed like the best candidate. However, even if it is true that sampling distributions are often normally distributed (and this may be true only for sampling distributions composed of very large samples), that does not mean population distributions also tend to be normally distributed. I return to this issue in Chapter 2 as well.

The final condition for using the sampling distribution of the mean is knowledge of the population standard deviation, usually symbolized by σ (Greek lowercase sigma). Because it has already been established that this intelligence test has a standard deviation of 15 in the general U.S. adult population, it might be reasonable to assume that the standard deviation in the population of adults who take the nutritional supplement treatment is also 15. In fact, Figure 1.3 was based on the assumption that the standard deviation for the population was 15.

This requirement that the population standard deviation is known often causes practical problems for using the sampling distribution of the mean. If we use 15 as our population standard deviation, we are assuming that the treatment does not affect the standard deviation of the scores, but what if the treatment makes scores more variable? If it does, then the correct standard deviation for the population of adults who receive the nutritional supplement is greater than 15. This will also affect the sampling distribution of the mean, and the number of samples with means of 102.5 or higher would be greater than five in 1,000. Furthermore, for many dimensional variables there may be no good estimate of the population standard deviation at all.

To summarize, four conditions were involved in using the sampling distribution of the mean:

1. The participants were randomly and independently sampled from the population.
2. The population was normally distributed.
3. There was some reasonable guess available for the value of μ.
4. There was some reasonable guess available for the value of σ.

This last condition is particularly problematic. If no good estimate of the standard deviation of the population is available, then the sampling distribution of the mean cannot be generated. Because σ is usually unknown, a more practical alternative to the sampling distribution of the mean was needed. That practical alternative was the *t* distribution.

The t *Distribution*

William Gosset, who published under the name Student, was a mathematician and chemist whose job it was to improve quality at the Guinness brewery in Dublin. In doing so, he confronted this issue of computing probabilities for means when the population standard deviation is unknown. In 1908, he offered a solution based on a new statistic, the *t* statistic (subsequently modified by Sir Ronald Fisher, an individual who will appear often in this story), and the corresponding sampling distribution, the *t* distribution.

There are several versions of the *t* statistic used for different purposes, but they all share the same sampling distribution. The *t* statistic formula relevant to the nutritional supplement study is

$$t_{\bar{Y}} = \frac{\bar{Y} - \mu}{\hat{\sigma}\sqrt{\dfrac{1}{N}}}, \tag{1.5}$$

where μ is the assumed population mean, $\bar{Y}$ is the sample mean, and N is the sample size. In the nutritional supplement example the assumed population mean has been 100, the sample mean has been 102.5, and the sample size has been 300. The formula also includes a new statistic, $\hat{\sigma}$, which is the best estimate of the population standard deviation (a caret is often used in statistics to mean "best estimate of") based on the sample. One formula for $\hat{\sigma}$ is

$$\hat{\sigma} = \sqrt{\frac{\displaystyle\sum_{i=1}^{N}(Y_i - \bar{Y})^2}{N - 1}}, \tag{1.6}$$

so another formula for $t_{\bar{Y}}$ is

$$t_{\bar{Y}} = \frac{\bar{Y} - \mu}{\sqrt{\dfrac{\displaystyle\sum_{i=1}^{N}(Y_i - \bar{Y})^2}{N(N - 1)}}}. \tag{1.7}$$

The new denominator of *t* involves taking each score in the sample, subtracting the sample mean, squaring the difference, summing those squared values, dividing the sum by $N(N-1)$, and then taking the square root of this value.

This formula highlights an important difference between the t distribution and the sampling distribution of the mean. Remember that the sample mean is an unbiased statistic: The expected value of the sampling distribution of the mean equaled the population μ. In the nutritional treatment example, if the treatment has no effect then the expected value of the sampling distribution of the mean would be 100. In contrast, the numerator for t is the difference between $\bar{Y}$ and the best guess for the population μ. So far, we have been using the value if the treatment has no effect for this μ, 100. If the nutritional treatment has no effect, on average $\bar{Y}$ will also equal 100, so the expected value of the t distribution will equal 0. For the t distribution, 0 represents the neutral point discussed in connection with noncentral distributions. To summarize this in terms of expected values, if the treatment has no effect then

$$E(\bar{Y}) = 100$$

$$E(t) = 0. \tag{1.8}$$

As I have noted already, the advantage of the t distribution over the sampling distribution of the mean is that the former does not require knowledge of the population standard deviation. However, this advantage comes at a cost. Whereas the shape of the sampling distribution of the mean was determined purely by the shape of the population distribution (if the sample was randomly and independently drawn from the population), the shape of the t distribution changes as a function of two variables. The first is the shape of the population distribution, and matters were again simplified by assuming the population from which scores were drawn is normally distributed.

The second variable that determines the shape of the t distribution is something called the degrees of freedom. Although degrees of freedom are an important component of many inferential statistics used in the behavioral sciences, the technical meaning of the term is pretty complicated. A reasonable definition for the **degrees of freedom** is *the number of observations used to estimate a parameter minus the number of other parameter estimates used in the estimation.* For example, Equation 1.6 estimates the parameter σ. You have $N = 300$ observations available from which to estimate that parameter. However, computing the estimate also requires using $\bar{Y}$ as an estimate of the population mean. So estimating σ involves N intelligence test scores and one parameter estimate, hence the degrees of freedom available for this estimate of the population standard deviation are $N-1$. As I said, it is a complex concept. In most instances all you need to know is that the degrees of freedom affect the shape of the sampling distribution.

As the degrees of freedom increase, the **standard error** of the *t* distribution gets smaller. Standard error is the term used to refer to *the standard deviation of a sampling distribution,* so as sample size (and degrees of freedom) increases there is less variability in the *t* statistic from sample to sample. You can see this pattern in Figure 1.5. With greater degrees of freedom, the tails of the sampling distribution are pulled in toward the center point, reflecting less variability, a smaller standard error, and less sampling error.

To summarize, using the *t* distribution involves meeting three conditions:

1. The participants were randomly and independently sampled from the population.
2. The population was normally distributed.
3. There was some reasonable guess for the value of μ.

FIGURE 1.5

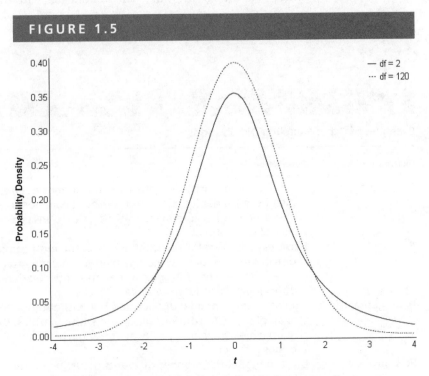

The *t* distributions for 2 degrees of freedom (*df;* solid line) and 120 *df.* Figure 1.5. The *t* distributions for 2 degrees of freedom (solid line) and 120 degrees of freedom (dotted line). Notice the distribution at 120 degrees of freedom is more concentrated around the mean of 0; there are fewer cases out in the tail. Also, the probabilities are very similar to those for the normal distribution in Figure 1.4.

Gosset was able to eliminate the fourth condition required for using the sampling distribution of the mean, a reasonable guess for σ, but doing so required dealing with degrees of freedom.

Because this book is about the logic rather than the mechanics of inference, I do not discuss additional sampling distributions in any detail. However, there are several others that are very commonly used in statistical inference and still others that probably should be used more frequently than they are to model psychosocial processes. Examples of some other sampling distributions are provided in Table 1.4. The list in this table is by no means complete. Statisticians have defined a number of sampling distributions relevant to modeling specific types of random events. Table 1.4 is simply meant to illustrate the various types of random events for which sampling distributions are available.

With this introduction to the *t* distribution you have enough statistical background to understand the quantitative models of inference that emerged in the 20th century. The story begins with the introduction of the significance testing model by Sir Ronald Fisher, which provides the topic for Chapter 2.

TABLE 1.4

Examples of Other Sampling Distributions

Distribution	Description
Chi-square	Used when the statistic of interest is the sum of a series of normally distributed variables. It is one of the most commonly used distributions in psychology because many statistical situations can be modeled as a sum of such variables.
F	Because of Sir Ronald Fisher, this is one of the most common sampling distributions used in psychology (and was named after him). It is used when the statistic of interest is the ratio of two variables that are sums of normally distributed variables.
Hypergeometric	Similar to the binomial distribution but without independence. For example, an urn contains black and white marbles. Drawing a black marble means the probability of drawing a black marble in subsequent draws is lower.
Poisson	Used to model the number of events occurring within a fixed time interval, such as the number of cars that pass a certain point each hour.
Weibull	This is a more complex and flexible distribution than others listed here. It is actually a family of distributions based on three parameters and so can take on a variety of shapes. It is used extensively to evaluate the reliability of objects and provides models for failure rates. However, it has many other uses.

Conclusion

In response to increasing concern about the problem of sampling error, scientists in the 18th century turned to a concept developed by mathematicians interested in probability theory called the sampling distribution. The sampling distribution provided the bridge between the population distribution, which is the true distribution of interest but unavailable to the researcher, and the sample distribution, which is available to the researcher but can inaccurately reflect the population. The sampling distribution provides information about the distribution of some statistic across samples of the same size. Using this information, it is possible to generate conclusions about the probability of a given value for a sample statistic assuming certain conditions. These conditions usually include random and independent sampling from the population but can include others, such as a normally distributed population.

For example, the binomial distribution is a sampling distribution that applies when a sample statistic is based on some variable that can take on only one of two values. The number of heads in a series of coin flips is an example of the type of statistic for which the binomial distribution is useful. In this chapter, I have demonstrated that the binomial distribution can be generated from just a couple of pieces of information without ever actually collecting data. The same is true for the other sampling distributions introduced here—the sampling distribution of the mean and the *t* distribution—although the amount of information needed to use each varies.

Ronald Fisher used the concept of the sampling distribution as the basis for a logical approach to making inferences about the population. His model of inference is the topic of Chapter 2.

Significance Testing 2

S ir Ronald Fisher probably had more of an impact on statistical methods in psychology, and the social sciences in general, than any other individual in the 20th century. At first blush that may seem odd given that his background was in agronomy and thus he was probably much more interested in manure than the mind. His influence reflects his willingness to apply his genius to any topic that touched on his field of study. For example, he completed the synthesis of Darwin's and Mendel's perspectives on the inheritance of traits, one of the most important achievements in the early history of genetics. Unfortunately, his genius was at times flawed by a tendency to disparage the conclusions of others who dared to disagree with him.

Among Fisher's contributions to inferential methods was the development of a bevy of new statistics, including the analysis of variance (ANOVA) and the formula for the t statistic now in common use. Perhaps most important, though, was a model he developed to use t and other statistics based on sampling distributions for purposes of drawing conclusions about populations. His model is commonly referred to as *significance testing,* and it is the focus of this chapter.

Fisher's Model

Significance testing is a procedure Fisher introduced for making inferential statements about populations. Note that significance testing is not in itself a statistical technique; it is not even a necessary adjunct to the use of statistics. It is *a logical model that Fisher proposed as a formal approach to addressing questions about populations based on samples.* It is a structured approach for comparing a sample statistic with the sampling distribution for that statistic, with the goal of drawing a conclusion about a population.

Significance testing consists of the following six steps, which I illustrate in this chapter using the example study of nutritional supplements and intellectual ability I described in Chapter 1:

1. *Identify a question about a population.* The question in this study is whether the nutritional supplement treatment enhances intellectual functioning.
2. *Identify the null state.* In the study described, the null, or no-effect, state would occur if the nutritional supplement has no effect on intellectual functioning.
3. *Convert this null state into a statement about a parameter.* If the nutritional treatment has no effect on intellectual functioning, then the mean intelligence test score in the population of individuals who complete the nutritional supplement treatment should be the same as it is in the general population. This is a conjecture about the population mean and so represents an example of a **null hypothesis**, *a mathematical statement of the null state in the population.* The mathematical statement of this null hypothesis for the nutritional supplement study is $\mu = 100$.

   The equals sign is an important element of the null hypothesis. In the procedure Fisher outlined, the null hypothesis always suggests an exact value for the parameter.
4. *Conduct a study that generates a sample statistic relevant to the parameter.* As I demonstrated in Chapter 1, some sample statistics that are relevant to this parameter are the sample mean and *t*. The latter has the advantage that the associated sampling distribution does not require knowing the standard deviation of intelligence test scores for the population of individuals who receive the treatment.
5. *Determine the probability (or probability density) associated with the sample statistic value if the null hypothesis were true.* It is possible to generate the *t* distribution that would result if the null hypothesis is true. As noted in Chapter 1, the mean value of the *t* distribution would have to equal 0 if the null hypothesis is true because on

average the sample mean would equal the value suggested by the null hypothesis. In a sample of 300, it is also known that the degrees of freedom are $N - 1 = 299$. Suppose the sample t value is 3.15. If the participants were randomly and independently sampled from the population, and if the population from which they were drawn is normally distributed, then it is possible to compute the probability density of a t value of 3.15 or greater based on those degrees of freedom.

6. *Draw a conclusion about the null hypothesis based on the probability of the sample statistic.* If the t distribution suggests that the sample value for t is very unlikely if the null hypothesis is true, then the result is what Fisher referred to as "significant" in that it suggests the null hypothesis is false. This finding would allow the researcher to reject the null hypothesis, an outcome that offers support for the existence of an effect in the population. If, on the other hand, the sample t value is close enough to 0 that it is likely to occur if the null hypothesis is true, then the result is not significant and the null hypothesis cannot be rejected. The latter outcome can be referred to as *retaining* the null hypothesis. Some textbooks refer to this as *accepting* the null hypothesis, but, as I discuss in Chapter 3, the latter terminology creates an incorrect implication about the outcome in significance testing.

If the sample of 300 taking the nutritional supplement produces a sample t value of 3.15, if the participants are randomly and independently sampled from the population, and if that population is normally distributed, Gosset's t distribution indicates that a t value of this size or larger has a probability of .0009 if the null hypothesis is true; that is, a t value of 3.15 or larger would occur in only nine out of every 10,000 samples of 300. Most people would agree that this is quite unlikely and would feel comfortable concluding that this is evidence for rejecting the null hypothesis. If instead the sample t value were 0.83, the probability of such a t value or larger is .20; that is, a t value of this size or larger could occur in one out of every five samples even if the null hypothesis is true. Most people would probably agree this is not enough evidence to justify rejecting the null hypothesis (see Figure 2.1).

To summarize, the probability density associated with the sample t value is computed assuming the null hypothesis is true. If it is a very unlikely event, the finding is taken as evidence for rejecting the null hypothesis. If the sample t value is reasonably likely to occur just because of sampling error, one cannot reject the null hypothesis; it must be retained. The obvious question here is how unlikely must a sample statistic be before it is considered reasonable to reject the null hypothesis.

The probability of a sample statistic used to determine whether or not to reject the null hypothesis is often referred to in significance testing as the **level of**

FIGURE 2.1

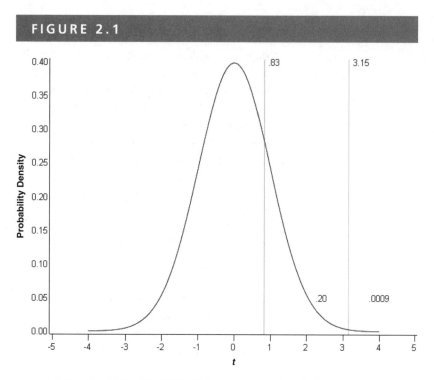

With *N* = 300 (*df* = 299), if the null hypothesis is true, a *t* value of .83 divides the top 20% of the sampling distribution from the bottom 80%; in other words, the probability of getting a sample *t* value if the null hypothesis is true is .20, or 1 in 5. So a sample *t* value of .83 can occur pretty easily because of sampling error if the null hypothesis is true. A value ≥ 3.15 would occur in only nine of every 10,000 samples if the null hypothesis is true. It is much less likely this result is due to sampling error, and so the researcher may feel justified concluding that the result is *significant* and rejecting the null hypothesis.

significance. In other words, the level of significance is the probability of a sample outcome (assuming the null hypothesis is true) at which one can reject the null hypothesis. The answer decides whether or not the results are seen as evidence for the presence of a treatment effect.

It was never Fisher's intention to provide a strict standard for the level of significance; it was instead his preference that significance would be a loose criterion and one that might vary across research contexts. Even so, Fisher (1925) at one point suggested that "it is a convenient convention to take twice the standard error as the limit of significance" (p. 102). Remember that the standard error is the standard deviation of a sampling distribution. In the sampling distribution of the mean, a value 2 standard deviations from the mean cuts off about 5% of the distribution. Fisher's comment was taken as suggesting .05 as a convenient standard for level of significance and rejecting the null hypothesis if the probability density associated with the sample statistic ≤ .05. Although he made this recommendation more than once (Fisher, 1935/1971), Fisher (1956/1973) ultimately opposed setting an absolute standard for significance. Instead he recommended that researchers report the exact p value (e.g., report "$p = .013$" rather than "$p < .05$"), but by then the use of .05 as the default level of significance was already established.[1] It is important to realize that there is absolutely no objective basis for the .05 standard for level of significance except tradition and people's desire for a standard that seems objective.

In summary, Gosset (Student, 1908) had introduced a new statistic and a new sampling distribution. It was Fisher who took that statistic (and other statistics with known sampling distributions, e.g., the chi-square and F statistics) and built a model for drawing inferences about populations based on those statistics. It was Fisher who turned the t statistic and the t distribution into the t test.

Fleshing Out the Model

With the basic logic of significance testing spelled out, it is worth lingering on some of the details of the model. In this section, I address four topics: (a) the distinction between nondirectional and directional null hypotheses, (b) the critical region, (c) the problem of fishing, and (d) the nature of test assumptions.

NONDIRECTIONAL AND DIRECTIONAL NULL HYPOTHESES

I mentioned earlier that the null hypothesis always includes an equals sign. By doing so, the null hypothesis suggests an exact value for the parameter.

---

[1] I should note two practical problems with Fisher's recommendation of reporting the actual p value. The p value is sometimes 0 when rounded to three, four, or however many decimal places. Because the probability of some sample outcome can never actually equal 0 if the null hypothesis is true, even when I am reporting exact p values I will use "$p < .001$" in cases in which the actual p value is so low that it rounds to zero. The SPSS/PASW statistical package incorrectly reports ".000"; other programs, such as SAS and R, handle this issue in more appropriate ways. Second, reporting exact p values can be inconvenient when results are being presented in a table. Using "$p < .05$" every time a result is significant avoids both of these problems.

This value is used to create the sampling distribution, which is then used to test whether the null hypothesis is true. The example used to make this point demonstrates the process. Based on a null hypothesis for our study of $\mu = 100$, each sample t value in the sampling distribution is created by subtracting 100 from the sample mean (see Equation 1.5). As a result, the mean of the t distribution will equal 0 if the null hypothesis is true and some other value if it is not.

However, notice that this particular null hypothesis is false if the true μ for people who take the supplement differs from 100 in either direction (either $\mu > 100$ or $\mu < 100$). In other words, this null hypothesis is false regardless of whether the nutritional supplement *improves* or *impairs* intellectual functioning. This is an example of a **nondirectional null hypothesis**, *a null hypothesis that would be false regardless of the direction of the effect.* If the true μ is greater than 100, or if it is less than 100, then the null hypothesis is false.

It is also possible to create a **directional null hypothesis**, *a null hypothesis that would be false only if the true parameter value lies in one direction from the parameter estimate included in the null hypothesis:* $\mu \leq 100$. Notice the null hypothesis still contains an equals sign, but the null hypothesis now includes a range of values for which 100 defines the upper endpoint. The null hypothesis is now false only if the true value for μ is > 100, in our example, only if the treatment enhances intellectual functioning.

Either the directional or nondirectional version could have served as the null hypothesis for the nutritional supplement study, but the two choices have different implications. In the case of the directional null hypothesis it is appropriate to reject the null hypothesis if the true parameter value is < 100 or > 100. In the nondirectional case it is appropriate to reject the null hypothesis only if the true value for μ is > 100. To explain how one tests a nondirectional versus directional null hypothesis it is first necessary to introduce the concept of the critical region.

THE CRITICAL REGION

Use of the directional null hypothesis $\mu \leq 100$ means the null hypothesis can be rejected only if the sample t value is greater than 0. This is true because a value for t that is less than 0 is perfectly consistent with the null hypothesis. To meet the standard criterion of a .05 level of significance, Figure 2.2 demonstrates the **critical region** for testing this null hypothesis, *the region of the sampling distribution that would allow rejection of the null hypothesis.* For the standard of .05 this is the set of scores that has a probability density of .05 if the null hypothesis is true.

The **critical value** is *the value of the sample statistic that serves as the dividing line between significance and nonsignificance;* that is, the critical value

FIGURE 2.2

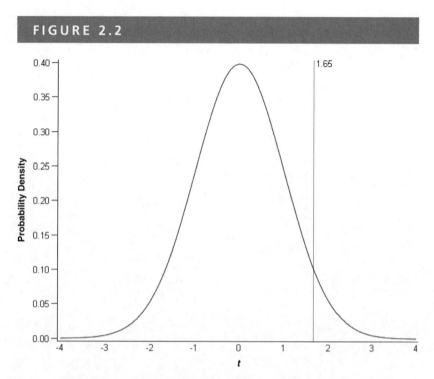

With 299 degrees of freedom, the total probability of a
t value ≥ 1.65 if the null hypothesis is true is .05. This serves
as the critical value for testing the null hypothesis μ ≤ 100.

is the endpoint of the critical region toward the middle of the sampling
distribution. There is no upper endpoint to the critical region, because
any sample *t* value that is greater than or equal to the critical value allows
you to reject the null hypothesis. In Figure 2.2 the critical value is 1.65;
that is, if the sample *t* value is ≥ 1.65 it falls in the critical region and
allows rejection of the null hypothesis at the .05 level of significance.
Many textbooks provide tables of critical values for statistics such as *t*.
The values in these *t* tables or chi-square tables are the critical values for
dividing the critical region from the rest of the sampling distribution
based on the desired level of significance and the degrees of freedom.

Suppose the researcher thought that the nutritional supplement
impairs rather than improves intellectual functioning. This would change
the direction of the null hypothesis as follows: μ ≥ 100.

Now only *t* values at the low end of the sampling distribution should
lead to rejection of the null hypothesis. Figure 2.3 indicates the critical
region in this case, with a critical value of −1.65. Notice that the critical
regions in Figures 2.2 and 2.3 each lie in one tail of the *t* distribution.
For this reason, when *t* is used to test a directional hypothesis it is

FIGURE 2.3

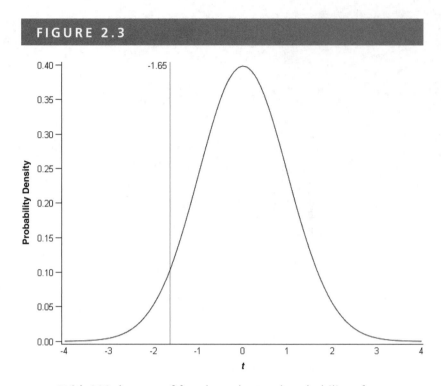

With 299 degrees of freedom, the total probability of a *t* value ≤ −1.65 if the null hypothesis is true is .05. This serves as the critical value for testing the null hypothesis μ ≥ 100.

sometimes referred to as a **one-tailed test**, *a test for which the critical region is in one tail of the sampling distribution.*

The nondirectional null hypothesis we have been working with is μ = 100, and this hypothesis is false if the true population mean is > 100 or < 100. To test this null hypothesis it becomes necessary to divide the critical region between the two tails; specifically, to use .05 as the level of significance, it means using a critical region in the lower tail that has a total probability of .025 if the null hypothesis is true and a critical region in the upper tail that has a total probability of .025 if the null hypothesis is true. The value that cuts off the extreme 2.5% of *t* values in both tails of the sampling distribution based on the null hypothesis is 1.968 in the upper tail and −1.968 in the lower tail. The two critical regions involved are indicated in Figure 2.4. Notice that 1.968 is farther out on the tails than 1.65. This shift should make sense, because the goal is to identify the top 2.5% of outcomes (assuming the null hypothesis is true) and the bottom 2.5%. This is an example of a **two-tailed test**, *a test in which the critical region is in both tails of the sampling distribution.* In this case, the critical

FIGURE 2.4

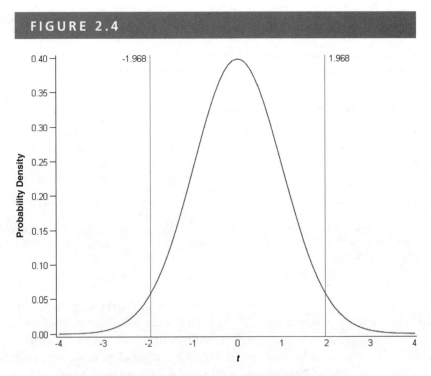

With 299 degrees of freedom, the total probability of a
t value ≤ −1.968 or ≥ 1.968 if the null hypothesis is true
is .05. These serve as the critical values for testing the null
hypothesis μ = 100.

value is ±1.968: A sample *t* value ≥ 1.968 or a sample *t* value ≤ −1.968
would allow rejection of the null hypothesis.

To summarize, the shape of the *t* distribution is determined by
the degrees of freedom. Once the shape of the distribution is known
(assuming the null hypothesis is true), the choice of the critical value
depends on the level of significance desired and whether the researcher
wants to test a directional or a nondirectional null hypothesis. A nondirectional null hypothesis contains only an equals sign and is tested
using a two-tailed *t* test. This involves setting a critical value in both tails.
Because the sampling distribution based on the null hypothesis is symmetrical around 0, this will always be the positive and negative values
of the same number (see Table 2.1).

A directional null hypothesis contains either ≥ or ≤ and is tested
using a one-tailed test. If it contains ≥ the critical region will be in the
lower tail of the distribution, so the critical value will be negative. If it
contains ≤ the critical region is in the upper tail, so the critical value will
be positive. The absolute value of the critical value will always be smaller

TABLE 2.1

Comparing Null Hypotheses for *t* Tests

	Null hypothesis		
If the null hypothesis . . .	μ = 23	μ ≤ 23	μ ≥ 23
is a:	nondirectional null hypothesis	directional null hypothesis	directional null hypothesis
the critical region lies in:	both tails of the sampling distribution	the upper tail of the sampling distribution	the lower tail of the sampling distribution

Note. All examples until now have used a null hypothesis parameter estimate of 100. In this table the value 23 is used instead simply to remind the reader that the value is not always 100; the value depends on whatever is the appropriate "no effect" value for the variables you are studying. The information provided in this table is specific to the *t* distribution. Other distributions have different characteristics.

for a directional null hypothesis (closer to 0) because it must cut off a larger portion of the tail. This is the information used to create the *t* tables of critical values typically found in the backs of statistics texts.[2]

Is it better to test directional or nondirectional null hypotheses? Remember that the original purpose of the study as described was to determine whether nutritional supplements enhance intellectual functioning, so there would seem to be some logic to testing the directional null hypothesis μ ≤ 100. Even so, I believe in most cases it is better to test nondirectional null hypotheses, for the following reasons:

- Even if the researcher is betting that the treatment has an effect in one direction, an effect in the opposite direction is also usually important. If the directional null hypothesis in the nutritional supplement study is tested and the results do not allow rejection of the null hypothesis, it is unclear whether the results mean the nutritional supplement has no effect or whether it actually impairs intellectual functioning. In contrast, if the researcher tests the nondirectional null hypothesis and gets significance, a positive *t* value provides evidence that the treatment improves performance, whereas a negative *t* value suggests the treatment interferes with performance. A directional null hypothesis is therefore justified only when results opposite in direction from what the researcher expects are of no importance.
- There are cases in which a directional hypothesis cannot be tested. When an *F* test is used to compare four groups, or a chi-square

---

[2]I have elected not to include tables of critical values for *t* and other statistics because you will typically conduct statistics on the computer.

statistic is used to test a confirmatory factor analysis, a set of comparisons is being evaluated simultaneously. In these cases, differences from the null hypothesis value always increase the value of the test statistic. For example, whether the mean of Group 1 is larger than the mean of Group 2, or vice versa, the larger the difference between them the larger the ANOVA F value will be (see Figure 2.5). As a result, the ANOVA F test is a one-tailed test, with the critical region falling in the upper tail, of a non-directional null hypothesis. Because any study can involve a combination of statistical tests, some of which can accommodate directional null hypotheses and some of which cannot, there is a tendency always to test nondirectional hypotheses for the sake of consistency.

FIGURE 2.5

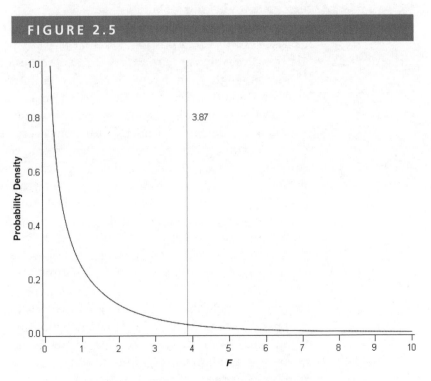

If the null hypothesis is true, this would be the analysis of variance F distribution for evaluating differences between two population means in a sample of 300 cases. Whether the mean of Group 1 is larger than the mean of Group 2 or vice versa, only a sample F value of 3.87 or greater would allow rejection of the null hypothesis at $p < .05$. This makes the analysis of variance F test a one-tailed test of a non-directional null hypothesis.

To summarize, nondirectional null hypotheses are probably best. For some statistics (e.g., t) this will mean a two-tailed test. For others (e.g., F and chi-square) this means a one-tailed test. Unfortunately, some statistical software sets the default for t to one-tailed tests. Sometimes the default is not the best choice.

MULTIPLE COMPARISONS

The discussion so far has focused on single significance tests, but most studies involve many variables in **multiple comparisons**, *the common term used for conducting multiple significance tests.* Treatment trials often involve multiple dependent variables, whereas a single study may report hundreds of correlations, each of which is associated with a significance test. There are two issues that arise in the context of multiple comparisons that you should know about.

A **fishing expedition** refers to *a research project involving multiple comparisons in which the researcher ignores or downplays nonsignificant results.* This practice is similar to *selective reporting* of results or to *capitalizing on chance*, although the different terms focus on different aspects of the problem. Suppose a researcher administers 15 questionnaires to workers that focus on perceived social support, job satisfaction, emotional distress, and other attitudinal variables. By correlating every questionnaire with every other questionnaire, the researcher is able to generate 105 unique correlations, and a t test can be computed for each correlation testing the null hypothesis that the corresponding population correlation equals zero. Let us suppose that six of the correlations turn out to be significant, and the researcher then publishes a study focusing on those six relationships and ignoring all the rest.

Fisher considered this type of selective reporting to be cheating, for the following reason. Imagine that in fact all 105 population correlations are equal to 0; in other words, all 105 null hypotheses are true. At a .05 level of significance, five or six of those correlations could be significant purely by chance because 5% of 105 significance tests equals 5.25. By focusing on only those six outcomes the researcher creates an illusion of consistent findings and ignores the alternative explanation that the results are all due to sampling error.[3]

---

[3]Discussions of this issue sometimes imply that all seven of those significant results *are* due to sampling error, but this is an incorrect conclusion. That would be the case only if all 105 null hypotheses are true. We usually do not know how many of those 105 null hypotheses are true—if we did, there would be no point to conducting the study—so we do not really know how many of those significant results are errors. What we do know is that looking at those seven in the context of 105 makes them look less impressive than looking at them in isolation.

The problem of selective reporting has returned to the forefront lately because of growing evidence that it is a common phenomenon in research on prescription medications. For example, Turner, Matthews, Linardatos, Tell, and Rosenthal (2008) recently reviewed company-funded studies that had been conducted to compare 12 antidepressants with a placebo. Only 51% of those studies found positive results, yet 94% of the published articles based on those studies presented positive findings. The difference reflected a failure to publish studies that did not find a difference, or in some cases focusing the article on a secondary analysis that was significant instead of a primary analysis that was not significant (see also Vedula, Bero, Scherer, & Dickersin, 2009). The federal government requires meticulous record keeping of all findings in drug studies. It is uncertain how often selective reporting occurs when researchers are not bound by this mandate.

The second issue has to do with probability in error with multiple comparisons. In the context of multiple comparisons, the level of significance can be thought of as the **per-comparison error rate**, *the rate of incorrect rejections across a set of analyses.* With multiple comparisons Fisher also thought it was important to consider the **familywise error rate**, *the probability of at least one incorrect rejection of the null hypothesis across multiple comparisons* (the word *family* here refers to the set of comparisons). To understand this concept a little better, return to the example of a fair coin flip. If the coin is flipped once, the probability of a head (*H*) is .50, as is the probability of a tail (*T*). If it is flipped twice, there are four possible outcomes with the following probabilities:

Outcome	Probability
HH	.25
HT	.25
TH	.25
TT	.25

The probability of *at least* one head has increased to $p(HH) + p(HT) + p(TH) = .75$.

Similarly, if you conduct a significance test at a .05 level of significance when the null hypothesis is true, then there is a .05 probability of an error. If you conduct two significance tests when both null hypotheses are true, each at a .05 level of significance, one can estimate that the probability that *at least* one of those two results will involve an incorrect rejection increases to .0975.[4] If you conduct 105 significance tests using a .05 level of significance, and all 105 null hypotheses are true, the probability of *at least* one incorrect rejection is estimated to be .995.

---

[4] The reason this is an estimate rather than an exact value is not really important to the discussion.

This number (.995) represents the familywise error rate for this family of 105 analyses. However, keep in mind that the familywise error rate of .995 applies only if every one of the 105 null hypotheses is correct (this is the same issue raised in footnote 1 of Chapter 1, this volume). Whether this is a realistic scenario is a separate question, which I discuss further in Chapter 4. For now, it is just important to know it is a problem that has troubled many statisticians over the years. In fact, one of the main reasons Fisher developed the ANOVA procedure was to have a means of controlling familywise error rate. I discuss other methods of controlling familywise error in Chapter 3.

TEST ASSUMPTIONS

One final topic having to do with the mechanics of significance testing warrants review: the issue of assumptions. The binomial distributions created in Chapter 1 were accurate only if coin flips were randomly and independently sampled. This seemed to be a pretty reasonable condition to accept because any coin flip is a random draw from the population, and coins rarely share their results with each other.

The *t* distribution when used with a single mean involved an additional condition: that the population was normally distributed. Gosset used this as a simplifying condition because if the population is known to be normally distributed, then the shape of the *t* distribution is determined solely by the degrees of freedom.

In the context of significance testing, these *conditions used for purposes of deriving the sampling distribution, and from that the critical value,* are referred to as **test assumptions**. The random and independent sampling assumption is probably the most common assumption in statistical tests based on sampling distributions. The normality assumption also is common. Other statistical procedures involve even more complicated assumptions.

The **normality assumption** is an example of *an assumption that refers to some characteristic of the population distribution.* Tests that require such assumptions are often referred to as **parametric tests**. In contrast, a significance test based on the binomial distribution would be an example of a **nonparametric test** because it does not require any assumptions about the population distribution shape. To be more precise, a nonparametric test is simply one in which parametric assumptions were not required to derive the sampling distribution underlying the test and the appropriate critical value. It is possible for aspects of the population distribution to affect the results in some other way, such as through the power of the test (which I discuss in Chapter 3, this volume), but the critical value is still accurate if the assumptions are accurate.

How reasonable are these assumptions, and how much do they matter? Consider the normality assumption. The assumption that most populations are normally distributed has become widely known and has even influenced discussions of social issues (e.g., Herrnstein & Murray, 1994; Taleb, 2007). However, the proposition that population values themselves stem from random events is itself a hypothesis that can be tested via large-scale sampling. Micceri (1989) identified 440 cases in which a very large sample of a population was available. Contrary to the common assumption, he did not find a single instance in which the population was normally distributed. Micceri compared the normal distribution with the unicorn, a phenomenon in which people once widely believed despite the complete absence of evidence that it actually exists.

If the assumptions of the test are not met, then you cannot be sure that the critical values found in textbook tables are accurate. For example, it is known that when the population is normally distributed and the null hypothesis is true, with 10 degrees of freedom a t value of 1.812 cuts off the top 5% of outcomes, and so 1.812 is the one-tailed critical value for 10 degrees of freedom and a .05 level of significance. When the population is not normally distributed, does 1.812 instead cut off the top 1% or 15% instead? There is no way to know the answer to this question unless one knows the degree to which the population is nonnormal.

Possible Solutions

Several solutions have been offered for this problem (for a review, see Erceg-Hurn & Mirosevich, 2008). To give this topic its due, I need to discuss some of these options in detail.

Meet the Robustness Conditions of Parametric Tests

The term **robustness conditions** can be used to refer to *the conditions under which a parametric assumption can be violated and still produce an accurate decision.* For example, I noted earlier that many sampling distributions, including the t distribution, are asymptotically normal: When the samples comprising the sampling distribution are large enough, the sampling distribution is still normally distributed even if the population distribution is not normal. This implies that if the sample size is large enough, then the results will be the same whether the population is normally distributed or not; that is, with a large enough sample, the t test is considered robust against violation of the normality assumption and the assumption can be ignored.

Statistics texts tend to recommend meeting robustness conditions as the solution to violations of assumptions. Unfortunately, there is good reason to believe that the robustness of parametric tests has been exaggerated. For example, a study published by Sawilowsky and Blair (1992) has been used to justify treating tests as robust to violations of the normality assumption in two instances: when (a) each group in the study consists of at least 25 to 30 people and (b) a two-tailed test is used.

However, others have noted that the conditions under which that conclusion holds are very unlikely. Looking at more extreme violations of assumptions, Bradley (1980) was far less sanguine, suggesting that samples of 500 to 1,000 were necessary before researchers may expect common tests to be robust to violations of parametric assumptions.

Transform the Data

Another option involves transforming data. For example, in some cases taking the logarithmic values of each score will generate data that look more normally distributed than the original data. These transformations complicate the interpretation of the findings in ways that many find undesirable, however, and they are not even particularly effective for purposes of correcting violations of assumptions. I am not a big fan of this option, and these methods seem to have waned in popularity.

Eliminate Extreme Scores

Extreme scores have a particularly strong influence on the results of parametric tests. For example, if all but one score on a questionnaire fall between 0 and 23, but one individual produced a score of 47, that single score substantially shifts statistics such as the mean and standard deviation that are sensitive to the exact location of every score in the distribution. If the score of 47 were eliminated from the sample the data would be less skewed and, assuming extreme scores are always eliminated, those statistics would be more reliable across samples.

Earlier discussions of this option recommended reviewing each variable and eliminating any **outliers**, *cases that are markedly discrepant from the rest of the data*. For example, if all the scores on a questionnaire vary between 0 and 12, but one score is 36, the researcher may choose to eliminate that score. The detection of individual outliers requires reviewing the distribution for each variable in the sample and deciding which values should be considered for elimination. Various criteria have been offered for detecting outliers, but none has emerged as a standard.

A more standardized option is offered by **trimming**, or winsorizing. Trimming involves *removing a preset percentage of the scores from each end of the distribution*. For example, suppose a data set consists of the following 10 values listed in size order:

1, 2, 5, 17, 26, 32, 45, 48, 52, 57.

Twenty percent trimming would remove the bottom 20% of scores (the lowest two scores) and the top 20% (the top two scores). In the present example, the resulting data set would look like this:

5, 17, 26, 32, 45, 48.

For reasons that will become clearer in Chapter 3, reducing the sample size can have undesirable consequences unless the sample is quite large to begin with. Another option is **winsorizing**, which *replaces trimmed scores with the most extreme scores left in the distribution.* In the present example the 20% winsorized data set would be:

5, 5, 5, 17, 26, 32, 45, 48, 48, 48.

The sample size remains the same; extreme scores shrink but are not removed.

A tool commonly used in the process of trimming and winsorizing is the box-and-whisker plot, an example of which may be found in Figure 2.6. This graph presents results for annual family income in a sample of 80 families. The box is the two squares, and the whiskers are the vertical lines that extend above and below the box. Each horizontal line in the plot is meaningful. In this example, the line that separates the two squares is set at the median (50th percentile, or second quartile).

FIGURE 2.6

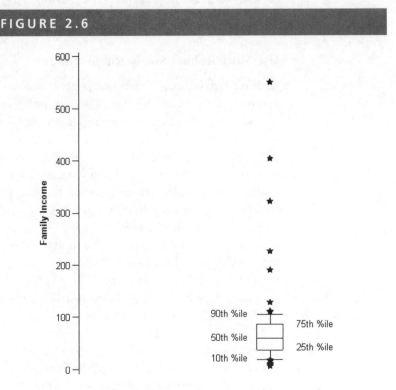

This box-and-whisker plot presents annual income data for 80 families, in thousands of dollars (e.g., 100 means $100,000 per year). Stars represent the bottom and top 10% of outcomes.

The top of the box indicates the 75th percentile value (the value that separates the bottom 75% from the top 25%), also called the third quartile. The bottom of the box is set at the 25th percentile value or first quartile (the value that separates the bottom 25% of incomes from the top 75%). The lowest and highest lines are set at the 10th and 90th percentile values, respectively. Scores outside that range are marked with stars; removing those scores would represent 10% trimming.

Reducing the effect of extreme scores should produce sample statistics that demonstrate less variability across samples, which is a valuable service, but if the parametric assumption is incorrect it does not necessarily address that problem. Also, many researchers are troubled by the idea of rejecting good data. In the case of the family incomes presented in Figure 2.1, for example, the outlying values represent an accurate representation of skew in the actual distribution of the variable in the population. Also, it is important to know there are special formulas for some statistics when using trimmed or winsorized data. Despite these caveats, eliminating outliers is an increasingly popular approach to dealing with possible violations of parametric assumptions.

Use More Robust Statistical Methods

Robust statistics are *statistical methods that are relatively insensitive to parametric assumptions.* By the 1950s, a number of significance tests had been developed that did not require parametric assumptions (Siegel, 1956). However, these early nonparametric alternatives often did not test the same question. Whereas a parametric test such as *t* might test whether two population means differ, the nonparametric alternative might instead evaluate whether the two population medians differ. This is a different question that can lead to different answers. Also, because the median uses less sample information than the mean (the mean is sensitive to the exact location of every score in the sample, whereas the median is not), some researchers thought that analyses based on medians ignored meaningful information in the sample. Finally, over time it became evident that the shape of the population distribution could still influence the results of these nonparametric alternatives.

In recent years, ready access to computers has made it possible to develop computationally intensive but truly robust nonparametric alternatives. A particularly important option uses a computational method called **bootstrapping** (Efron & Tibshirani, 1986), which involves *generating a large number of bootstrapped samples of equal size by randomly sampling with replacement from a target sample.* In our sample of 10 cases, a bootstrapped sample can be generated by randomly sampling from the original sample with replacement. The concept of replacement is important here: Subject 3's score can be drawn several times for one bootstrapped sample, not at all for another. From the original sample,

1, 2, 5, 17, 26, 32, 45, 48, 52, 57,

here are three bootstrapped samples that might be generated:

52, 2, 52, 32, 48, 5, 5, 5, 2, 32
32, 32, 52, 17, 32, 5, 52, 57, 17, 57
57, 1, 1, 52, 1, 52, 1, 48, 26, 45.

Because the bootstrapped samples are created by sampling from the target sample, only values in the original sample will appear in the bootstrapped samples, and values that appear more frequently in the target sample will also tend to appear more frequently in the bootstrapped samples (e.g., if the value 7 appears 20 times in the original sample and a value of 12 appears only once, then 7 will appear more often in the bootstrapped samples than 12 does). A computer can generate thousands of bootstrapped samples of equal size and then compute the sample statistic of interest (e.g., the mean or t) for each sample. These sample statistics are then used to generate a sampling distribution with which the statistic from the original sample can be compared. If the original sample value for the statistic is unusual enough across the distribution created from the bootstrapped samples, the researcher concludes it is significant just as with the standard t distribution. It may seem an odd approach, but research demonstrates that the results can be quite accurate. Although bootstrapping offers a particularly valuable alternative to parametric tests, especially now that computers can handle the grunt work, it unfortunately remains an uncommon choice solely because most psychologists are unfamiliar with the methodology.

Assume the Population is a Hypothetical Entity

One final way of addressing the problem of parametric assumptions has to do with the conceptual understanding of significance tests. In psychology, participants are rarely if ever randomly and independently sampled from the population that really interests the researcher. Furthermore, there are no robustness conditions under which it is acceptable to violate the random and independent sampling assumption. This is a pretty odd state of affairs, in which most studies use significance tests yet every study violates the most basic assumption underlying the use of those tests. Fisher (1955) offered a clever solution to this problem. He suggested treating the population from which the sample is randomly and independently sampled as a fiction created simply for the purposes of conducting the test itself. There was some discussion in Chapter 1 suggesting that the population may be hypothetical. Fisher was suggesting something more radical, that the population is *usually* hypothetical. Even in this fictional landscape, whether or not you are able to reject the null hypothesis is thought to provide interesting information about whether the effect is large enough to consider it reliable (Frick, 1998; Gold, 1969).

Because most researchers ignore the issue of assumptions completely, in practice it is this last option that tends to represent the status quo. The reader may feel justified at this point asking, "So all of significance testing may be based on a lie?" In response to this I can only refer you back to the discussion in the Introduction on the potential value of invented models. It would seem to me fair to characterize Fisher's significance testing model as having been historically useful but clearly invented. In the coming chapters I consider whether there are better alternatives available.

The Good, the Bad, and the Alternative

The previous paragraph may lead you to wonder why it was that anyone thought significance testing was such a good idea in the first place. To appreciate why significance testing became so popular in psychology, and in the social sciences in general, it is important to understand some of the method's positive attributes. Before the advent of significance testing there was no set standard for dealing with sampling error. Early experimental research relied on large numbers of replications before publication, a method of control that was popular in the physical sciences as well. This approach became less practical as research dealt with more complex issues such as personality structure, educational interventions, and social processes.

Significance testing offered a general framework for reducing the impact of sampling error, and it had two important positive features. First, if you look back at the description of significance testing you will notice sample size is barely mentioned. It is true that for some significance tests, such as t, the critical value changes as the sample size changes (although for other significance tests, e.g., chi-square, the critical value is often unrelated to sample size). It is also true that as the sample size increases, the results become more reliable, a characteristic of significance tests Fisher (1925) acknowledged. However, neither of these factors affects a researcher's ability to use the test. In terms of the mechanics of significance testing, it is possible to establish the desired level of significance no matter how small the sample is. The significance testing model described by Fisher allows researchers to draw conclusions about populations with some control over sampling error even with only a handful of observations.

Second, significance testing allowed the researcher to draw a con-clusion about the truth or falsehood of the null hypothesis on the basis of a single analysis, without needing to replicate the findings. Given these two useful features it is not surprising to find that, beginning in the 1940s, and increasingly during the 1950s and 1960s (Gigerenzer & Murray, 1987), significance testing became the dominant inferential strategy in psychology, education, medicine, and most sciences that reg-ularly struggled with small sample sizes (Brenner-Golomb, 1993).

To appreciate what happened next in the development of inferential methods, though, it is important to understand one of the most serious flaws of significance testing: its odd asymmetry. If the null hypothesis is rejected, this finding presumably supports the conclusion that the null hypothesis is false and that an effect does exist in the population. If the null hypothesis is retained, the meaning of the finding is unclear. It is not considered sufficient evidence for concluding the null hypothesis is true; other factors could explain the failure to achieve significance. It is for this reason that *retaining the null* is more accurate terminology than *accepting the null* in the context of significance testing, although Fisher did equivocate at times on the implications of nonsignificance (Gigerenzer, 1993).

This asymmetry did not seem to concern Fisher much because he correctly recognized that researchers are usually more interested in concluding that the null hypothesis is false than concluding it is true. Jerzy Neyman and Egon Pearson, two contemporaries of Fisher's, were quite concerned by this asymmetry. They suggested a revision of signif-icance testing that attempts to provide clear evidence either that the null hypothesis is true or false (Neyman & Pearson, 1933). In doing so, they evoked Fisher's ire but also initiated an important change in psychologists' preferred model of inference.

Conclusion

Fisher offered a formal logical model of inferential decision making based on sampling distributions, a model that has come to be known as *significance testing*. Significance testing involved six steps: (a) identifying a question about a population; (b) identifying the corresponding null (no-effect) state; (c) converting this null state into a statement about the value of a parameter, which has come to be called the *null hypothesis;* (d) computing some sample statistic related to the parameter; (e) deter-mining the probability of the sample value for that statistic if the null hypothesis were true; and (f) making a decision about whether or not to reject the null hypothesis given the probability of the sample outcome.

Other components of the model include the distinction between directional and nondirectional significance tests, defining the critical region and critical value, and dealing with multiple comparisons and test assumptions.

Fisher rejected the concept of a strict dividing line between a significant and nonsignificant result. Even so, he suggested multiple times that a sample outcome occurring in less than 5% of samples if the null hypothesis were true is sufficiently unlikely that it would justify rejecting the null hypothesis. From this informal guideline .05 emerged as the standard level of significance that allows rejection of the null hypothesis.

That significance testing permitted the researcher to conduct a test of a hypothesis about the population regardless of the sample size was initially seen as a tremendous boon to psychological research. Research with humans has always been and will always be afflicted by the shortage of data points, and Fisher seemed to offer a means of avoiding the problem.

However, Jerzy Neyman and Egon Pearson (1933) quickly recognized Fisher's emphasis on rejecting the null as asymmetrical, in essence ignoring the implications of failing to reject or retaining the null hypothesis. Their efforts to address this imbalance ultimately set the stage for a revised inferential model for testing null hypotheses.

Null Hypothesis Significance Testing 3

N eyman and Pearson's (1933) efforts to address the basic asymmetry in significance testing led them to develop an alternate mode that has come to be called *hypothesis testing*, in contrast to Fisher's significance testing. Although Fisher (1955) was quite negative about their work, for reasons I discuss later, the two approaches share a number of similarities (Lehmann, 1993). For the sake of expediency, instead of describing hypothesis testing independently of significance testing I will jump ahead and discuss the inferential strategy that subsequently emerged incorporating elements of both approaches, often called *null hypothesis significance testing* (NHST). Whether NHST is a reasonable compromise or a patchwork mess is a topic of much debate, as I discuss in Chapter 4. Whatever one's opinion, this inferential model is the one most commonly discussed in statistics texts today.

The Decision Matrix

Remember that Fisher's significance testing is all about the null hypothesis. The researcher acts as if the null hypothesis is true in order to determine the probability of a sample outcome under that assumption. Neyman and Pearson (1933) introduced the concept of the **alternative hypothesis**, *a mathematical statement that complements the null hypothesis.* So, if the null hypothesis suggests two population means are equal,

$$\mu = 100,$$

the alternative hypothesis would suggest they are not,

$$\mu \neq 100.$$

Similarly, the directional null hypothesis $\mu \leq 100$ implies the alternative hypothesis $\mu > 100$, and the directional null hypothesis $\mu \geq 100$ suggests the alternative hypothesis $\mu < 100$. Notice that the alternative hypothesis does not contain an equals sign; no specific value is implied for μ.

NHST also involves deciding whether or not to reject the null hypothesis; however, it builds on significance testing by requiring that the researcher consider the implications for the analysis if the null hypothesis is true *and* the implications if the alternative hypothesis is true. Where significance testing is purely a test of the viability of the null hypothesis, NHST is more of a horse race between two competing statistical hypotheses. In considering the implications of assuming both hypotheses to be true, Neyman and Pearson (1933) developed a method that both built on Fisher's work and differed from it markedly.

For Fisher, there were two possible outcomes of a significance test: (a) reject the null hypothesis or (b) retain the null hypothesis. Neyman and Pearson (1933) noted that there are actually four possible outcomes of a decision to reject or retain the null hypothesis. These are illustrated in Figure 3.1. The thick line running down the middle of the exhibit is

FIGURE 3.1

		Fact	
		Null hypothesis (H_0) is true	Alternative hypothesis (H_1) is true
Statistical decision	Reject	Incorrect rejection (Type I error) $p(incorrect\ rejection) = \alpha$	Correct rejection $p(correct\ rejection) = 1 - \beta$ (power)
	Retain	Correct retention $p(correct\ retention) = 1 - \alpha$	Incorrect retention (Type II error) $p(incorrect\ retention) = \beta$

Four possible outcomes of a decision to reject or retain the null hypothesis.

important because it indicates that in any analysis only the left-hand "Fact" column or the right-hand "Fact" column applies; that is, either the null hypothesis or the alternative hypothesis is factually true, because they are complementary hypotheses. In any analysis only the outcomes in the first column can occur, or only the outcomes in the second column can occur. Unfortunately, because you do not know which column applies to your analysis—if you knew whether or not the null hypothesis is true, why do the study?—Neyman and Pearson considered it important to plan for all four possible outcomes.

If the null hypothesis is true, then there are two possible outcomes for the study:

1. The researcher rejects the null hypothesis. This decision represents *an incorrect rejection of the null hypothesis,* which Neyman and Pearson (1933) labeled a **Type I error**. Ideally, one would never want a Type I error to occur, but to avoid Type I errors completely would require never rejecting the null hypothesis, a decision unlikely to advance science very much. The researcher must therefore set an acceptable probability of a Type I error, which Neyman and Pearson symbolized using the Greek lowercase letter alpha (α). This is the same quantity Fisher referred to as the *level of significance.*

2. The researcher retains the null hypothesis. This decision represents *a correct retention of the null hypothesis* (no special name for this one). If the null hypothesis is true and the probability of a Type I error is set at α, then the probability of a correct retention is $1 - \alpha$.

If these are only two of the four possible outcomes, why is it that the probabilities you allow for these two outcomes equal 1.0? This occurs because these are **conditional probabilities**, *probabilities of some event given another event has occurred.* If the null hypothesis is true (the first event), there are only two possible outcomes: (a) incorrect rejection or (b) correct retention. If the null hypothesis is false, then the two outcomes described so far cannot occur, and the quantities α and $1 - \alpha$ are meaningless.

If the alternative hypothesis is true, the two possible outcomes are as follows:

1. The researcher retains the null hypothesis. This decision represents *an incorrect retention of the null hypothesis,* more commonly referred to as a **Type II error**. Ideally, one would never want a Type II error to occur, but the only way to avoid Type II errors completely would require never retaining the null hypothesis. The researcher must therefore set an acceptable probability of a Type II error, which Neyman and Pearson (1933) symbolized with the Greek lowercase letter beta (β).

2. The researcher rejects the null hypothesis. This decision represents *a correct rejection of the null hypothesis.* If the alternative hypothesis is true and the probability of a Type II error is set at β, then the probability of a correct rejection is $1 - \beta$. *The probability of a correct rejection or Type II error* is also referred to as the **power** of the analysis.

If the alternative hypothesis is false, then these two outcomes cannot occur, and the quantities β and $1 - \beta$ are meaningless.

The concepts just introduced can seem confusing, but you probably are already familiar with a very similar system of logic. The set of outcomes described by Neyman and Pearson (1933) is much like the set of outcomes that occur within the English–American criminal justice system:

1. The defendant is either guilty or innocent. These are considered complementary factual possibilities: Either one or the other is true.
2. At first, the defendant is assumed to be innocent. This is similar to the assumption that the null hypothesis is true.
3. The jury must make a decision to reject or retain this assumption of innocence. In the criminal justice system the decision to reject the assumption of innocence is referred to as *conviction,* the decision to retain the assumption as *acquittal.* Regular viewers of legal dramas on television know that conviction is not the same thing as guilt and acquittal is not the same thing as innocence. Guilt and innocence are real-world factual states. Conviction and acquittal are decisions made by members of a jury about whether or not they have sufficient evidence to justify rejecting the assumption of innocence.
4. In theory, the jury can reject this assumption only if the case for guilt has been made beyond a reasonable doubt. The criterion of reasonable doubt parallels the requirement that the null hypothesis is rejected only if the sample outcome is unlikely if the null hypothesis is true.

This last characteristic is an extremely important one in that it biases the system toward acquittal. A system that assumes guilt, such as that in France, instead biases the system toward conviction. A system that makes no preliminary assumption presumably lies somewhere in between. The American civil court system, for example, theoretically treats guilt and innocence of the defendant as equally likely. It is for this reason that a person may be acquitted of a crime in criminal court but then be found liable for damages resulting from that crime in civil court.

Any criminal trial can therefore result in one of four outcomes, as depicted in Figure 3.2. The thick line running down the middle of the

FIGURE 3.2

Fact

		Defendant is innocent	Defendant is guilty
	Convict	Incorrect rejection (Type I error)	Correct rejection
Jury decision			
	Acquit	Correct retention	Incorrect retention (Type II error)

Four potential outcomes of a criminal trial.

exhibit indicates that, in fact, either the defendant is innocent or the defendant is guilty. Unfortunately, because the guilt or innocence of the defendant is unknown, all four possibilities must be considered.

Convicting an innocent defendant is like an incorrect rejection of a true null hypothesis, or a Type I error. Acquittal of an innocent defendant represents a correct retention of the null hypothesis of innocence. Acquitting a guilty defendant is like an incorrect retention of a false null hypothesis, a Type II error. Conviction of a guilty defendant represents a correct rejection of the assumption of innocence.

Controlling the Outcomes

One of the weaknesses of the English–American criminal justice system is the ambiguity of the term *reasonable doubt*. Different juries may come to different decisions based on exactly the same evidence because they disagree on whether their doubts can be considered reasonable. NHST has an important advantage over the criminal justice system in that it attempts to set an objective criterion for a decision.

Fisher introduced the method used to control α and $1 - \alpha$, although he did not use those symbols. They are controlled by adjusting the critical value as necessary to achieve the desired level of significance. If the acceptable probability of a Type I error is .05, and if the researcher chooses a .05 level of significance, then the null hypothesis is rejected only if the sample *t* value falls within the .05 critical region. This is the meaning of the ubiquitous "$p < .05$": The probability of the sample outcome is less than the alpha level, which in this case is .05.

Now let us assume the alternative hypothesis is true rather than the null hypothesis. The goal becomes minimizing the probability of a Type II error and maximizing the power of the analysis. How does the researcher control the power of the study? This is a more complicated issue than controlling the probability of a Type I error.

It should make some sense that any factor that increases the probability of rejecting the null hypothesis also increases power. Most textbooks suggest there are three such factors: (a) the alpha level, (b) the effect size, and (c) the sample size.[1]

AS THE ALPHA LEVEL INCREASES, POWER INCREASES

If alpha is set at .05 and there are 60 degrees of freedom, the critical value for the *t* test of a nondirectional null hypothesis is ± 2.00. If alpha is instead set to .10, the critical value changes to ±1.658, an easier standard to meet. This would increase the probability of rejecting the null hypothesis, and if the alternative hypothesis is true then the power of the study is increased. However, this strategy for increasing power is risky. If the null hypothesis is true rather than the alternative hypothesis, then increasing the alpha level instead increases the probability of a Type I error. Because increasing the alpha level has undesirable consequences if the null hypothesis is true, this is not commonly used as a method for increasing power.

AS THE EFFECT SIZE INCREASES, POWER INCREASES

The term *effect size* is a new one, and it will soon prove to be an extremely important one, so I discuss it in some detail. Because this section is lengthy, I start by outlining the three key topics to be addressed here: (a) the definition of effect size, (b) the definition of an effect size statistic, and (c) the problems involved in using the effect size to control power.

Consider the coin-flipping studies I described in Chapter 1. Suppose you believe a coin has been fixed, so the probability of a head is not .50 but something higher. Your hypothesis is easier to support if the coin is fixed so the probability of a head is 1.0 (so that every coin flip results in a head) than if it is fixed to a probability of .60 (so it produces a head 60% of the time).

---

[1]Note that for certain analyses power can be affected by other factors, including the relative size of subgroups and restriction of the range of scores (Aguinis, 1995; McGrath & Meyer, 2006). However, this point is not really central to the current discussion.

This example provides an intuitive introduction to the concept of effect size. In Chapter 2, I described significance testing as a logical model for evaluating whether an effect exists. Once the issue of power is considered, however, it turns out that the probability of finding evidence that an effect exists depends in part on how large the effect is, or how far the true parameter differs from the null hypothesis value for the parameter. So, an **effect size** refers to *the size or strength of an effect.*[2] In the context of NHST, if the null hypothesis is true then there is no effect or relationship. The larger the effect or relationship, the greater the difference from the null state and the easier it will be to reject the null hypothesis. In turn, the easier it is to reject the null hypothesis, the greater the power of the study.

The simple example study in which American adults are administered an intelligence test after receiving a nutritional supplement treatment can be used to present the concept a little more formally. Significance testing only deals with what happens when the null hypothesis is assumed to be true, in which case the mean for the population would be 100. Now it is time to consider what happens when the alternative hypothesis is assumed to be true. If it is true, then the population mean must be some value other than 100 and the *t* distribution is noncentral.

Consider two possibilities that are consistent with the alternative hypothesis being true. In one case, the nutritional supplement on average increases intelligence test scores by only 1 point, so the true mean for the population that receives the treatment is 101. In the other case, the nutritional supplement on average increases test scores by 10 points, so the population mean is 110. For the moment, we are dealing with three possibilities: (a) the null hypothesis is true and $\mu = 100$, (b) the alternative hypothesis is true and $\mu = 101$, and (c) the alternative hypothesis is true and $\mu = 110$. Figure 3.3 depicts sampling distributions of the mean for each of these scenarios.

The critical value is set on the basis of the null hypothesis sampling distribution. If we want to conduct a one-tailed test (which we will do in this case to simplify matters) with $\alpha = .05$, the critical value is the value that separates the top 5% of sample means that would occur if the null hypothesis were true. This value turns out to be 103.29, so a sample mean of 103.29 or greater will allow us to reject the null hypothesis. Now imagine the alternative hypothesis is true, but the population mean is only 101. Because the alternative hypothesis is true, the concepts of Type I error and correct retention are no longer meaningful, and what matters are the Type II error and correct rejection rates.

---

[2]I should warn the reader that in some early literature on estimating the size of effects, a statistic to be discussed shortly as *d* was called the *effect size.* Just to confuse things, the term is still occasionally used in this way.

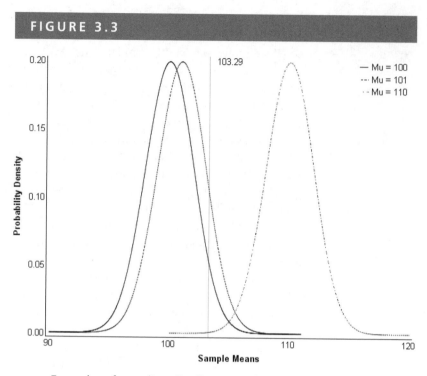

FIGURE 3.3

Examples of sampling distributions of the mean that would result for μ = 100, 101, and 110 and standard error = 2.0 (values chosen for convenience). Based on Fisher's significance testing, the critical value is set based on the sampling distribution for the null hypothesis μ = 100. The critical value is 103.29, the value that cuts off the top 5% of the null hypothesis sampling distribution (using a one-tailed test to simplify matters). In other words, if the alternative hypothesis is true, the significance test will only produce a correct decision (reject the null hypothesis) if the sample mean is at least 103.29. If μ = 101, most sample means (87%) are actually less than 103.29, so the majority of samples will result in a Type II error. If μ = 110, however, most samples (> 99%) will result in rejection of the null hypothesis.

Figure 3.3 indicates that if the effect of the treatment increases intelligence test scores on average by 1 point, only 13% of sample means will equal 103.29 or greater. Using Neyman and Pearson's (1933) terminology, the power of this study is only .13, whereas the probability of a Type II error is .87. Stated another way, if the alternative hypothesis is true but the true μ is 101, the null hypothesis will be incorrectly retained in 87% of samples. This is pretty poor odds of uncovering the truth.

Alternatively, if the nutritional supplement treatment on average increases intelligence test scores by 10 points so that the population mean is 110, almost every sample mean exceeds the critical value of 103.29. The power of the study is quite high, exceeding .99, and the Type II error rate is only .01: Ninety-nine percent of samples will result in correctly rejecting the null hypothesis. A larger effect size means greater power, all other factors being equal.[3]

An **effect size statistic** is *a descriptive statistic or parameter that reflects the size or strength of an effect;* that is, any descriptive statistic intended to indicate the size of an effect, or distance from the null hypothesis value, may be used as an effect size statistic. It may not be surprising to find that effect size statistics are often scaled to equal 0 when there is no effect or relationship, that is, when the null hypothesis is true. Looking back at Figure 3.1, a useful effect size parameter would equal 0 if the null hypothesis is true, some value less than 0 if the true value for μ is < 100, some value greater than 0 if the true value for μ is 101, and some even greater positive value if $\mu = 110$.

This relationship between the null hypothesis value and the effect size statistic has led some authors (e.g., Rosenthal, Rosnow, & Rubin, 2000) to define effect sizes specifically in terms of their role in hypothesis testing; however, effect sizes are increasingly recognized as important pieces of information in their own right, as one factor in understanding the practical or theoretical importance of a finding. Accordingly, the American Psychological Association's (2010) publication policy indicates that all studies should provide effect size statistics, and many journals now require the reporting of effect sizes for key analyses regardless of whether NHST is used.

One might suggest that something as simple as the difference between the null hypothesis mean and the true value for μ would make a useful effect size parameter, and there are circumstances in which the difference between two means can be a useful effect size statistic (C. F. Bond, Wiitala, & Richard, 2003). However, look at Figure 3.4. This figure consists of two curves, one based on the null hypothesis that $\mu = 100$ and one based on $\mu = 110$. In this case, the sampling distributions of the mean demonstrate more variability than in Figure 3.3: They spread out more from the central point of the distribution. In fact, the standard errors for the

---

[3]The concept of effect size also helped me understand something that was confusing to me for years, which is why in the case of a directional null hypothesis, such as $\mu \leq 50$, the null hypothesis sampling distribution was based on the value $\mu = 50$ and all the other null hypothesis possibilities (e.g., $\mu = 36$, $\mu = 29$) were ignored. Because 50 represents the dividing line between the null and alternative hypotheses being true, if the result is significant assuming $\mu = 50$, then a significance test based on $\mu = 36$, $\mu = 29$ or any other null hypothesis value would be associated with an even larger effect size and therefore would be even more powerful. The test of $\mu = 50$ represents the toughest test of the null hypothesis.

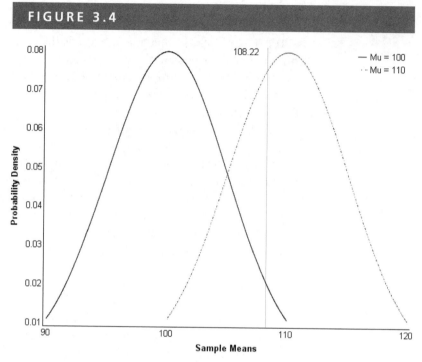

FIGURE 3.4

This figure differs from Figure 3.1 in two important ways. First, the curve based on μ = 101 is eliminated to simplify the presentation. Second, the remaining curves show more variability than in the previous figure. The critical value has increased to 108.22. The sampling distribution on the right is based on a population mean of 110, but now only 64% if samples will allow rejection of the null hypothesis.

sampling distributions in Figure 3.4 are 2.5 times those used for the sampling distributions in Figure 3.3. As a result, the critical value for setting the probability of a Type I error increases to 108.22. Even if the true μ is 110, the probability of rejecting the null hypothesis is only .64 rather than the .99 reported for Figure 3.1. In other words, increased variability in the sampling distributions reduces the power of the study.

The role of variability in NHST is explicit in some significance test formulas. For example, consider the formula for t provided in the following equation:

$$t_{\bar{Y}} = \frac{\bar{Y} - \mu}{\sqrt{\dfrac{\sum\limits_{i=1}^{N}(Y_i - \bar{Y})^2}{N(N-1)}}}. \tag{3.1}$$

The denominator is based on differences between each score and the mean. The more variability there is in the scores, the larger these differences are, the smaller t will be, and the harder it will be to reject the null hypothesis. In contrast, less variability in the scores increases the value of t and therefore increases the power of the study.

In recognition of the role variability plays in establishing the power of the study, most popular effect size statistics take variability into consideration in some way. For example, many studies involve comparing two groups at a time, such as a treatment and a control group. The independent-groups t test provides a reasonable significance test for such comparisons. The most popular effect size statistic in such studies is probably the standardized mean difference (Cohen, 1988; symbols based on McGrath & Meyer, 2006). At the level of the population, the appropriate formula for the standardized mean difference is

$$\delta = \frac{\mu_1 - \mu_2}{\sigma},$$ (3.2)

which divides the difference between the population means by the standard deviation of either population, which are assumed to be equal (when *population variances—and therefore standard deviations—are assumed to be equal*, this assumption is referred to as **homoscedasticity**). The lowercase Greek letter delta (δ) can be estimated in the sample by

$$d = \frac{\bar{Y}_1 - \bar{Y}_2}{\hat{\sigma}}.$$ (3.3)

For example, a d value of .50 means the difference between the means is one half of the corresponding standard deviation.[4] Thus, d can be referred to as a **metric-neutral effect size statistic**, in that *the effect size is scaled in units that are considered comparable across measurement devices.*[5] Because it is metric neutral it makes no difference whether the original dimensional variable was measured in feet, or meters, or points on a questionnaire: The results are converted to what seems to be a common scale, in this case standard deviation units. The concept of "metric neutral" is not specific to effect size statistics. Many of the important statistics in psychology, including most significance tests, are metric neutral. One way to tell whether

---

[4]Several formulas are available for computing standardized mean differences. One variant is appropriate for comparing pretest and posttest means; another can be used when one group represents a control condition. I have seen too many studies in which the incorrect formula for d is used; make sure you know what you are doing before using this statistic!

[5]This characteristic of d has also been referred to as *metric free* or *standardized*, but the term suggested here is technically more accurate.

a statistic is metric neutral (although this is not a perfect indicator) is that the no-effect value is always the same. In the case of z, t, d, the log odds ratio, and r, for example, the no-effect value is always 0, whereas for the F statistic and the odds ratio 1.0 represents the no-effect value.

As the previous example indicates, it is possible to discuss effect size as a characteristic of a population or a sample descriptive statistic. This section began with the statement that power increases as effect size increases. It is important to realize that this statement refers to the *population* effect size. In the case of the standardized mean difference, larger differences in the population μs or smaller population σs mean greater power for the analysis.

There are some things you can do that can affect the population effect size. The less variability there is in the populations from which participants are drawn, the larger δ will be. For example, research on cognitive functioning is sometimes limited to right-handed individuals, because people who are left-handed introduce greater variability, and historically, many medications have been tested first on males to avoid the variations that result from women's menstrual cycles. The latter strategy can have serious drawbacks in terms of generalizing the results. It can also raise ethical questions if medications are not tested sufficiently on females before they are distributed to the public.

You can also draw from populations that maximize differences between the population means. For example, consider a drug trial in which a new antidepressant is to be compared with a placebo. On the basis of preliminary research, the minimally effective dosage is believed to be 10 mg, and 30 mg is believed to be the maximum dosage that will be fully metabolized. A researcher interested in demonstrating that this drug is more effective than a placebo would be wise to use a dosage of 30 mg instead of 10 mg because the drug's effect is likely to be greater when 30 mg is given rather than 10 mg.

Unfortunately, a researcher's ability to maximize differences between population means and minimize population variability is quite limited. As a parameter, the population effect size is essentially a fixed quantity. Furthermore, the true population effect size is rarely known, and the power of the study cannot be precisely determined unless the effect size can be estimated. The problems involved in estimating power proved to be a serious obstacle to the adoption of NHST over significance testing for many years. Before I turn to the issue of estimating population effect sizes, however, I must review the role of sample size in power.

AS SAMPLE SIZE INCREASES, POWER INCREASES

I began the section on effect size by suggesting that it is easier to identify a fixed coin when it is set to produce heads 100% of the time than when it is set to produce heads 60% of the time. Similarly, it is more effective to demonstrate that a coin is fixed by flipping it 500 times than by flipping it twice; that is, as sample size increases, power increases.

This principle can again be demonstrated using the formula for t in Equation 3.1. As $N(N-1)$ increases, the value of t increases. The larger the value of t, the easier it will be to reject the null hypothesis.

What we have learned so far is that (assuming the alternative hypothesis is true) power increases as alpha increases, the effect size increases, and the sample size increases. Increasing alpha has the drawback that it increases the probability of a Type I error if the null hypothesis is true while the researcher has limited control over the population effect size. Using larger samples is therefore seen as the best way to achieve control over Type II errors while not giving up control over Type I errors.

The Good, the Bad, and the Alternative

The failure to teach psychologists that there are two competing and partly incompatible models of inference operating in psychology has caused a great deal of confusion and bad research practice. To help clarify this matter, at this point I offer a brief summary of the differences between the two:

- The emphasis on the null hypothesis over the alternative hypothesis is a residual influence of significance testing.
- Significance testing implies that sample size is not an important consideration in research. It has been suggested that this implication in part explains the success of significance testing. NHST, in contrast, suggests that setting the sample size is as important as choosing the level of significance.
- Although the idea can be traced to Fisher, only NHST mandates choosing an exact p value for rejecting the null hypothesis. Setting α to .05 or .01 is attractive because it reduces the decision to significant–not significant. In contrast, Fisher's later recommendation to report the exact p value leaves the conclusion of the test more ambiguous.
- Remember the distinction I made in the Introduction between invented and realistic models. Significance testing and NHST are invented models of inference, with the purpose of testing whether a certain model of reality is justified. Significance testing evaluates

whether a single model of reality, that no effect exists in the population, is justified by the data. NHST instead compares two models of reality and evaluates which is better supported by the data. On the other hand, significance testing and NHST can both be distinguished from other models of inference in that they focus on a dichotomous either–or decision rather than an estimate of parameters. Both the distinction between methods that evaluate goodness of fit for a single model and relative fit of multiple models, and the distinction between dichotomous decisions and parameter estimates, appear multiple times in this book.

▪ If the researcher retains one or more null hypotheses and does not consider power as a possible cause of that outcome, then the researcher is using significance testing rather than NHST. The failure to consider power as the cause of nonsignificant results remains common in psychological research articles, for reasons that should become clearer in Chapter 4.

There are notable advantages to NHST in theory. It offers a more symmetrical model for testing hypotheses. In significance testing the researcher either rejects or retains the null hypothesis, and retention is an equivocal finding. Neyman and Pearson (1933) outlined a method in which both rejection and retention have potentially clear implications about the truth of the null hypothesis.

Once NHST was introduced, it also allowed statisticians to compare alternative significance testing methods in terms of their relative power (Neyman & Pearson, 1933). It turns out that some statistical methods make it easier to reject the null hypothesis than others when the alternative hypothesis is true without changing the probability of a Type I error. For example, in Chapter 2, I described Fisher's concern with the problem of familywise error rate. He created a procedure called the **least significant difference** (LSD), *a multistep method for controlling familywise error using an omnibus null hypothesis.* Suppose a researcher is interested in testing mean differences in five groups. That would allow 10 significance tests of differences between two means. The LSD begins with a test of the omnibus null hypothesis: $\mu^1 = \mu^2 = \mu^3 = \mu^4 = \mu^5$.

An **omnibus null hypothesis** is *a null hypothesis that combines a set of more specific null hypotheses. A test of an omnibus null hypothesis is often* called an **omnibus test.** According to the LSD, comparisons of pairs of means are permitted only if the omnibus test is significant.

It turns out that the LSD procedure has its problems. Sometimes it results in too many Type I errors and sometimes in too many Type II errors. However, omnibus tests continue to appear regularly in the literature, another example of researchers preferring the familiar over the optimal. Other methods of controlling familywise error were subsequently introduced, such as the Tukey test, the Newman–Keuls test, and the Bonferroni procedure. In recent years, a method described by Benjamini and Hochberg (1995) has become the preferred option, for two reasons:

1. Many procedures developed to control familywise error, such as the Tukey test, are specific to comparisons of means. The Benjamini–Hochberg procedure is applicable to any significance test: chi-square tests, tests of whether a population correlation equals 0, or whatever.

2. The Benjamini–Hochberg procedure controls the false discovery rate instead of the familywise error rate. Remember that the latter has to do with the probability of at least one Type I error if all null hypotheses are true. The **false discovery rate** is *the proportion of true null hypotheses that are falsely rejected.* It considers the possibility that at least some of the null hypotheses are false. By doing so, the control is not quite as stringent, and the power for each analysis is greater, sometimes substantially greater, than is true for analyses that control the familywise error rate.

Despite its advantages, several problems were quickly identified with Neyman and Pearson's (1933) hypothesis testing and, by extension, the modern NHST model. The Pearson–Neyman approach has been criticized conceptually for requiring fixed values for alpha and beta, a practice Fisher ultimately rejected. As Rosnow and Rosenthal (1989) famously put it many years later, "Surely God loves the .06 nearly as much as the .05" (p. 1277). A strategy whereby one hundredth of a point can make the difference between concluding there is and is not an effect is troubling.

The other problems with the method were more practical. Estimating the power of a study often requires noncentral sampling distributions (e.g., *t* distributions in which the expected value is something other than the neutral value 0), although computers have now resolved this problem. The more serious issue was the estimation of the population effect size. There is a chicken-and-egg issue here. Before you can conduct research, you have to decide how many participants to include. Before it is possible to set the number of participants, an estimate of the population effect size is needed. Before a defensible estimate of the population effect is possible, you must conduct research. For many years, statistics texts dealt with this problem by assuring the reader that it is important to control the probability of a Type II error but then offering no advice about how to do so (Huberty, 1993). Practical guidelines for power analysis did not emerge until 30 years after the introduction of hypothesis testing, thanks to the work of Jacob Cohen, whose work provides the starting point for Chapter 4.

Conclusion

Neyman and Pearson (1933) introduced a model for testing hypotheses similar to Fisher's significance testing but also quite different. They charged the researcher with the task of attending both to the implications of assuming the null hypothesis is true and the implications of assuming the alternative hypothesis is true. Assuming the null hypothesis is true, the researcher must control the probability of incorrect rejection (Type I error) and correct retention. Assuming the alternative hypothesis is true, the researcher must control the probability of correct rejection (the power of the study) and incorrect retention (Type II error).

The probabilities of correct rejection and incorrect retention depend on three factors: (a) the alpha level, (b) the effect size, and (c) the sample size. Of these, the sample size is the factor most under the researcher's control. Unfortunately, determining the sample size needed to achieve a desired level of power also depends on having an estimate of the effect size. This practical obstacle remained unresolved until Jacob Cohen addressed the issue beginning in the 1960s, as I describe in Chapter 4.

Practical Issues in Null Hypothesis Significance Testing

4

n 1962, Cohen published a study that set the stage for the replacement of significance testing by the hybrid model called *null hypothesis significance testing* (NHST). To evaluate the implications of assuming the alternative hypothesis for psychological research, he collected sample sizes from a year's worth of articles in one of the premier psychology journals of the time. He assumed reasonably that researchers in psychology tend to use an alpha level of .05. Now all he needed was an estimate of the effect size in the population from which the samples in those articles were drawn before he could start looking at the power of the research. Unfortunately, researchers did not regularly provide the information needed for such estimates at that time because effect size was not an important issue in significance testing.

His solution was to identify an appropriate effect size statistic to correspond to each of the significance testing statistics used in the studies he reviewed. He then established tentative benchmarks for what could be considered small, medium, and large effects for each statistic. For example, the correlation coefficient is one of the best known effect size statistics among psychologists, one for which a value of 0 means no effect. He assumed that a correlation of .20 represents a small relationship, a correlation of .40 is medium sized, and a correlation of .60 is large (in later work he revised these benchmarks). He was then able to estimate what the power of these studies would be if the effects were on average small, on average medium sized, or on average large.

What he found was troubling. If the average population effect size for significance tests reported in the journal was small, the average power of the analyses he reviewed was only .18; that is, even when the null hypothesis was wrong and the correct decision of the significance test would be to reject the null hypothesis, the null hypothesis would be rejected only 18% of the time, and 82% of the significance tests would result in Type II errors. When he assumed the average effect was medium, the average power increased only to .48. This suggested that more than half of significance test outcomes would still be incorrect in analyses in which the null hypothesis was wrong. It was only when the mean effect was assumed to be large (and correlations of .60 are not that common in the behavioral literature) that the mean power of the analyses increased to a more acceptable .83. Even then, though, 17% of significance tests with a true alternative hypothesis would result in Type II errors.

The implications of this study were clear. Behavioral scientists trained in Fisher's significance testing focused solely on the control of Type I error and ignored the very real potential for Type II errors. More recent reviews in a variety of research areas suggest that although there are exceptions, behavioral research continues to be plagued by the problem of insufficient power (e.g., Cashen & Geiger, 2004; Kazdin & Bass, 1989; Sedlmeier & Gigerenzer, 1989; Woods et al., 2006; Woolley, 1983). Sedlmeier and Gigerenzer (1989) even reported a decline in the power of significance tests in the same journal reviewed by Cohen 30 years later largely because researchers were increasing their use of more conservative tests intended to control the familywise error rate (see Chapter 2, this volume); that is, to reduce the likelihood of at least one Type I error when multiple significance tests were being conducted, more conservative statistical procedures were being used that increased the probability of a Type II error if the alternative hypothesis is true. The irony is that, as the following discussion suggests, there is good reason to believe the alternative hypothesis is usually if not almost always the true hypothesis. Under these circumstances, it is Type II error that is the more troubling issue than Type I error.

In the remainder of this chapter I focus on three topics that have been widely discussed in the statistical literature in response to Cohen's (1962) seminal article. The first is an introduction to Cohen's practical approach to power analysis. The second topic is a brief summary of some of the reaction in the literature to the problems that have been identified with the power of behavioral research. The chapter ends with the third topic, some recommendations for how to practice and read research in light of the problems identified.

Practical Power Analysis

Cohen recognized that the situation would never get any better unless procedures became available for making power analysis practical. In a classic book on the topic, Cohen (1969, 1988) proposed a variety of procedures for simplifying the process. As noted previously, power analysis requires establishing the acceptable risk for both Type I and Type II errors. Where the acceptable risk of a Type I error is usually set at .05, he recommended setting the standard risk for a Type II error to .20 (power = .80).

At first blush the reader may consider this standard too liberal, allowing an error to occur 20% of the time if the alternative hypothesis is true. No one could disagree with this perception, but consider the following. First, given reason to believe the Type II error rate could be above .50 in some fields of psychology, .80 power would be a tremendous improvement over the status quo. Second, remember that increasing power requires increasing the sample size, and increasing the sample size is not always easy. Furthermore, the increase in power that comes from adding to the sample gets smaller as the sample gets larger, so reaching .80 can sometimes require sample sizes well beyond the resources of all but the most generously funded researchers.

For example, suppose a researcher sets alpha to .05 (two tailed) and believes δ is .50 (i.e., the difference between two population means is one half the standard deviation of either population). This is the value Cohen (1988) considered a medium or typical effect for the standardized mean difference. Table 4.1 provides some examples under these circumstances of the power associated with various sample sizes for the independent-groups t test. A total sample of 64 means there are 32 participants in each of two groups. This is not a particularly large sample,

TABLE 4.1

Sample Sizes and Corresponding Levels of Power for the Independent-Groups t Test

Total sample size	β	$1 - \beta$ (power)
64	.50	.50
128	.20	.80
172	.10	.90
192	.07	.93
210	.05	.95

Note. These examples are based on assuming $\delta = .50$ and $\alpha = .05$ (two-tailed).

but there are circumstances in which even a sample this large can tax the researcher's resources, and many published studies in certain research areas historically involve substantially smaller samples than this (see Fletcher & Fletcher, 1979; Kazdin, 1986).

Although this might be a large sample in some research areas, a sample size of 64 is associated with power of only .50 for a medium-sized population effect. Achieving power of .80 requires doubling the sample again to 128. Because of diminishing returns, achieving a .05 standard for the Type II error probability would require a sample of at least 210 participants (105 per group). These are sample sizes few researchers can afford unless participants are readily accessible, which is one reason why psychology sometimes seems to be a science of rats and college freshmen. Given the issues, Cohen considered a Type II error rate of .20 to be reasonable.

Once the researcher sets the desired level of power, the next step involves estimating the population effect size. In recent years, this burden has to some extent been ameliorated by the development of **meta-analysis**, a term used to refer to *a variety of statistical procedures that have been developed for purposes of aggregating statistical results across research studies.* I discuss meta-analysis in more detail in Chapter 5, but for now a simple example will suffice. Suppose 25 studies have been conducted that have compared the effectiveness of a certain medication for attention-deficit/hyperactivity disorder with a placebo pill in adults. If Cohen's *d* statistic is computed for each of the 25 samples, and those *d* values are averaged, the result is an estimate of the overall effectiveness of the medication when compared with a placebo (see my discussion of publication bias in Chapter 5, this volume, for some caveats about this method).

One can often find a meta-analysis that can be used to provide information about effect sizes for future research, even if not directly on point. For example, Faraone, Spencer, Aleardi, Pagano, and Beiderman (2004) found that a common medication for attention-deficit/hyperactivity disorder was on average associated with a *d* value of .90 when compared with a placebo in adults. Any new medication for the disorder should demonstrate an effect as least as strong as the existing medications, so it would be reasonable to assume a population *d* value of .90.

Even when there is no meta-analysis specific to a research area, several general meta-analyses can provide guidance. Lipsey and Wilson (1993) aggregated results from meta-analyses having to do with the effectiveness of educational, behavioral, and psychological interventions. They found that in studies in which participants were randomly assigned to an experimental treatment or to some comparison treatment, the mean *d* value was .46. Similarly, Hemphill (2003) reviewed meta-analyses summarized by Meyer et al. (2001) concerning psychological tests and found that the middle third of correlations with criteria were in the interval from .21 to .30. New scales should be expected at the least to demonstrate similar levels of validity.

Cohen (1988) suggested an alternative method if, after all that, the researcher is still unable to estimate the population effect size. As in his 1962 article, Cohen offered benchmarks for small, medium, and large effects for various effect size statistics. In some cases he updated the values, for example, recommending a correlation of .10 be considered small, .30 medium, and .50 large. Although he recommended that researchers develop benchmarks specific to their research area, his general guidelines have been widely adopted.

In cases in which no empirical estimate of the population effect size is available, Cohen (1988) recommended assuming that the population effect size is equal to the smallest effect size that is likely to indicate an important effect. Some examples of how his benchmarks could be used to estimate the smallest important effect size may be found in Table 4.2.

Cohen (1988) offered tables for identifying the necessary sample size once the researcher has set the desired level of power (usually .80) and the desired alpha level (usually .05), and an estimate of the population effect size is generated. Software is now also available that automates

TABLE 4.2

Recommendations for Setting the Smallest Important Effect Size

The smallest important effect	When
Small effect	A small, barely noticeable effect can be important when a treatment has potential benefits that clearly outweigh the risks or costs. For example, Willard et al. (1992) examined whether taking aspirin can reduce the rate of heart attacks. Chronic aspirin use can cause complications, but it is a relatively low-risk medication. It is also low cost, and the benefits that would result from avoiding heart attacks are obvious. For these reasons, even a small effect would be socially valuable.
Medium effect	A medium effect is important if a typical effect size is worth detecting. This might also be appropriate when studying the effectiveness of some treatment that demonstrates both marked risks or costs and marked potential benefits.
Large effect	Any phenomenon that should be grossly obvious suggests a large effect. Also, only a large effect would be important when studying the effectiveness of some treatment regarding which there is controversy over whether the potential benefits outweigh the risks or costs, such as electroconvulsive therapy for severe depression (American Psychiatric Association Committee on Electroconvulsive Therapy, 2001).

Note. If no prior empirical evidence is available for estimating the population effect size, a last-resort alternative is to base the estimate on the smallest population effect size that would suggest an important effect.

this process. In recent years I have relied heavily on a program called G*Power (Erdfelder, Faul, & Buchner, 1996) that has one particularly compelling feature: It is free to download. The accompanying website (http://www.psycho.uni-duesseldorf.de/aap/projects/gpower/) also offers extensive information about power analysis.

Two points are worth making about Cohen's practical approach to power analysis. First, because both sample size and effect size are positively related to power, there is a trade-off between the two in terms of achieving a desired level of power. The larger the effect size, the smaller the sample size needed to achieve power of .80 or whatever standard you set. For example, with alpha (two-tailed) set to .05, assuming δ is large means a sample of 52 is needed to achieve power of .80 for the *t* test. As Table 4.1 indicates, a medium effect size requires a sample size of 128, whereas a small effect would require a whopping 788 participants! Clearly, it is not surprising that Cohen (1962) found the power to detect small effects in psychological research was so low. It is rarely the case that behavioral researchers can afford the samples that would be needed to achieve a desired level of power for studies examining small effects.

Second, this trade-off has implications for using Table 4.2 to generate an estimate of the population effect size. Suppose a researcher is evaluating a treatment with relatively low costs and risks and potentially dramatic benefit, such as using aspirin to avoid heart attacks. In this situation the default is to assume a small effect. This decision will require gathering, as has been shown, almost 800 participants. The benefit of doing so, though, is that if the treatment is in fact better than placebo the researcher is likely to find the result significant even if the effect is small. What if the effect of using aspirin is instead medium sized or large? Then the large sample means the power of the study is even greater than .80. This can mean the researcher will collect far more participants than are actually needed to achieve adequate power. It has been suggested that the problem can be mitigated by analyzing the data intermittently as they become available and terminating the study when the effect becomes significant (but see Strube, 2006).

The contrasting situation involves a treatment with significant risks, such as a medication that occasionally causes debilitating side effects. The researcher may assume that the effect must be large, because only a large effect would justify the medication's use, and so that researcher conducts the study with only 52 participants. If the effect in fact is not large, then power will be less than the targeted .80. If the effect is in fact medium sized, for example, the power declines to .42; that is, even if there is a difference in efficacy between the medication and placebo most analyses with this sample would result in retaining the null hypothesis. Although the outcome is inaccurate, failing to reject the null hypothesis in this case at least suggests that the medication will not be recommended, which is not a bad outcome given that the actual effect may not be large enough to justify the medication's use. To summarize, use prior research to generate a reasonable estimate of effect size if you can. If prior research offers no guidance, you can base the estimate on whatever would be the smallest effect size that would suggest an important effect.

The Significance Testing Controversy

Another response to the evidence that power is consistently insufficient in psychological research has been to question whether NHST is an inherently flawed statistical method. Cohen (1994) ultimately seems to have come to this conclusion, as have many others. This topic has been discussed in great detail (e.g., Chow, 1988; Hagen, 1997; Meehl, 1978; Rozeboom, 1960), with several whole books devoted to it (Harlow, Mulaik, & Steiger, 1997; R. B. Kline, 2004; Morrison & Henkel, 1970; and my personal favorite, Oakes, 1986). The debate is complex and detailed and often revolves around technical issues that can make your head spin. In the following sections I ignore the technical issues and instead focus on two practical issues that have to do with how the reliance on NHST has shaped psychological research practices and theory development.

OBSTACLES TO THE ACCUMULATION OF KNOWLEDGE

Schmidt (1996) made a forceful case for the complete abandonment of significance testing on the grounds that NHST undermines efforts to accumulate knowledge about behavioral processes. His argument proceeds as follows.

As behavioral theory becomes more sophisticated, it is reasonable to expect that researchers will focus less of their research on true null hypotheses. Perhaps 70 years ago, when little was known about cognitive processes or mechanisms of change, researchers were frequently evaluating ineffective treatments or invalid theories, but the understanding of psychological phenomena has presumably advanced since then. This creates the potential for a troubling paradox in which growing sophistication in theory renders a true null hypothesis increasingly unlikely and an empirical strategy that focuses on the null hypothesis increasingly irrelevant. On a side note, Meehl (1990) argued that the null hypothesis is unlikely simply because "in the social sciences and arguably in the biological sciences, 'everything correlates to some extent with everything else'" (p. 204), a principle he labeled the *crud factor*. Whether behavioral scientists have become better at avoiding no-effect situations or whether they rarely existed in the first place, the emphasis on Type I error would appear to be misguided.

Schmidt (1996) then considered how researchers reviewing the results of significance tests are likely to interpret those results. Reviews of the literature based on significance tests traditionally consider the proportion of tests that were significant. Imagine a situation in which five studies have been conducted to test the same null hypothesis. This null hypothesis happens to be false, but the power of the studies is only .50 on average. Using the binomial formula, we can generate the following probabilities for the results of the five significance tests:

Outcome of test	Probability
0 out of 5 significant	.03125
1 out of 5 significant	.15625
2 out of 5 significant	.31250
3 out of 5 significant	.31250
4 out of 5 significant	.15625
5 out of 5 significant	.03125

In other words, in cases such as this the probability of no significant outcomes is .03, the probability that fewer than half the tests will be significant is $(.03125 + .15625 + .3125) = .50$, and the probability that at least one test will be nonsignificant is $(1 - .03125) = .96875$.

Finding that fewer than half of the tests were significant is likely to be interpreted as evidence that there is no effect in the population. However, considering I already stated that the null hypothesis is false, this is clearly an incorrect conclusion. Alternatively, if there is a record of both significant and nonsignificant outcomes across studies, a common practice is to introduce additional variables that could account for the differences. For example, if an educational intervention is significantly better than placebo in some studies but not in others, someone reviewing the literature might conclude the effect is observed only when the intervention is administered by experienced teachers, or to highly verbal children. Researchers often do the same thing, attempting to account for differences between their own results and those of previous studies with ad hoc explanations based on additional variables, such as differences in the sample or the measures used, when those differences may reflect nothing more than the natural result of insufficient power. Writing in a similar vein, Meehl (1978) noted that the history of psychology is littered with concepts such as level of aspiration, androgyny, and locus of control that at one time were the object of extensive study but eventually faded away because inconsistencies in the results led to an increasingly complex model and ultimate frustration with the concept. The pattern is unfortunate because inconsistencies in the outcomes of significance tests are more simply understood as the result of inadequate power. The reliance on underpowered significance testing as a criterion for determining whether an effect exists has potentially compromised the gradual development of models for psychological phenomena.[1]

Jones and Tukey (2000) suggested that the problem lies in our interpretation of significance test results. They offered an alternative interpretive strategy that takes into consideration the low probability that the null hypothesis is true and the inadequate power of many significance tests. Suppose a researcher computes a correlation coefficient and then computes a *t* test for that correlation. If the test is significant and the correlation is positive, the result provides evidence that the population correlation is positive. If the test is significant and the correlation is negative, the result supports the conclusion that the population correlation is negative. If the test is nonsignificant, then the direction of the population correlation is indeterminate; that is, the results are uninterpretable. Although reasonable, this approach is unlikely ever to become popular, primarily because researchers do not want to present equivocal results. It can also be criticized for excluding the possibility that the null hypothesis really is true, a possibility some would not want to surrender completely (e.g., Hagen, 1997).

FAMILYWISE POWER

I noted in Chapter 2 that significance testing was in part attractive to behavioral scientists because of the perception that the results of a single significance test provided reliable information about a hypothesis. In the preceding section I made a strong case that this perception can be incorrect and that underpowered tests actually interfere with the straightforward accumulation of knowledge. You may therefore wonder why researchers continue to conduct underpowered studies. One factor would seem to be the high cost of achieving an acceptable level of power. On more than one occasion I have seen students really come to understand the problem of power, conscientiously conduct a power analysis for their next study, and throw their hands up in distress when they see how many participants would be needed to achieve a power of .80. At that point, power is seen as an impractical ideal best ignored. In a sense,

---

[1] I have noted a related mistake in articles that present a series of studies, in which significance test results from one study are assumed to be accurate and determine the methodology for the subsequent studies. For example, in Study 1 the researchers found no effect for Variable *X* and so omitted Variable *X* from Studies 2 through 4. This is also a subtle overestimation of the accuracy of significance tests: No decision should be based on a single analysis. I invite you to look for examples of this phenomenon in your own reading of multistudy articles.

psychologists overtly treat NHST as their primary inferential model but covertly often continue to rely on the significance testing model that ignores issues of sample size.

If power is so poor, how is it then that so many studies result in significant outcomes? Maxwell (2004) offered a clever analysis of how research practice in psychology has evolved in such a way as to compensate for low power.

Researchers have addressed the problem of insufficient power by conducting studies that involve multiple significance tests. A researcher studying aggressiveness and social skills in children might use five different measures of aggression and three different measures of social skills. This allows 15 different relationships between a measure of aggression and a measure of social skills, each of which can be the target of a significance test. Similarly, a study involving three treatments for autistic behavior might involve four different behavioral measurements, for a total of 12 significance tests.

Even if the power of each analysis (assuming all alternative hypotheses are true) is quite poor—in other words, the probability of a correct rejection is low for any one analysis—the probability of *at least one* correct rejection can be quite high. To use a concept traditionally associated with Type I error, it is possible to think in terms of the *familywise power* of a set of analyses, the probability of at least one significant outcome. For example, Maxwell (2004) provided one instance in which the power for each of three analyses was only .35 but the probability that at least one of them would be significant was .71. Similarly, if 12 analyses are conducted with a power of .40 and all the alternative hypotheses are true the researcher can still expect about five of the analyses to be significant ($.40 \times 12 = 4.8$ outcomes). By collecting substantial numbers of variables, researchers have created a research model in which some analyses will almost inevitably be significant, and administering a variety of measures is a much more cost-effective means of ensuring significant results than gathering more participants.

When discussing the results, there is even an unintentional bonus that accrues to the researcher when some tests are significant but others are not. I noted in the preceding section that when the same analysis is significant in some studies but not in others psychologists often introduce additional variables to account for the discrepancy, such as suggesting that the effectiveness of a treatment depends on participants' language skills, or is greater in middle-class participants. The individual researcher gets to engage in a similar process when similar analyses within a single study result in different outcomes, for example, using some ad hoc explanation to understand why it was that Job Satisfaction Scale A correlated significantly with Social Support Scale B but not with Social Support Scale C. These sorts of discrepancies can make the results of the study seem more interesting or revealing, but the reader may well be better served if the researcher acknowledged there was only a 50–50 chance of getting significance in the first place.

Living With Significance Tests

I do not blame you if you are feeling some confusion, disappointment, or even distress at this point. On the one hand, NHST is the only inferential model taught to many students of the behavioral sciences, and it seems to remain the most popular in psychological research (Cumming et al., 2007). On the other hand, NHST just does not perform in practice as you may have been led to expect.

Given the controversial nature of NHST, it is inevitable that behavioral researchers will increasingly rely on alternative inferential strategies. I briefly outline some of these strategies in Chapter 5. For now, though, the behavioral science professionals continue to rely heavily on significance tests as a basis for inferences. This section is intended to provide you with some recommendations about how to operate in an environment that relies on significance testing given what you now know about such tests. A handy summary of these recommendations can be found in Exhibit 4.1.

CONDUCTING RESEARCH

When conducting research in which you intend to use significance tests, two recommendations are appropriate. First, always start with a power analysis. Realize that there is a reasonable likelihood that when you see how many participants would be required you will experience some distress. Even so, this is a good practice; at the least, it will force you to think more clearly about how many participants would be desirable. It may encourage you to consider how to gather a larger sample, for example, by collaborating with colleagues at other sites. It will also help you avoid the trap of assuming that nonsignificant outcomes are due to other factors not considered in the design. G*Power can be used to generate a graph of the relationship between various sample sizes and power so you can make a judgment about the sample size that offers the best trade-off between power and pragmatics.

Second, the latest *Publication Manual of the American Psychological Association* (American Psychological Association, 2010) indicates that "for the reader to appreciate the magnitude or importance of a study's findings, it is almost always necessary to include some measure of the effect size" (p. 34) but offers no situation in which it would not be

---

EXHIBIT 4.1

Summary of Recommendations for Living With Significance Tests

Conducting Research
- Begin all research studies with a power analysis to set the sample size.
- Report an effect size estimate for every substantive significance test.
- When reporting significance test results, use a single asterisk (in tables), or present the exact *p* value (in text).

Statistical Versus Practical Significance
- Always keep in mind that statistical significance does not ensure practical significance.
- If an effect exists, statistical significance depends on three factors:[a]
  1. Alpha level
  2. Population effect size
  3. Sample size
- Practical significance depends on four factors:
  1. Population effect size
  2. Potential benefits
  3. Costs
  4. Potential risks

Reviewing the Literature
- Meta-analysis is always preferable to a review of significance test outcomes.
- Prior research tends to support the presence of an effect in the population if the following characteristics are present:
  - Half or more of tests are significant.
  - A substantial majority of the effects are in the same direction.
  - The probability of significance increases as a function of sample size.
- Prior research tends to support the absence of an effect in the population (or a very small one) if the following characteristics are present:
  - A quarter or less of the tests are significant.
  - Effects are approximately equally divided in terms of direction.
  - The probability of significance is unrelated to sample size.

---

[a]Other factors can affect power in specific situations, but the three factors listed in this exhibit matter under all circumstances.

necessary. My advice is to report a sample effect size statistic for every substantive significance test in the study. Substantive tests include those that bear directly on the research questions addressed by the study. For more peripheral tests, such as a preliminary analysis to investigate whether the groups differ on certain demographic variables, effect sizes are still desirable but less essential.

A growing number of journals require the reporting of effect size estimates for all substantive analyses (McGrath & Meyer, 2006). Some authors elect to include effect size statistics only if the associated hypothesis test is significant, on the grounds that a significant outcome at least provides evidence of a nonzero effect in the population. This practice does not make sense given the poor power of behavioral research. For example, suppose the population correlation between two variables is .40. Sample estimates of this population correlation should vary, with about half of them greater than .40 and about half less than .40. If the average power of these studies is only .50, then only those sample estimates that are greater than .40 will result in rejecting the null hypothesis. Only reporting the sample correlation when the null hypothesis is rejected means that a later meta-analysis of this literature is likely to conclude that the population correlation is larger than .40, perhaps .45 or higher, because those sample estimates that fell below .40 were not available (Schmidt, 1996). The moral of this is to provide a sample effect size estimate whenever it is reasonable to assume that someone might later want to use that estimate in a review of the literature.

To make room for these new statistics, a strong case can be made that there is no point to reporting significance test statistics such as t or F. These statistics are computed for one purpose only, which is to evaluate whether the result is significant. This outcome can just as easily be presented by identifying which of the effect size estimates were associated with a significant test result, using the standard asterisking or some other notation. This is already the standard for the presentation of correlational results, which usually involves a matrix of the effect size statistics (the correlation coefficients) with asterisks or changes in the font (e.g., boldface formatting) used to identify those statistics associated with significant test results.

STATISTICAL VERSUS PRACTICAL SIGNIFICANCE

It is important to understand the difference between the statistical and practical (sometimes called *clinical*) significance of an effect (Kirk, 1996; Thompson, 2002). *Statistical significance* is traditionally about nothing more than whether or not a population effect equals some null value. It is an attempt to state a fact about a population, recognizing of course the potential for error. As you have learned already, the probability of a statistically significant outcome is affected by several factors, including

- the alpha level, which affects the probability of both a Type I and Type II error;
- the effect size, which is relevant only to Type II error and power; and
- the sample size, which has important effects only on Type II error and power.

Whether an effect equals 0 or not is an important question, but research intended for use in applied settings, such as employee selection research or evaluations of educational or clinical interventions, should address a second question: Should I care? This is the issue of the practical importance of an effect.

For example, suppose a new treatment is introduced for weight control. A study is conducted that compares this treatment with a relatively neutral intervention, such as having overweight volunteers simply track their weight. At the end of treatment, the mean weight loss is determined for the two groups.

It is likely that any well-structured treatment will be better than the comparison, and with a sufficiently large sample there should be a significant outcome. Suppose the sample difference is small, though, which Cohen (1988) defined as a *d* value of .20. Remember what this means if we assume this is an accurate estimate of the population δ. Imagine two populations of overweight individuals, one of which consists of individuals who participate in the new treatment and another that comprises individuals who simply weigh themselves. If the standard deviation for each of these populations is 10 pounds (4.5 kg), there is only a 2-pound (0.9-kg) difference between them on average after treatment. If the new treatment requires 5 hr per week to complete, is this difference large enough to be important?

It is this issue of importance that really interests the consumer of this research. However, *statistical significance says nothing about an effect's importance*. In fact, if you consider the discussion of NHST up until this point you will realize that the topic of practical importance has been raised only once, and that was as a basis for estimating a population effect size when absolutely no other method was available (see Table 4.2).

All statistical significance indicates is whether there is evidence that the effect differs from the null value in the population. Users of significance tests sometimes mistakenly treat them as though they could reveal information about importance. For example, I have sometimes heard it argued that the low power of behavioral research is acceptable because a nonsignificant result reduces the chances that an unimportant effect will turn out to be significant. This sort of assertion is misleading, because it ignores the very real possibility that in certain circumstances even a small effect can be important (e.g., Willard, Lange, & Hillis, 1992).

For example, the practice of using different numbers of asterisks for different levels of significance seems to have evolved at least in part as a way of trying to use significance test results to say something about the relative importance of the findings, with more asterisks suggesting more substantive effects. This practice is misleading, because it ignores the possibility that a small effect can be more important than a large effect if the small effect is a treatment that, for example, reduces death rate, and the larger effect is associated with a treatment of less compelling impact. Furthermore, if the significance tests reported in the table involve different numbers of participants, then interpreting the number of asterisks as evidence of relative importance is remarkably poor practice, because differences in the number of asterisks can indicate nothing more than differences in sample size (as the discussion of power analysis indicated, significance tests based on larger samples will tend to be associated with more asterisks than tests based on smaller samples).

How, then, do you judge the practical significance of an effect? Practical significance is primarily a function of four variables:

1. The effect size: the larger the effect size the more practically significant a finding, all other factors being equal.
2. The potential benefits of the technique: the larger the potential benefit, the more practically significant a finding, all other factors being equal.
3. The cost of the technique, such as time spent or actual price to the consumer: the greater the cost the less practically significant a finding, all other factors being equal.
4. The potential risks of the technique, such as side effects: the greater the potential risks, the less practically significant a finding, all other factors being equal.

For example, a treatment or prediction strategy with a small effect size can be important if costs and risks are low and potential benefits are high. As costs and risks increase, or potential benefits decrease, larger effect sizes will be needed before the effect can be considered important (these conclusions are consistent with the recommendations offered in Table 4.2). Unfortunately, the process of estimating the practical importance of an effect is not as mathematically straightforward as setting the power of a significance test because it is often difficult to quantify the costs, risks, and benefits of a treatment.

There are several reasons why statistical and practical significance tend to be confused. The fact that effect size influences both the probability of statistical significance, if an effect exists, and the practical significance of an effect, can lead one to believe they are more related than is actually the case. The use of the term *significance* in the context of NHST also contributes to this confusion because it implies a significant result is important. Users of significance tests must keep in mind that this term, when used in the context of NHST, refers to nothing more than whether there is evidence to reject the null hypothesis.

Some authors (e.g., Gold, 1969) have even argued that statistical significance is at least a precondition for concluding that an effect is practically significant. According to this argument, the failure to establish statistical significance leaves open the possibility that the effect does not exist in the population. The case for this argument would be stronger if power were sufficient to ensure that practically important effects consistently generated significant outcomes, however. Even so, one can reasonably argue that a researcher conducting a study has no business interpreting an effect if the effect is not associated with a significant NHST outcome. That being said, it important to realize that practical and statistical significance are overlapping (because effect size plays a role in both) but quite distinct issues.

REVIEWING THE LITERATURE

Meta-analysis has been increasingly accepted as the optimal strategy for integrating results across prior studies for drawing general conclusions about a research question. However, even now it is not uncommon for researchers to review the results of significance tests from previous studies. Several recommendations can be offered for reviewing prior evidence from significance tests in light of the power problem.

The prior research tends to support the presence of an effect under the following conditions:

- A substantial number of the NHSTs are significant. Given that the power for any one analysis is typically about .50, if more than half of the published reports indicate a significant effect, there is reasonable evidence of a nonzero effect. This is only a very rough rule of thumb, however, because there is a well-established bias toward the publication of studies that report significance (Dickersin, 2005).[2]
- Almost all effects, whether significant or not, are in the same direction (see Jones & Tukey, 2000, for a rationale). For example, if every study finds that the mean improvement in the experimental treatment is greater than the mean improvement in the comparison treatment, these findings suggest a nonzero effect *even if not one of the significance tests is significant,* because it is extremely unlikely that the effect would consistently fall in the same direction if there is no effect. The consistent failure to find significance may suggest a small effect, which in turn has implications for the practical significance of that treatment, but it says nothing about whether the effect exists.
- If the number of studies evaluating a certain null hypothesis is fairly large, it becomes possible to look at the relationship between sample size and the probability of significance. If studies with relatively large samples consistently find a significant effect, but

---

[2]The article by Maxwell (2004) discussed earlier implies that this bias may not distort the literature as much as might be expected, as long as nonsignificant tests of a null hypothesis are embedded in studies in which other analyses proved significant.

studies with small samples do not, the pattern suggests that the alternative hypothesis is true.

The following are signs that the null hypothesis may be true. Keep in mind that any of these could also indicate a very small effect, however:

- Relatively few of the NHSTs are significant. Again, it is difficult to provide a defensible standard given publication biases and low power. If fewer than 25% of tests are significant, this should raise a red flag.
- Effects are approximately equally distributed in terms of direction. If the correlation between two variables is positive in some samples and negative in about the same number of samples, then the case is stronger for no effect.
- The probability of getting a significant result is unrelated to sample size. Sample size has no effect on the probability of a Type I error, so if sample size does not predict the rate at which tests prove significant there is reason to suspect that the null hypothesis is true.

None of these recommendations is foolproof, but at least they will help you avoid falling into the trap of assuming that nonsignificance inevitably means the null hypothesis is true. The consumer of research who is knowledgeable about power realizes that simplistic interpretations of NHST results are likely to be incorrect.

Conclusion

What a mess! Beginning with Cohen's (1962) seminal article, researchers have grown increasingly concerned about the issue of power. At a practical level, it is often unrealistic to ensure a reasonably low probability of a Type II error should the alternative hypothesis be true. This creates tremendous problems in terms of the interpretation of significance tests, and unless one considers power when reviewing the literature it is easy to draw conclusions that are very likely to be incorrect (Schmidt, 1996). This perplexing status quo is allowed to continue because researchers have adapted to conditions of limited power by conducting studies with large numbers of significance tests, thereby ensuring that at least some of tests are likely to be significant (Maxwell, 2004). However, this strategy ignores the real possibility that most of the nonsignificant tests are also associated with nonzero effects and that the question of whether or not an effect exists is generally a trivial question.

Some authors have suggested many of the problems of NHST result from our misperceptions about what the model is capable of achieving (e.g., Hagen, 1997). For example, the problem of insufficient power is not inherent to NHST but the result of how psychologists use NHST. At the same time, it is important to recognize Fisher was partly to blame for minimizing the importance of sample size.

Alternatively, it is reasonable to conclude that NHST is simply not the best choice for an inferential model, and it is not surprising to find that some commentators have argued for eliminating NHSTs completely from behavioral research (McGrath, 1998; Schmidt, 1996). What are the best alternatives? Read on!

Alternatives to Null Hypothesis Significance Testing

5

nference at the level of the individual analysis has traditionally been accomplished via null hypothesis significance testing (NHST), whereas inferences based on the literature as a whole involve counting the number of significant and nonsignificant findings (sometimes called a *box score*). Although NHST remains influential in the behavioral sciences, its weaknesses have encouraged psychologists to pursue other models of inference. In this chapter, I outline the most important alternatives. Some researchers (e.g., Schmidt, 1996) have suggested that confidence intervals provide a better inferential strategy for single analyses, whereas meta-analysis provides the optimal approach to integration of the literature.[1] The first two sections of this chapter focus on these strategies.

---

[1] I will mention another option suggested for single-sample inferences, which involves testing a "good-enough" null hypotheses (Serlin & Lapsley, 1985). Instead of testing a no-effect null hypothesis, this would involve testing whether an effect is trivial. For example, if an intervention is important only if the population mean exceeds 10, then test the null hypothesis $\mu = 10$ rather than $\mu = 0$. A significant result would then indicate not only that an effect exists but also that it is worth studying further. For students of NHST this may have some intuitive appeal, but I do not know of any technical advantages to this approach over confidence intervals and can think of several disadvantages. If we are going to do things differently, it makes sense to go with the best option.

In the third section, I introduce Bayesian methods as an alternative to NHST. These three alternatives involve changing the central inferential question. Whereas NHST has to do with dichotomous questions about parameters (effect exists–effect does not exist; effect is positive–effect is negative), the strategies discussed here have to do with modeling the size of parameters.

Interval Estimation

In Chapter 2, I described a hypothetical study in which 300 American adults received a nutritional supplement treatment. After 6 months, their mean score on a standard intelligence test was 102.5 rather than the 100 that is typical in the general population. You breathe a sigh of relief to find the result is significant and prepare the results for publication.

Let me throw a damper on your revelry. This significance test supports the conclusion the population mean is *not* 100, but it has told you nothing else about what it actually *is*. This can seem like a very unfulfilling outcome, a meager increase in the amount of information you have after so much work. One response is to say, "But we do have some information about what μ might be: Because the sample mean is an unbiased estimate of the population mean, we have 102.5 as the best sample estimate of the population mean." This is not a bad response, but it ignores a very important consideration. Although 102.5 is our best estimate possible of μ in this sample it is unclear, given sampling error, just how good an estimate it is.

Neyman (1937) formalized interval estimation as a means of addressing this problem, although the basic concept preceded his work. **Interval estimation statistics** are *inferential statistics that use sample statistics to estimate an interval of scores in which a parameter is likely to fall*. Once again, I will use the nutritional supplement study to demonstrate the concept.

As Equation 5.1 indicates, the formula for *t* when there is one group is

$$t_{\bar{Y}} = \frac{\bar{Y} - \mu}{\hat{\sigma}\sqrt{\dfrac{1}{N}}}. \tag{5.1}$$

This same formula can be used to generate information about an estimate for μ; specifically, in a sample of 300 people ($df = 299$), if the value for μ used in Equation 5.1 is correct, and the assumptions identified earlier for the *t* test apply, then the value that isolates the outermost 5% of the t distribution is ± 1.968 (see Figure 2.4). That is why, if the null hypothesis is true, a value ≥ 1.968 or a value ≤ -1.968 was considered evidence that the null hypothesis value for μ is incorrect, because such a value for t would occur less than 5% of the time if that value for μ is correct.

Another implication of this formula is that 95% of sample estimates of μ (i.e., 95% of the sample means) will fall in the interval

$$\mu \pm 1.968\left(\hat{\sigma}\sqrt{\frac{1}{N}}\right). \tag{5.2}$$

If 95% of sample means will fall in this interval, then the reverse is also true: In 95% of the samples μ will fall within the following interval:

$$\bar{Y} \pm 1.968\left(\hat{\sigma}\sqrt{\frac{1}{N}}\right). \tag{5.3}$$

This interval is called a **confidence interval**, *an interval of sample values in which some parameter is likely to fall with an established probability.* More specifically, this is a 95% confidence interval. In 95% of samples, μ should fall within the 95% confidence interval for that sample. If the quantity

$$\hat{\sigma}\sqrt{\frac{1}{N}} \tag{5.4}$$

equals 2.7 in this sample with a mean of 102.5, then the 95% confidence interval for the nutritional supplement sample is

$$102.5 \pm (1.968 \times 2.7) = [97.19, 107.81]. \tag{5.5}$$

The bracket here is a mathematical convention that means the interval begins at 97.19 (the lower limit) and includes all successive values up to and including 107.81 (the upper limit). Sometimes the interval is presented with a dash, 97.19–107.81, but I find the brackets to be a less confusing option because sometimes the limits of the confidence interval are negative numbers.

Many students find the implications of the confidence interval confusing, so I will state it in another way. Using interval estimation statistics, it is possible to create an interval of values called the *95% confidence interval* for the sample. Suppose an infinite number of samples of equal size are randomly and independently sampled from the population. If the 95% confidence interval is generated for each of these samples, one can demonstrate using the sampling distribution of the mean that μ will fall within this 95% confidence interval in 95% of samples.

I use the rest of this section to briefly introduce a series of core concepts in confidence intervals. These topics include the meaning of the term *confidence* in the context of confidence intervals, changing the confidence level, the relationship between confidence intervals and significance tests, and problems with interval estimation.

THE MEANING OF THE TERM *CONFIDENCE*

In the example I have provided it is not appropriate to say, "There is a 95% chance that μ falls within the interval 97.19 to 107.81" or that "I can be 95% confident or certain that μ falls in that interval." The population mean (i.e., μ) is fixed in the population, and it either falls or does not fall within the interval. The only appropriate interpretation of the 95% confidence interval is that μ will fall within the 95% confidence interval in 95% of samples. For this reason I think the term *confidence* is misleading here, but that is the tradition and we are stuck with it. I raise this subtle point later in this chapter in my discussion of Bayesian methods.

CHANGING THE CONFIDENCE LEVEL

The 95% confidence interval parallels the standard .05 level of significance in NHST in an important way. The .05 level of significance results in a correct decision 95% of the time if the null hypothesis is true, and the 95% confidence interval will include μ in 95% of samples, so in both cases the error rate is 5%. For this reason it is the 95% confidence interval that is typically computed. However, you could choose to compute the 90% confidence interval instead, or the 99% confidence interval, 50% confidence interval, even the 1% confidence interval if you wanted to, although making sure you are right only 1% of the time would not be particularly useful. Changing the level of confidence requires only that one change the value drawn from the *t* distribution in Equation 5.3. For the 95% confidence interval, the value that separates the middle 95% of scores from the most extreme 5% of *t* values is ±1.968. For the 90% confidence interval, ±1.650 cuts off the outer 10% of sample values from the middle 90%:

$$90\% \text{ confidence interval}: 102.5 \pm (1.650 \times 2.7) = [98.05, 106.96]. \quad (5.6)$$

For the 99% confidence interval, ±2.592 demarks the outer 1% of *t* values:

$$99\% \text{ confidence interval}: 102.5 \pm (2.592 \times 2.7) = [95.50, 109.50]. \quad (5.7)$$

Compare the three sets of confidence intervals computed so far:

Level of confidence	Lower limit	Upper limit	Size of interval
90%	98.05	106.96	8.91
95%	97.19	107.81	10.62
99%	95.50	109.50	14.00

The size of the interval provided here is simply the difference between the upper and lower limit. Notice that the 90% confidence interval is narrower than the 95% confidence interval, whereas the 99% confidence interval is wider. This occurs because achieving a 99% level of confidence (so μ will fall within the confidence interval in 99% of samples) means that only 1% of confidence intervals will involve an error, so you need a wider interval. If you are willing to settle for a 90% level of confidence, with errors 10% of the time, then the interval can be smaller. To achieve a higher level of confidence requires accepting a larger set of possible values for μ. *The higher the desired level of confidence that the parameter is included in the interval, the wider the confidence interval will be.*

By far, 95% represents the most commonly used confidence level. I have even seen studies that failed to mention the level of confidence, in which case it can be assumed the 95% level was used. However, it is probably best always to state the level explicitly.

CONFIDENCE INTERVALS AND SIGNIFICANCE TESTS

There is an important relationship between confidence intervals and NHST. I noted previously that the 95% confidence interval parallels the .05 level of significance. In fact, the *t* value used to compute the 95% confidence interval is the same *t* value that provides the critical value for α = .05 (two-tailed), ± 1.986 (see Equation 5.3). Similarly, the *t* value used for the 90% confidence interval is the same *t* value that would be used for the critical value if α = .10 (two-tailed),[2] whereas the critical value for α = .01 (two-tailed) and *df* = 299 would be 2.592, the same value used to compute the 99% confidence interval.

There is another parallel between the level of significance and the level of confidence. Remember that the nutritional supplement study involved testing the null hypothesis μ = 100. Notice that the 95% confidence interval [97.19, 107.81] includes the null hypothesis value 100. This finding indicates that the two-tailed test of this null hypothesis with α = .05 would not be significant because the confidence interval suggests that 100 is a reasonable guess for the value of μ. Suppose the

---

[2]In fact, if you look back at Figures 2.2 and 2.3, you will see that the *t* value of 1.65 was identified as the value that cut off the highest 5% of *t* values and the lowest 5% of *t* values in the *t* distribution if the null hypothesis is true.

95% confidence interval was instead [101.9, 103.1], so 100 is omitted. In this case, the test would be significant because 100 is not a reasonable guess at the value of μ. If you are not able to reject the null hypothesis at α = .05 (two-tailed), then the null hypothesis value for the parameter will fall within the 95% confidence interval; if you are able to reject the null hypothesis at α = .05, then the null hypothesis value for the parameter will not fall within the 95% confidence interval. This relationship applies to any level of confidence and the corresponding alpha level, so long as the test is two-tailed: If the null hypothesis value falls within the 99% confidence interval you will not be able to reject the null hypothesis at α = .01, for example.[3] Finally, note that, at least in the example discussed here, the confidence interval and significance test involve the same assumptions (random and independent sampling and normality) and robustness conditions.

A confidence interval therefore offers as much information as a significance test but does more. Where NHST often indicates only what the value of the parameter is not, the confidence interval provides information about what it *might be*. In addition, the width of the confidence interval provides some sense of the precision of the mean as an estimate of μ. The wider the confidence interval, the less precision is available. In fact, there are several factors that affect the width of the confidence interval:

- As the desired level of confidence increases (or the acceptable error rate decreases), the interval becomes wider.
- As the standard deviation of the scores decreases, the interval becomes narrower.
- As the sample size increases, the interval becomes narrower.

If you are someone who loves the challenges of statistics, you may want to consider the similarities with and differences from the factors that influence power. For everyone, the lesson to be learned is that larger sample sizes improve precision in confidence intervals, just as they increase power (Maxwell, Kelley, & Rausch, 2008).

One other benefit of confidence intervals over significance testing is worth noting. Users of NHST often assume that finding a significant outcome in one study suggests a reliable finding and thus subsequent studies will also tend to find significance. As the discussion of power in Chapter 4 attests, this assumption is untrue in practice. Cumming (2008) went further, suggesting that even the *p* value associated with the sample significance testing statistic is not a particularly reliable value and can vary dramatically from one study to the next. The unreliability of significance

---

[3]It is possible to create one-tailed confidence intervals, but they tend to be of little practical interest for the same reasons as one-tailed tests.

tests thoroughly undermines the case for their use. In contrast, confidence intervals generate much more reliable conclusions about the parameter of interest.

In general, then, confidence intervals represent a better inferential strategy than NHST. I have not been surprised that some well-known commentators in statistics for the behavioral sciences have recommended replacing NHST completely with confidence intervals (e.g., Cohen, 1994; Schmidt, 1996), and the sixth and latest edition of the American Psychological Association's *Publication Manual* (2010) strongly encourages their use. There has been growing interest in the development of confidence intervals specifically for effect size descriptive statistics, and Bonett (2008) compellingly argued that reporting effect sizes without a confidence interval is a questionable inferential strategy. A related development is the increased use of error bars in figures presenting parameter estimates such as group means (see Figure 5.1 for an example).

FIGURE 5.1

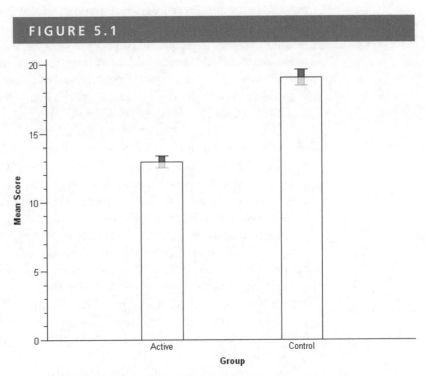

This figure provides an example of the use of error bars. The vertical bars indicate the mean score for the Active group was 13.1, while the mean for the Control group was 19.3. The error bars indicate that the 95% confidence interval for the mean of the Active group was [12.6, 13.6], while that for the Control group was [18.7, 19.9].

PROBLEMS USING INTERVAL ESTIMATION

Recommendations to increase the use of confidence intervals have started to have an effect. This has been particularly true in medical research, where confidence intervals have become commonplace (Fidler, Thomason, Cumming, Finch, & Leeman, 2004). Even so, many behavioral researchers still rely almost exclusively on significance tests. Why is this the case? Several factors seem to play a role, but most of these are not particularly compelling. One is that many behavioral scientists have received substantially more training in NHST than in interval estimation and so simply may not feel as comfortable using confidence intervals (e.g., Belia, Fidler, Williams, & Cumming, 2005). Compounding this discomfort is the tendency of popular statistical software to emphasize significance tests over confidence intervals, although that has started to change and many resources are now available to help one automate the process.[4]

A second factor contributing to their relative unpopularity is the potential for confidence intervals to embarrass the researcher in a way significance tests cannot. A sample correlation coefficient of .30 will be significant in a sample of 100 people because the significance test evaluates whether there is evidence to suggest that the population correlation is some value other than 0. The goal of the confidence interval is grander: to provide information about the actual value of the population correlation. Suppose the 95% confidence interval in this situation proves to be [.111, .468]. The confidence interval supports the conclusion to reject the null hypothesis, because 0 does not appear within the interval. However, as an estimate of the true value for the population correlation this interval is troublingly imprecise. As with power analysis, achieving precision in confidence intervals can require larger samples than is common in behavioral research.

A third factor is that no-effect null hypotheses allow the use of sampling distributions centered on the neutral point; in contrast, the computation of confidence intervals requires the use of noncentral distributions (see Chapter 1, this volume), and for some statistics these distributions are substantially more complicated than the no-effect variants. In some cases this means that no formula for a confidence interval has even been generated, including for some of the newer effect size statistics.

A solution exists to this problem. Bootstrapping (see Chapter 2, this volume) can be used to compute the confidence interval for a sample without any information about the population distribution

---

[4]In particular, the MBESS package available for the free R statistical programming language (http://nd.edu/~kkelley/site/MBESS.html) can generate confidence intervals for many of the most commonly used effect size statistics.

from which the sample was drawn. In regard to our target sample of 300 intelligence test scores, bootstrapping would involve generating perhaps 500 subsamples of 300 scores each. To repeat what I said earlier, bootstrapping involves drawing scores *with replacement* from the target sample to create bootstrapped samples. The mean would then be computed for each bootstrapped sample, and the interval that encompasses 95% of these values (excluding the top and bottom 2.5% of the bootstrapped sample means) can be treated as a 95% confidence interval. As I noted in Chapter 2, bootstrapping does not require knowledge of the population distribution, so it is possible to compute bootstrapped confidence intervals even for statistics for which the nature of the population distribution has not been widely studied, including recently developed effect size statistics. Given the widespread availability of powerful computers, the infrequent use of bootstrapping as a general solution to the estimation of confidence intervals owes far more to the factors discussed earlier—lack of familiarity and embarrassing imprecision—than to any failings of the method.

One common error in the use of confidence intervals should be noted before we move on. In Figure 5.1, the 95% confidence interval for the mean of the "Active" group is [12.6, 13.6] and that for the control group is [18.7, 19.9]. Because the 95% confidence intervals do not overlap, you might assume the difference would be significant. This is not *necessarily* the case. To make sure there is a significant difference between two means, you must compute the confidence interval for the difference between the means. In this case, the 95% confidence interval for the difference between the means is [−6.617, −5.143], so the results would allow rejection of the null hypothesis. However, because this is not always the case, you cannot just compare confidence intervals for groups and decide the results are significant (Belia et al., 2005; Schenker & Gentleman, 2001).

Meta-Analysis

I briefly discussed meta-analysis in Chapter 4 as a source of population effect size estimates for power analysis, but now I discuss it in a broader context. Although meta-analysis was first described only 35 years ago (Glass, 1976), it has radically changed the way behavioral scientists integrate prior findings to draw summative conclusions.

The first published meta-analysis demonstrated the method's power. For many years, the discussion of whether psychotherapy is an effective intervention for psychological disorders was dominated by a single review of the literature by Hans Eysenck (1965), who concluded that psychotherapy is no better than receiving no treatment at all. One serious problem with this review is that it was based on results from significance tests that compared people who received therapy with others who did not. In the days before substantial federal funding of mental health research, however, studies of something as complicated as psychotherapy often involved samples of 30 or fewer. This is not surprising given the ignorance of power issues at the time and the general neglect of issues of sample size fostered by significance testing. The circumstances created exactly the sort of problem Schmidt (1996) criticized (see Chapter 4, this volume), in which underpowered studies easily contributed to the belief in the absence of an effect.

M. L. Smith and Glass (1977; M. L. Smith, Glass, & Miller, 1980) instead have computed a variant of the d statistic for each of hundreds of psychotherapy studies and averaged them to get a best estimate of δ, the population standardized mean difference. They concluded that psychotherapy was not only effective but that it also improved outcomes on average by about two thirds of a standard deviation. Since then, meta-analysis has become the standard for integrating results from prior studies.

OUTLINE OF A META-ANALYSIS

All good meta-analyses tend to share certain features (Moher, Liberati, Tetzlaff, Altman, & The PRISMA Group, 2009):

- The analysis begins with a review of the relevant literature. The authors must first set criteria for the selection of studies, although these criteria often evolve as the study progresses. The most obvious criterion has to do with selecting studies relevant to the meta-analysis, but some meta-analyses require certain methodological elements before a study can be included. Some are limited to a specific time frame for publication, or to certain journals, to reduce the studies used to a manageable number. The literature review is often a lengthy process because some studies may be difficult to find. Cooper (2009) provided helpful tips for designing and conducting the literature search. During the course of reading the literature it may be possible to define criteria for excluding some studies because of concerns about the methodological quality of the study. For example, some meta-analysts exclude unpublished material, such as analyses presented only at conferences or in dissertations, or establish other criteria for determining whether the rigor of the study is sufficient to merit including it. In some cases, multiple reviewers evaluate each study and come to a consensus about its merit.
- Each of the studies selected for inclusion in the meta-analysis is reviewed for methodological characteristics. These might include

the sample size, the measures used, the types of treatment groups, aspects of the design of the study, characteristics of the population represented, ratings of the study's methodological rigor, and so on. Again, having multiple raters review each article can enhance the reliability of the ratings.

- An effect size is computed for each relevant analysis in each study. There is a tremendous literature available on how to do this, and many effect size statistics have been developed for this purpose, but most meta-analyses rely on some variant of the correlation coefficient, the standardized mean difference, or a statistic used with dichotomous variables called the *odds ratio*. The goal is to reduce all analyses to a single metric-neutral effect size statistic so that direct comparisons of effect size can be made across studies. If one study includes multiple relevant analyses (e.g., a single study that examined the effectiveness of some employee intervention may have evaluated several measures of job satisfaction), it is best to use the mean or median effect size estimate from that study for the meta-analysis so the results of the meta-analysis are not affected by the number of analyses conducted in any one study. You can think of a meta-analysis as a type of research in which the data consist not of variables collected on N research participants but instead of statistics collected from k previous research studies.

- These effect size estimates are then aggregated in some way. Usually, this involves an average weighted by some statistic related to the sample size. Most commonly this is the inverse of the statistic's variance (Fleiss, 1993), so that the sample size is in the numerator of the weight. This means that the impact of any one study on the results of the meta-analysis increases as the sample size increases.

- Many meta-analyses also include an evaluation of whether the effect sizes are homogeneous across studies. The issue here is whether variability in the effect sizes can be accounted for purely by sampling error and measurement error or whether the effect size is affected by other aspects of the study, such as variations in the treatment or how some variable is measured. Statistics have been developed specifically for the purpose of detecting heterogeneity in the effect size estimates across studies and for detecting possible causes for heterogeneity if it is present. For example, M. L. Smith and Glass (1977) found evidence of heterogeneity in their estimates of the effectiveness of psychotherapy, and additional analyses suggested that psychotherapy was more effective in samples in which the intelligence level seemed higher than the average, such as college students. Ironically, these statistics are often significance tests, so that even in the context of meta-analysis researchers have to worry about Type I and Type II errors.

If you are interested in conducting a meta-analysis it is always a good idea to begin by reviewing one of the standard textbooks on how to conduct one (e.g., Borenstein, Hedges, Higgins, & Rothstein, 2009; Cooper, 2009; Hunter & Schmidt, 2004; Lipsey & Wilson, 2000; Schulze, 2004).

As a method of integrating prior research results, there is no doubt that meta-analysis is a superior alternative to counting the number of significant versus nonsignificant test results. In fact, I believe the introduction of meta-analysis has done more than any other factor to enhance the quality of inferential modeling in the social and behavioral sciences, for the following reason: Ultimately, final conclusions about real-world models must involve some aggregation of results across studies. Basing those conclusions on the frequency of significant results meant insufficient sample sizes led to aggregate conclusions that were often incorrect (Schmidt, 1996). In contrast, although there are reasons to believe that small-sample studies on average overestimate the size of effects (Kraemer, Gardner, Brooks, & Yesavage, 1998), meta-analysis offers an alternative that reduces the effect of small sample size on the conclusions. In fact, as the story of the first psychotherapy meta-analysis illustrated, the advantages of meta-analysis are particularly compelling when samples are smaller than desirable. The success of meta-analysis has in turn shifted attention from the significance-testing question of whether an effect exists, or its direction, to the more interesting question of how large that effect is. Whereas effect size statistics were originally introduced for the primary purpose of making power analysis practical, thanks to meta-analysis they have become important in their own right as a means of estimating the size of population effects.

A relatively recent innovation in meta-analytic techniques, the *forest plot,* is particularly pleasing to me. The forest plot gets its name from its capacity to present both the forest and the trees in a meta-analysis. The effect size estimate from each study is plotted with its confidence interval on a common scale. As demonstrated in Figure 5.2, the forest plot visually indicates whether each study indicates an effect, the direction of the effect, relative sample size, and all sorts of good stuff. The forest plot can get unwieldy with large numbers of studies, but for smaller meta-analyses it is a great way to present a tremendous amount of information efficiently.

PROBLEMS USING META-ANALYSIS

Of course, as with any statistical method, there are problems with the use of meta-analysis. Perhaps the most serious is the effect the researcher's choices can have on the outcome. For example, some researchers have argued that unpublished research should be included in meta-analyses, for the following reason. If, as I suggested in Chapter 4, there is a bias

FIGURE 5.2

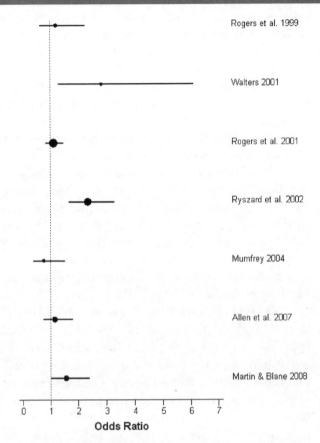

Rogers et al. 1999

Walters 2001

Rogers et al. 2001

Ryszard et al. 2002

Mumfrey 2004

Allen et al. 2007

Martin & Blane 2008

Odds Ratio

This is a forest plot for a meta-analysis. The metric-neutral effect size statistic used here is something called the *odds ratio*. For the odds ratio a value of 1 means no effect, while a value between 0 and 1 indicates an effect in an opposite direction from expectation (e.g., controls did better than those in the active treatment). For each study the circle indicates the sample estimate of the odds ratio. A circle to the left of the dotted line (< 1) means an effect in the wrong direction, one directly on the line would mean no effect, and circles to the right of the line are in the expected direction. The size of the circle indicates relative sample size, while the horizontal line running through each circle indicates the 95% confidence interval for the sample odds ratio. You can expect that larger circles, indicating larger samples, will tend to be associated with narrower intervals. If the confidence interval line crosses the dotted line, it means the value 1 falls within the interval and the null hypothesis cannot be rejected in that study at α = .05 (two-tailed). I love how much information the forest plot can present in one picture.

toward the publication of significant rather than nonsignificant outcomes (Dickersin, 2005), and most studies are underpowered, then effect size estimates in the published literature will tend to be too large. Why is that? Imagine that for some effect the true standardized mean difference is $\delta = .30$, which Cohen (1988) considered a small-to-medium effect. If studies generally use α (two-tailed) $= .05$, and the average sample size is $N = 100$, then the mean power of studies looking for this effect is only .32: Only 32% of analyses will be significant. Which analyses are significant is not random, though. Remember, there is sampling error associated with sample estimates of the population effect, so one study may produce a d value of .30, another study a d of .23, another .42, another .67, and so forth. Only the highest 32% of sample estimates of δ will produce significant results. If only those estimates are published, or if studies in which the test was not significant do not report effect size estimates, then the meta-analysis based on published articles may tend to suggest 251658240(the best estimate of δ) $= .50$. As an alternative to seeking out unpublished literature, Kraemer et al. (1998) suggested omitting published studies with low levels of power because these are the studies most likely to overestimate the population effect.

The problem of selective reporting, which I described in Chapter 2 in the "Multiple Comparisons" section in my discussion of fishing expeditions, can also play a role in misestimation of effect sizes based solely on published literature. Turner, Matthews, Lindardatos, Tell, and Rosenthal (2008), in their study of selective reporting on the effectiveness of medications, found that effect sizes reported in published articles were on average 32% larger than those provided in the research reports generated by the company that funded the study (see also Vul, Harris, Winkielman, & Pashler, 2009). On the other hand, unpublished research does not undergo critical review and so may be of poorer quality.[5] Researchers also face similar choices about which effect size statistic to compute, the method of weighting effect size estimates, methods of dealing with and evaluating effect size homogeneity, and many other factors.

A second instance of a choice that can have profound implications for the findings has to do with the statistical methods used. Different texts offer different conclusions about how best to analyze a meta-analysis,

---

[5]One compromise in this situation involves estimating the effect size on the basis of the published literature and then conducting analyses that estimate the potential effect of additional unpublished data with different results on the estimate of the population effect size. For example, a meta-analysis demonstrating a large effect for some intervention might estimate how much additional unpublished data that suggest a smaller effect would be needed to offset the conclusion of a large effect. Such approaches to the "file drawer problem" (Rosenthal, 1979), so called because the unpublished data are presumably sitting in researchers' file drawers, often demonstrate that the number of unpublished data points needed to change the conclusions would be so substantial as to seem unrealistic.

and normative practices are still evolving. Even the choice of an effect size to analyze can have profound implications. McGrath and Meyer (2006) found that the correlation coefficient and standardized mean difference, two of the most commonly used effect sizes in meta-analysis, can lead to very different conclusions about the size of an effect under certain conditions.

The various choices made in reviewing the literature—deciding which analyses to include, selecting a statistical method, identifying possible predictors of heterogeneity, and so forth—can also change the results of the meta-analysis. To cite just one example, Parker, Hanson, and Hunsley (1988) and Garb, Florio, and Grove (1998) came to completely different conclusions about the validity of a psychological test using exactly the same set of studies. The only difference was the set of choices they made about the analyses.

A particularly current statistical issue in the meta-analytic literature has to do with whether to use a fixed-effects or random-effects model of the parameter being estimated. A **fixed-effects meta-analysis** is *a meta-analysis that assumes all the samples in the meta-analysis come from the same population,* that is, the parameter underlying all the studies is fixed. A **random-effects meta-analysis** is *a meta-analysis in which it is possible that different studies involved different populations with different values for the parameter.*

Both fixed-effects and random-effects meta-analyses ultimately generate a single estimate of δ or whatever population statistic is being estimated. In the case of the fixed-effects meta-analysis, though, this estimate is assumed to apply to a single population. Variations in sample estimates of δ are assumed to be the result of sampling error only. In the random-effects meta-analysis the overall estimate is assumed to be the mean δ across a series of populations. Variations in sample estimates of this mean δ are assumed to be the result of differences in the δ values for the populations studied as well as sampling error.

The latter is the more conservative option, not only because it does not assume a single population but also because the statistical methods associated with random-effects models tend to be more conservative. For example, they produce wider confidence intervals for parameter estimates (Schmidt, Oh, & Hayes, 2009), and as we have seen, narrower confidence intervals are more desirable to researchers. This factor is not a very good justification for using fixed-effects models, but it helps explain their continuing popularity.

A related problem occurs when researchers fail to consider heterogeneity in the effect sizes. A meta-analysis of 100 studies on the impact of homework on educational outcomes might combine results that are based on a variety of populations, homework models, and measures of educational outcomes. Although there is a temptation to do so, these findings demonstrate the danger in assuming that a meta-analysis provides information about *the* effect size for some treatment or test. If the researchers report a single estimate of the population effect, and do not evaluate heterogeneity in the findings, it is probably best to think of the results as a helpful summary of the existing research on a topic rather than as a characteristic of some population.

Supporting this conclusion is a study by LeLorier, Grégoire, Benhaddad, Lapierre, and Derderian (1997) in which they identified 40 instances in which a meta-analysis evaluating a medical intervention could be compared with results from a subsequent large-sample study (1,000 or more participants) on the same intervention. There were no cases in which the two approaches resulted in opposite conclusions, that is, when one approach suggested a treatment was helpful and the other found it harmful. However, in 33% of their comparisons one approach suggested the treatment was effective and the other suggested it was ineffective. The authors discussed how a meta-analysis can produce an inaccurate estimate of the population effect, including the tendency, discussed previously, for the published literature as a whole to overestimate effect sizes.

A final issue of concern has to do with the quality of the meta-analysis. As with any other procedure that crunches information, the rule is "Garbage in, garbage out." To the extent that a meta-analysis relies on studies of dubious quality, the results must be viewed with caution. Because a meta-analysis can include anywhere from dozens to hundreds of studies there is simply not enough room in the research report of a meta-analysis to list all the troubling elements of the studies reviewed; suffice it to say that almost every study has its flaws and quirks. In an effort to improve the quality of meta-analyses, the PRISMA (Preferred Reporting Items for Systematic Reviews and Meta-Analyses; Moher et al., 2009) guidelines, a list of 27 issues that should be addressed in any report summarizing results of a meta-analysis, were developed.[6]

These issues should not be taken as evidence against the value of meta-analysis; they would be at least as problematic for any method used to integrate existing literature. By providing a formal model for drawing inference from multiple studies, meta-analysis has simply provided the context in which such issues can be discussed and possibly addressed. It is a powerful tool and one that increasingly plays a central role in drawing final conclusions about research questions.

---

[6]Although not relevant to the current discussion, I should mention that similar guidelines are available for the conduct of clinical trials, the CONSORT standard (CONsolidated Standards Of Reporting Trials; http://www.consort-statement.org/), and for diagnostic classification studies, the STARD standard (STAndards for the Reporting of Diagnostic accuracy studies; http://www.stard-statement.org/).

FIGURE 5.3

Fact

		Null hypothesis (H_0) is true	Alternative hypothesis (H_1) is true
Statistical decision	Reject	Incorrect rejection (Type I error) $p(incorrect\ rejection) = \alpha$	Correct rejection $p(correct\ rejection) = 1 - \beta$ (power)
	Retain	Correct retention $p(correct\ retention) = 1 - \alpha$	Incorrect retention (Type II error) $p(incorrect\ retention) = \beta$

Four possible outcomes of a decision to reject or retain the null hypothesis.

Bayesian Methods

In Chapter 3, I described the NHST model as modeling statistical decisions in terms of four possible outcomes, depicted again in Figure 5.3. Remember that alpha refers to the probability of rejecting the null hypothesis if the null hypothesis is true. So, with $\alpha = .05$, the researcher can assume there is only a 5% chance of rejecting the null hypothesis if the null hypothesis is true. It is often the case that users of significance tests assume it follows that if the null hypothesis is rejected there is very little chance that the null hypothesis is true. However, this is a false assumption that confuses what may be referred to as the *frequency and subjective models of probability*.

FREQUENCY AND SUBJECTIVE MODELS OF PROBABILITY

Read the following two phrases:

1. The probability of rejecting the null hypothesis if the null hypothesis is true is .05.
2. The probability the null hypothesis is true if the null hypothesis is rejected is .05.

Statement 1 reflects alpha. It is the information that a significance test provides you when the null hypothesis is rejected. If you think about it,

Statement 2 is probably more along the lines of what you would actually like to know: Given that you have rejected this null hypothesis, how likely is it that the null hypothesis is true?

It is easy to think the two statements are saying the same thing, especially given the belief fostered by NHST that rejecting the null hypothesis in itself is an important event. In fact, these two statements are not equivalent. To use a parallel, consider the following phrases:

3. The probability you are human if you are a U.S. citizen.
4. The probability you are a U.S. citizen if you are human.

The probability of being a citizen of the United States if you are a human (Statement 4) is about .04, meaning that approximately 4% of the human population consists of U.S. citizens. The probability of being a human if you are a U.S. citizen (Statement 3), on the other hand, is 1.0.

To state the difference between the two statements more formally, it is important to recognize that the term *probability* is being used in two different ways. One use, defined way back in Chapter 1, is purely mathematical and has to do with *the expected frequency of some outcome across a series of events*. If some event occurs multiple times, the probability of Outcome A is the proportion of events expected to result in Outcome A. If you play American bingo, in which 75 balls with letter–number combinations are drawn in random order until a winner is declared, the probability that the first ball selected will be I27 can be computed as 1/75, or .0133; the probability it will be the second ball selected is 1/74, or .0135, because the first ball has been removed; and so forth. This can be referred to as the **frequency model of probability**, and it provides the traditional understanding of probability used in statistics since the 17th century. In fact, NHST and confidence intervals rely exclusively on the frequency model.

The second model instead uses the term *probability* to refer to *a subjective level of belief in the truth of a statement*. This is often referred to as the **subjective model of probability**. In contrast to the frequency definition, mathematicians did not really begin to address whether a formal approach to the study of subjective probabilities was possible until well into the 20th century, although some of the mathematical underpinnings of this approach appeared hundreds of years earlier.

Complicating matters is that the intended use of the word *probability* is not always immediately clear. Consider this statement:

The probability of life on other planets is about .50.

From the frequency perspective, this statement would imply that if one could inspect many planets, life would be found to exist on about half of them; that is, from a frequency perspective life on other planets is true about half the time. From the subjective perspective, the statement instead implies there is a 50–50 chance that life exists somewhere else in the universe. I suspect you will agree with me that the speaker probably intended the latter meaning, which is a subjective estimate of the probability that the statement is true. Notice that in the previous sentence even the use of the word *probably* implies the subjective definition of probability. In common language use the subjective approach to probability is far more popular than the frequency approach.

This distinction has important implications for the inferential models discussed so far in this book. Suppose you are a particularly obsessive researcher and decide to conduct exactly the same study 100 times, each with $\alpha = .05$ and $1 - \beta = .80$. In the first 99 replications, 95 significance tests were not significant and four were significant. Now you have just completed the 100th replication, and the finding is significant. Because in this 100th study you have rejected the null hypothesis at .05, does that mean there is only a 5% chance the null hypothesis is true? That would be a ridiculous conclusion because examining all 100 outcomes provides pretty strong evidence that this is one of those rare cases in which the null hypothesis is true. The problem is that NHST has no built-in mechanism that allows you to aggregate results across significance tests to make a final judgment about the truth of the null hypothesis.[7]

The difference between the two probabilities can also be used to expand on the earlier section about confidence intervals titled "The Meaning of the Term *Confidence*." The word *confidence* is usually used as a synonym for *subjective probability*. It is not surprising, then, to find that even savvy statistics users sometimes fall into the trap of assuming they can be 95% confident (assume a .95 subjective probability) that the parameter they are estimating falls within the 95% confidence interval for their sample. Imagine, though, that in every previous study conducted on this topic the 95% confidence interval for the mean was in the range [107, 126]. If the 95% confidence interval for your sample proves to be [97, 101], would you really be 95% confident that your interval is correct?

The problem here is the odd use of the word *confidence*. What we know about a 95% confidence interval is that in 95% of samples the parameter being estimated should fall within the interval. This is a frequency-based approach to probability. It does not by itself tell us anything about how confident we should be that the 95% confidence interval for *this* sample is accurate, only about expectations over the long haul.

I know this is a tough distinction. I have to remind myself about the difference between "the probability of rejecting the null hypothesis if it

---

[7]Methods have been developed for combining NHST *p* values (Whitlock, 2005), but these methods are not inherent to NHST.

is true" and "the probability the null hypothesis is true if it is rejected" every time I think about it, and I have thought about it a lot (though I promise I am not nearly as boring as I sound). It may help you feel better about it to know that Oakes (1986) listed examples of published literature in which the author got this distinction wrong, some even by very well-known statisticians. I hope you can see from the previous examples that it is an important distinction, though.

In trying to come to grips with the subjective approach to probability, statisticians have generated an alternative set of inferential statistics collectively referred to as *Bayesian methods*. A thorough discussion of Bayesian methods is far beyond what can be accomplished here. If you are interested in learning more about Bayesian methods, see Iversen (1984) and Bolstad (2007), both of whom have provided particularly readable introductions. Here I simply provide a couple of examples to show how Bayesian methods can work in the context of testing null hypotheses, general decision making, and interval estimation.

MAKING DECISIONS ABOUT NULL HYPOTHESES

In Figure 5.3 is, once again, what you have learned so far about the possible outcomes of a significance test. To understand Bayesian methods, it is necessary to introduce some new ways of thinking about the probabilities depicted in Figure 5.4. The four probabilities in the cells of the figure are now stated as **conditional probabilities**, *the probability of one*

FIGURE 5.4

		Fact		
		Null hypothesis (H_0) is true	Alternative hypothesis (H_1) is true	
Statistical decision	Reject	$p(incorrect\ rejection) = \alpha$ $= p(R|H_0)$	$p(correct\ rejection) = 1-\beta$ $= p(R|H_1)$	$p(R)$
	Retain (not reject)	$p(correct\ retention) = 1 - \alpha$ $= p(NR|H_0)$	$p(incorrect\ retention) = \beta$ $= p(NR|H_1)$	$P(NR)$
		$p(H_0)$	$p(H_1)$	

Conditional probabilities.

event given the occurrence of another event. For example, the probability of a Type I error is the probability of rejecting the null hypothesis given that the null hypothesis is true, $p(R|H_0)$. Similarly, the power of the study is the probability of rejecting the null hypothesis given that the alternative hypothesis is true, $p(R|H_1)$, whereas the probability of a Type II error is the probability of retaining (not rejecting) the null hypothesis given the alternative hypothesis is true, $p(NR|H_1)$.

In addition, I have added the overall probabilities (usually called the **unconditional probabilities** or the **marginal probabilities**, because they are in the margins of the figure) of rejecting the null hypothesis, $p(R)$, the unconditional probability the null hypothesis is true, $p(H_0)$, and so forth.

"But wait a second!" the savvy reader will say. "How do I know the probability the null hypothesis is true, when the point of the study is to figure out whether the null hypothesis is true?" You are a very clever reader, indeed! The answer is that to use Bayesian methods you must have some *prior* guess about how likely it is that the null hypothesis is true, as well as the probability the alternative hypothesis is true. These values are referred to in Bayesian analysis as **prior probabilities**, *the subjective probabilities associated with some inference prior to considering a new outcome.* It may seem silly to say that you must have a subjective probability that some statement such as the null hypothesis is true before you can use new information to estimate the subjective probability of that statement, and opponents of Bayesian methods have at times focused on just this issue. In response, I point out that, first, when you think about it, this procedure is no sillier than assuming the null hypothesis is true in order to find evidence it is false, and, second, as you will see shortly, there are reasonable methods for estimating these prior probabilities. Using some conditional probabilities and the estimated prior probabilities, you can use new results to generate **posterior probabilities**, *the subjective probabilities associated with some inference after considering a new outcome.*

Suppose you conduct a study of a brand-new null hypothesis, one that has never been tested before, using $\alpha = .05$ and $1 - \beta = .85$, and the null hypothesis is rejected. What is the probability that your null hypothesis is in fact false? The Rev. Thomas Bayes introduced a formula to address this question that has since come to be called **Bayes' theorem**, *the formula presented by Bayes that came to serve as the basis for Bayesian methods,* although the basic concept underlying the theorem was discovered independently by several others. For answering the current question, Bayes' theorem can be stated as follows:

$$p(H_0|R) = \frac{p(R|H_0)p(H_0)}{p(R)} = \frac{p(R|H_0)p(H_0)}{p(R|H_0)p(H_0) + p(R|H_1)p(H_1)}. \tag{5.8}$$

The goal of this formula is to compute the probability that the null hypothesis is true *given* that it was rejected, $p(H_0|R)$. This is the inverse of the probability $p(R|H_0)$, which is the probability of a Type I error in NHST, and so Bayesian methods are sometimes described as generating "inverse probabilities from direct probabilities." These terms are considered anachronistic (notice I did not set them in bold) because the term *direct* implies that the NHST conditional probabilities such as $p(R|H_0)$ are more direct or straightforward, a pejorative implication Bayesians would not accept. These terms still occasionally appear in the literature, however.

This goal of estimating $p(H_0|R)$ makes no sense in the context of NHST: Either the null hypothesis is true or it is not, so the probability that the null hypothesis is true is either 0 or 1 and cannot change on the basis of data. From a frequency perspective, $p(R|H_0)$ represents an acceptable conditional probability because it is possible to conduct the same study many times and determine how frequently the null hypothesis is rejected.

Equation 5.8 also requires the prior probabilities for the possible outcomes: your degree of faith that the null hypothesis is true before the study and your degree of faith that the alternative hypothesis is true. Because we are assuming this is a new null hypothesis never tested before, and you have no prior information about its truth or falsehood, it would be reasonable to start by assuming the following:

$$p(H_0) = 50$$
$$p(H_1) = .50; \tag{5.9}$$

that is, start by assuming that the possible fact states are equally likely. This is sometimes referred to as being *indifferent* to or *agnostic* about the probability of the different possible fact states. These two values can be thought of as the distribution of prior probabilities, the subjective probabilities you attach to each possible outcome before data are collected.

To summarize, we know the following:

- The null hypothesis was rejected.

- $\alpha = p(R|H_0) = .05$ and $1 - \beta = p(R|H_1) = .85$.

- The most reasonable prior probabilities for the null hypothesis, $p(H_0)$, and alternative hypothesis, $p(H_1)$, were both .50.

According to Bayes' theorem,

$$p(H_0|R) = \frac{p(R|H_0)p(H_0)}{p(R|H_0)p(H_0) + p(R|H_1)p(H_1)}$$

$$= \frac{(.05 \times .50)}{(.05 \times .50) + (.85 \times .50)} = .37. \tag{5.10}$$

Similarly, we can compute the probability the alternative hypothesis is true from the following:

$$p(H_1|R) = \frac{p(R|H_1)p(H_1)}{p(R|H_1)p(H_1) + p(R|H_0)p(H_0)}$$

$$= \frac{(.85 \times .50)}{(.85 \times .50) + (.05 \times .50)} = .63. \qquad (5.11)$$

I hope you see that these two posterior probabilities must sum to 1.00 because there are only two possibilities: Given that the null hypothesis has been rejected, either the null or alternative hypothesis must be true.

Before gathering the data we had no reason to believe the null hypothesis was more or less likely than the alternative hypothesis: Both of our prior probabilities for the two possible hypotheses were .50. Knowing that we rejected the null hypothesis with a certain alpha level and power, we can estimate a new posterior probability that each hypothesis is true. The fact that we rejected the null hypothesis increases our subjective probability that the alternative hypothesis is true to .63 and reduces our subjective probability that the null hypothesis is true to .37.

One of the nice features of Bayesian analysis is that it also allows for cumulative decision making across studies. Imagine that we replicate this study with a new one, except this time $\alpha = .05$ but $1 - \beta = .52$. This time we fail to reject the null hypothesis. Now how much faith should we have in the null hypothesis?

Because the first study was already completed, now we can treat .37 as the prior probability that the null hypothesis is true and .63 as the prior probability that the alternative hypothesis is true. Bayes' theorem now suggests the following:

$$p(H_0|NR) = \frac{p(NR|H_0)p(H_0)}{p(NR|H_0)p(H_0) + p(NR|H_1)p(H_1)}$$

$$= \frac{(.95 \times .37)}{(.95 \times .37) + (.52 \times .63)} = .52. \qquad (5.12)$$

The failure to reject the null hypothesis increases the subjective probability that the null hypothesis is true; however, because the power of the two studies differed they did not perfectly offset each other. Over many replications, the probability that the null hypothesis is true should stabilize. In this way, Bayesian analysis is like meta-analysis in its ability to accumulate evidence across studies.

GENERAL DECISION MAKING

It is important to understand that Bayesian methods are the basis for a complete alternative inferential strategy to NHST, as I attempt to demonstrate in this and the next two sections. Even Bayes' theorem has more general utility than the previous example suggests. For example, take the case of a mammogram, which is an X-ray of the breast that can accurately detect breast cancer about 90% of the time. In addition, the result is negative for about 95% of women who do not have cancer. On the basis of these numbers, the National Cancer Institute recommends that all women 40 and older receive a mammogram every 1 to 2 years. The rate of breast cancer for women in this age group is about 0.2%. This means that if all women age 40 and older receive mammograms, then only two in every 1,000 women who get a mammogram will actually have breast cancer. This situation is outlined in Figure 5.5, with the statistics presented so far in boldface type.

We know that the prior probability of cancer before a mammogram, $p(C)$, is .002, whereas the prior probability for not having cancer is .998; that is, the bottom row of the figure indicates the distribution of prior probabilities. Using Bayes' theorem, it is possible to compute the posterior probability a woman has cancer if she has a positive mammogram as follows:

$$p(C|P) = \frac{p(P|C)p(C)}{p(P|C)p(C) + p(P|NC)p(NC)}$$

$$= \frac{(.90 \times .002)}{(.90 \times .002) + (.05 \times .998)} = .035; \qquad (5.13)$$

that is, if all women 40 and older regularly had mammograms, less than 4% of those who have positive results would actually have cancer; the posterior probability of not having cancer would be about .965.

FIGURE 5.5

		Fact	
		Cancer (C)	No cancer (NC)
Mammogram results	Positive (P)	$p(P|C) = .90$	$p(P|NC) = .05$
	Negative (N)	$p(N|C) = .10$	$p(N|NC) = .95$
		$p(C) = .002$	$p(NC) = .998$

Probabilities related to mammogram results and breast cancer. Numbers in boldface type are discussed in the text.

If a woman has a negative mammogram, the posterior probabilities would instead be

$$p(NC|N) = \frac{p(N|NC)p(NC)}{p(N|NC)p(NC) + p(N|C)p(C)}$$

$$= \frac{(.95 \times .998)}{(.95 \times .998) + (.10 \times .002)} > .999, \qquad (5.14)$$

and the posterior probability of having cancer would be $p(C|N) < .001$.

If a hypothetical woman, Angela, has a mammogram and receives a positive result, and if Angela completed the mammogram only because it has been recommended that all women do so (in other words, if she had no symptoms that increased her prior probability of cancer), this analysis suggests that it is reasonable to assign the hypothesis that Angela has cancer a subjective probability of only .035. This is likely to be very different than the information Angela received from her physician, however. Most troubling of all, even when provided with similar statistical information about mammograms, 60% of gynecologists thought a positive mammogram was accurate 80% to 90% of the time (Gigerenzer, Gaissmaier, Kurz-Milcke, Schwartz, & Woloshin, 2007). Notice that a positive mammogram does produce a dramatic increase in the probability one should attach to Angela's having cancer: Whereas the prior probability was .002, the posterior probability is .035. Even so, the test is far more often wrong than right because the large majority of women over 40 do not have cancer.

I hope you can see that this can be a very useful formula in any decision-making situation. A whole set of statistics has been developed in conjunction with understanding decision making that I do not discuss here but that can be found in Figure 5.6. I should also note that Bayes' theorem can handle situations involving more than two fact statements (e.g., no cancer, early-stage cancer, or late-stage cancer) and more than two outcomes (e.g., positive, negative, or indeterminate).

PARAMETER ESTIMATION

The Bayesian model is not limited to the decision-making case in modeling; it can also be used for parameter estimation. Let us return again to the hypothetical nutritional supplement study in which the sample of 300 had a mean score of 102.5 and the mean for the general population on this test is $\mu = 100$ with a standard deviation of $\sigma = 15$. The solid line in Figure 5.7 represents the proposed distribution of prior probabilities. This can be compared with the two previous examples used to demonstrate the Bayesian model. In the cancer example we knew from population data that the probability of breast cancer in women over

FIGURE 5.6

Fact (Y)

		Positive (Y+)	Negative (Y−)	
Test result	Positive (X+)	$p(X+Y+) = .09$	$p(X+Y−) = .10$	$p(X+) = .19$
(X)	Negative (X−)	$p(X−Y+) = .01$	$p(X−Y−) = .80$	$p(X−) = .81$
		$p(Y+) = .10$	$p(Y−) = .90$	

Sensitivity	$p(X+|Y+) = p(X+Y+)/p(Y+) = .90$
False negative rate	$p(X−|Y+) = p(X−Y+)/p(Y+) = .10$
Specificity	$p(X−|Y−) = p(X−Y−)/p(Y−) = .89$
False positive rate[a]	$p(X+|Y−) = p(X+Y−)/p(Y−) = .11$
Positive predictive power (or value)	$p(Y+|X+) = p(X+Y+)/p(X+) = .47$
False alarm ratio[b]	$p(Y−|X+) = p(X+Y−)/p(X+) = .53$
Negative predictive power (or value)	$p(Y−|X−) = p(X−Y−)/p(X−) = .99$
Frequency bias	$p(X+)/p(Y+) = 1.90$
Base rate	$p(Y+) = .10$
Selection ratio	$p(X+) = .19$
Correct fraction	$p(X+Y+) + p(X−Y−) = .89$

Terminology for decision-making research. Warning: Different research literatures use different names for these statistics, sometimes in ways that are confusing. I have seen both the sensitivity and the correct fraction referred to as the *hit rate*. The figure provides what I thought was the most generally useful name for each statistic. When reading research about decision making make sure you know which statistic is being referenced; do not expect to be able to rely exclusively on the names. The examples provided in the figure are arbitrary and were included solely so you can verify how these statistics are computed should you wish to do so. Within each cell, notation such as $p(X+Y−)$ refers to the probability that a person is both positive on the test and negative for the condition being identified. This is a smaller quantity than a conditional probability, such as the probability a person is positive on the test *given* they are negative for the condition, $p(X+|Y−)$. Statistics in boldface type are listed in the Index, to help you find brief descriptions of statistics in the future when reading research.
[a] In the context of null hypothesis significance testing, this ratio also represents the per-comparison error rate (see Chapter 2, this volume).
[b] In the context of null hypothesis significance testing, this ratio also represents the false discovery rate described by Benjamini and Hochberg (1995; see Chapter 3, this volume).

FIGURE 5.7

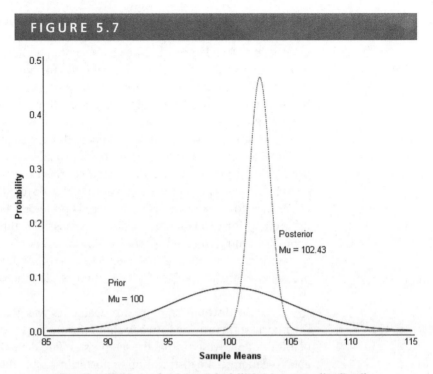

The distribution of prior probabilities is normally distributed around the best estimate of μ prior to data collection,
which is 100. The sample with $\bar{Y} = 102.5$ shifts the distribution of posterior probabilities so that the most probable
value for μ (the value associated with the highest subjective probability) is 102.43. The distribution of posterior
probabilities also becomes narrower, indicating a smaller
range of probable values.

40 is approximately .002, whereas the probability of not having cancer
is .998. In the other example, in which we attempted to estimate the
probability that the null hypothesis is true, we started from the agnostic
or indifferent position, assigning the same probability (.50) to both the
null and alternative hypotheses. If we generated prior probabilities in
the present case agnostically we might assign an equal prior probability
to every possible value of μ within what would seem to be a reasonable
range, perhaps from 85 to 115. This choice would imply that we expect
that the supplement changes intelligence by at most 15 points but have
no preconceived notion of how much change we will see. The distribution
of prior probabilities would then look like a horizontal line. *A distribution
in which every value has the same probability* is often referred to as a **uniform**
or **rectangular distribution**, so the agnostic approach would lead us
to suggest a rectangular distribution of prior probabilities.

That would be an acceptable choice, but a third option seems better in this case. We might expect that a smaller effect is more likely than a larger effect. That logic would suggest assigning higher prior probabilities to values around 100 and lower probabilities to values further from 100. If we follow this strategy, a normal distribution can be used to provide a reasonable model of the subjective probabilities we assign to different possible μ values.

To summarize what has just happened, I am suggesting that there are at least three ways to estimate prior probabilities. One is based on prior data. If prior data are not available, then the prior probabilities must be set logically (a process similar to that used to estimate population effect sizes for power analysis). If there is no logical basis for assigning different prior probabilities to different possible outcomes, then the agnostic or indifferent approach of assigning every possible outcome the same prior probability is acceptable. However, other distributions of prior probabilities are acceptable so long as there is a logical basis for the values that are assigned.

Once the distribution of prior probabilities was generated, and using the information provided already about this study (I had to add one piece of information, which is that the sample standard deviation was 10), I was able to generate the distribution of posterior probabilities in Figure 5.3. Do not worry about the mathematics of this process; the important point is this: It was possible (based on logical argument in this case) to generate a set of prior probabilities for possible values of μ in the population of people who use the supplements. After collecting data, I amended that distribution. Notice that the value with the highest probability in the posterior distribution (102.43) is quite close to the sample mean (102.5). This is because the sample size was quite large. Also, the distribution is much narrower, reflecting the decline in uncertainty that comes with using data to estimate the subjective probabilities.

One advantage of Bayesian methods over NHST is that additional information can be incorporated quite easily. Suppose a second study is conducted, and in this one we find that $\bar{Y} = 104.9$, and $2\hat{\sigma} = 18$, but the sample size is only 25. On the basis of this additional information the posterior distribution shifts slightly, so that the most probable value is now 102.81 (the value changes very little because of the small sample size), and the distribution becomes even narrower (because more information always reduces uncertainty further).

A Bayesian alternative to confidence intervals has also been suggested that is often referred to as **credibility intervals** or **Bayesian confidence intervals**. Because these are even less familiar to researchers than confidence intervals, I do not discuss them in detail, except to note two things:

1. Unlike confidence intervals, credibility intervals do allow for interpretation in terms of subjective belief; that is, one can hold a .95

probability that the parameter falls within the 95% credibility interval. On the basis of the discussion of the meaning of the word *confidence,* as the subjective probability that something is true, credibility intervals are probably more deserving of the name *confidence intervals* than the methods described earlier in this chapter, but tradition often trumps logic.

2. As a practical matter, if prior probabilities are set on the basis of indifference, credibility intervals and confidence intervals tend to produce very similar results. The two tend to differ more as information about the credibility interval is aggregated across studies.

CRITICISMS OF BAYESIAN METHODS

Bayesian methods are not without their critics. It should be clear that the subjective model of the term *probability* is more slippery than the frequency model. The justification for the distribution of prior probabilities can appear pretty subjective, especially when compared with the purely objective definition of probability used in NHST. Fisher (1925) did not even think subjective probabilities were valid, indicating that the study of such quantities was "founded upon an error" (p. 10). It is noteworthy that the state of Nevada has a law based on similar concerns that in essence restricts gambling to activities that comply with the frequency definition of probability.

Others have disagreed with Fisher about the folly of studying subjective probabilities, for one very important reason: Few things in life are certain, and people frequently have to make a decision about whether a statement is true or false in circumstances in which the information is less than perfect. Improving decision making in the context of imperfect information is a very important goal for science and mathematics. Only the subjective approach to probability makes it possible to create quantitative models of those situations.

In fact, Fisher (1922) himself introduced a concept he called **maximum likelihood**, *a method for choosing between the possible estimates of a parameter based on their relative likelihood of being correct.* Here is how it works. Suppose I have the following sample:

27, 18, 23, 24, 17, 21, 19, 19, 24, 22.

The sample mean is 21.4. I would like to estimate the population mean (ignore for now that you already know that the sample mean is the best estimate of the population mean). For the purposes of this example I will assume the variable is normally distributed in the population with $\sigma = 3.0$. On the basis of the sample values it is reasonable to assume that μ falls somewhere in the interval [18.0, 27.0]. We start by assuming that the population mean is 18.0. If that is true, then values closer to 18 will be more probable than values further from 18, and we can use the normal distribution with a standard deviation of 3.0 to compute the probability of each value. A statistic called the likelihood is then computed:

$$L(\mu = 18.0) = \prod_{i=1}^{N} p(x_i|\mu) = p(27|\mu = 18) \times p(18|\mu = 18)...$$

$$= 18.5195 \times 10^{-15}. \tag{5.15}$$

The resulting likelihood in this case is a very small number, so I divided it by 10^{15} to make it easier to read. The Π (Greek uppercase letter pi) symbol may be new to you. It parallels the Σ operator. Whereas Σ means "sum across all the values," Π means "multiply across all the values." Multiplying thousands of numbers can tax even computers. Multiplying numbers is equivalent to summing their logarithmic values, so to simplify the computations the values are first transformed using the natural logarithm and then can be summed rather than multiplied. As a result, you will frequently see references to the *log likelihood*.

The likelihood can then be computed for 18.1, for 18.2, and every value up to 27.0. Here are three. In each case L is divided by 10^{15}:

Estimate of μ	L
18.0	18.5195
21.4	11,396.3220
27.0	0.0003

Of all the values tested, 21.4 has the highest likelihood and so represents the most likely value for μ given this sample. In fact, the ratio of the likelihood of two estimates of μ provides their relative likelihood of being true:

$$\frac{L(\mu = 21.4)}{L(\mu = 18.0)} = \frac{11396.3220}{18.5195} = 615.37. \tag{5.16}$$

Given these data, the population mean is far more likely to be 21.4 than 18.0.

One nice feature of maximum likelihood is that it allows estimation of multiple parameters simultaneously. For example, instead of assuming $\sigma = 3.0$, I could have computed likelihoods for all possible combinations of values for μ from 18.0 to 27.0 and values for σ from 1.5 to 5.5. It is therefore used frequently in connection with complex models in which many parameters are being estimated simultaneously. One problem with maximum likelihood estimation is that it requires knowledge of the population distributions for all the variables involved.

Like Bayesian methods, maximum likelihood estimation generates a best guess about the value of a parameter. It differs from Bayesian estimation in that it provides no estimate of how probable it is that the estimate is correct. This is as Fisher wanted it, and why he used the term *likelihood*, because such an estimate would represent a subjective probability. Despite the differences between the two, it is not unusual for maximum likelihood and Bayesian methods to be used together, a turn of events that may have Fisher rolling in his grave.

Bayesian methods have other, less philosophical weaknesses. Whereas power analysis is a relatively well-defined procedure, no similar standard exists for setting sample sizes in Bayesian analyses. Another concern is a potential sense of arbitrariness in the choice of prior probabilities. Despite the problems, Bayesian methods are playing a growing role in psychological research.

Conclusion

Given the problems with NHST, statisticians have considered a variety of alternative options. In this chapter, I have summarized the three options that have received the most attention: (a) confidence intervals, (b) meta-analysis, and (c) Bayesian inference. Each has its particular strengths and problems, but they all demonstrate advantages over an inferential strategy based on NHST alone. The emerging consensus seems to be that a combination of effect sizes with confidence or credibility intervals at the level of the primary study and meta-analysis at the level of research integration represents the best alternative to traditional methods. In fact, meta-analysis has already become the dominant approach in integration, and the number of studies that report effect sizes and/or confidence intervals is increasing. This is not to say that inferences that involve a choice between two conclusions will ever disappear completely, however. Sometimes what matters more than anything else is a decision about whether or not some effect exists. In the context of inferential decisions, NHST is likely to remain an important tool.

MODELS OF MEASUREMENT II

Models of Measurement Error 6

P art I of this book told a kind of story about the strategies psychologists have used for dealing with the problem of sampling error. The chapters in Part II are different in that each focuses on a relatively discrete topic. What these topics have in common is their relevance to **psychometrics**—*quantitative models of psychological measurement.* You will also notice a difference in style. Whereas null hypothesis significance testing and the other models of inference represent general strategies applicable to all sorts of statistics, from here on the modeling methods I describe are usually connected to certain statistical techniques. As a result, more of the tables and footnotes represent resources and advice when working with those techniques.

Problems in psychological measurement can often be traced to the difficulties psychologists face when they are measuring concepts that cannot be directly observed. I use the terms **latent variable** or **construct** to refer to *an attribute of individuals or organisms that cannot be directly observed.* Examples of such variables include feelings of anxiety (which are phenomenological) or group cohesion (which is an abstract social concept). To enhance consistency in the discussion I also generally use the term **indicators** to refer to *instruments used to measure variables.* This term encompasses measurement devices as diverse as psychological tests such as the Beck Depression Inventory (BDI; Beck, Steer, & Brown,

1996), ratings of behavioral frequency, and functional magnetic resonance imaging scans. An indicator is a structured method of measurement that often produces a quantitative variable.

True-Score Theory

My discussion of inference in Chapter 1 began with an introduction to the problem of error. The chapters in Part I focused specifically on various strategies for dealing with sampling error as an obstacle in drawing inferences about populations from samples. A second type of error that needs to be considered—in fact, the type of error that first concerned astronomers—is **measurement error**, *error that occurs in the act of measuring some attribute*. There are really two types of measurement error. I find a bathroom scale is a particularly effective example for demonstrating the nature of measurement error. Balzac gets on his bathroom scale and finds that his weight is 192 pounds (87 kg). He gets off the scale and, just to be sure, tries it again. This time he gets a reading of 235 pounds (107 kg). Checking again a moment later, he finds that his weight is now 213 pounds (97 kg). Clearly, this is not a trustworthy indicator because it is not *reliable*.

Alternatively, each time Balzac gets on the bathroom scale he finds his weight is 192 pounds (87 kg). Unfortunately, several other weight scales in the recent past have indicated that his true weight is about 225 pounds (102 kg). His scale is reliable, but it is not particularly accurate or *valid*.

Similarly, the study of measurement error can be divided into the study of reliability and the study of validity. The first has to do with *random errors* in measurements of an attribute, that is, errors that change from measurement to measurement. The second has to do with *systematic errors* or consistent inaccuracies in indicators. I define these terms more formally later in this chapter.

Suppose your psychology graduate program of choice rejects you because your Graduate Record Examination score on the Quantitative section is 600, whereas that of the candidate they chose is 630. How would you argue with this decision? You might claim that the difference is so small that it could be due to chance; this would represent an argument made from the perspective of random error or reliability. You might also try to claim that the Quantitative score is not a very effective predictor of graduate school performance, arguing your case in terms of systematic error or validity. This example is intended to demonstrate that poor reliability or validity can have real-world implications when psychological tests are used to make decisions about people.

The traditional approach to understanding random error in measurement is called *true-score theory*. As you will see, this theory is another example of a clever and mathematically sophisticated model with some serious flaws when applied to real-world circumstances. To begin the discussion of this model, note that Balzac's test of the reliability of his bathroom scale required two conditions. First, he had to measure his weight multiple times. If he weighed himself only once, he would not have enough information to evaluate whether the scale is reliable. Second, it is reasonable to assume that his true weight was consistent. If he weighed himself once in January, once in February, and once in August, a fair amount of the variations in the results could reflect actual changes in his weight. Instead, he weighed himself three times in a matter of minutes because it is reasonable to assume weight is constant in that short a time span.

Any method of evaluating reliability requires these two features: (a) repeated measurements of some attribute that (b) should be consistent across those measurements. These conditions are so fundamental that some discussions of reliability measurement do not even mention them, but they are always necessary. True-score theory is a specific approach to reliability evaluation that represents a mathematical model based on several additional definitions and assumptions.

The BDI can be used to demonstrate the process of estimating reliability in psychological instruments. The BDI consists of 21 items, each of which is scored on a scale from 0 to 3. For example, the first item asks respondents to rate how sad they feel, on a scale on which a 0 indicates no feelings of sadness and a 3 indicates feeling so sad or unhappy "I can't stand it." In the context of true-score theory, these 21 items are treated as repeated measurements of the attribute depression.

If a sample of 100 people is administered the BDI, a data matrix can be created in which the columns represent BDI items and rows represent members of the sample. This table of 21 columns and 100 rows might look like the unshaded portion of Table 6.1. In the context of true-score theory, the members of a sample are frequently referred to as the *targets* of the measurements because the objects of measurement are not always people. These data can be used to demonstrate many of the key concepts of true-score theory.

DEFINING RELIABILITY

True-score theory (also called *classical test theory* or *reliability theory*) is *a mathematical model of test reliability based on the concept of a true score.* As formalized by Lord and Novick (1968), true-score theory is founded on two definitions. The first defines an individual's true score on some indicator as $T_i = E(X_{ij})$,

TABLE 6.1

Sample Data for an Internal Reliability Analysis of the Beck Depression Inventory

Person	| Item									
	1	2	3	4	5	...	20	21	*M*	Score
1	1	0	0	1	0		1	2	0.71	15
2	2	2	3	1	0		2	2	1.52	32
3	2	2	1	1	0		3	1	1.05	22
...										
100	1	0	0	0	1		0	0	0.38	8
M	1.13	0.92	0.76	0.81	0.49		0.91	1.01	**0.89**	18.7

Note. In an analysis of the reliability of a scale the individual items serve as the multiple measurements of the attribute for each member of the sample. The total score each target receives on the Beck Depression Inventory is the mean score per item multiplied by the number of items (21). The value in boldface type (0.89) is the mean of all 21 item means and also the mean of the 100 target means, or the mean for all measurements in the sample.

where X_{ij} refers to the j measurements for individual i and T_i is a parameter that represents individual i's true score. This formula uses the concept of expected value (see Chapter 1, this volume). In this context, it refers to the mean of the population of measurements for this person; that is, a target's **true score** can be defined as *the mean of the population of measurements for a target.*

In Table 6.1, the first measurement for the first member of the sample is that person's score on the first BDI item: $X_{11} = 1$. That person's score on the second measurement is $X_{12} = 0$, and so forth, across the row. Person 1's mean score across the 21 items, $T_1 = 0.71$, represents the best estimate of the person's true score. The total BDI score is generated by summing instead of averaging scores on the items, so it equals the best estimate of the true score multiplied by the number of items. This value is provided in the last column of the table.

The term *true score* in this setting is potentially very misleading. The word *true* can easily lead you to believe this is the correct, accurate, or valid score, the best estimate of how depressed this person is. That conclusion would be incorrect. We determined that our best estimate of Balzac's true score on the reliable bathroom scale was 192 pounds (87 kg), and the fact that the same result occurred each time indicates that 192 pounds (87 kg) is his true score according to this bathroom scale. However, in fact he weighs 225 pounds (102 kg), so his *true* score on this scale is also an *incorrect* score. The true score can be thought of as the most valid score possible with *this* indicator, but a different indicator might produce a more valid score. When you see references to the true score in relation to reliability you should always keep in mind the fact that this term refers to the *reliable* or *consistent* score for *this* indicator, not the *correct* score.

The second term defined in true-score theory is measurement error (*e*):

$$e_{ij} = X_{ij} - T_i. \tag{6.1}$$

This formula defines the error in measurement *j* of person *i* as the difference between measurement *j* and the person's true score. Remember that because *T* is a parameter, values of *e* can only be estimated. For Person 2 in Table 6.1 the true score is estimated to be 1.52. The first measurement for Person 2 (score on Item 1) is 2, so the error in this target is estimated to be

$$e_{21} = X_{21} - T_2 = 2 - 1.52 = 0.48. \tag{6.2}$$

True-score theory represents a quantitative model of measurement error. Measurement error is defined mathematically as the difference between a measurement and the true score, where the true score is defined as the population mean of those measurements. One characteristic of a mean is that differences from the mean will sum to 0. Because the true score is the population mean of the measurements, it follows that for any target the sum of the true errors will equal 0.

Combining the definitions and conditions described so far, we can draw three conclusions: (a) A person's true score on an indicator is a fixed value, (b) multiple measurements will vary around the true score, and (c) that variation represents measurement error. To this point the discussion has focused on individual members of the population, but on the basis of the concepts that have been introduced so far it is also possible to define several statistics relevant to the entire population.

The first is the total variance of the measurements in the population,

$$\sigma_X^2 = \frac{\sum_{j=1}^{k}\sum_{i=1}^{N}(X_{ij} - \mu..)^2}{N \times k}, \tag{6.3}$$

where *N* is the number of targets in the population, *k* is the number of measurements of each target, and $\mu..$ is the population mean of all measurements for all targets. If the data presented in Table 6.1 represent a complete population, then $\mu.. = .89$ and the total variance equals

$$\sigma_X^2 = \frac{(1 - .89)^2 + (0 - .89)^2 + \ldots (0 - .89)^2 + (0.89)^2}{100 \times 21}. \tag{6.4}$$

To state the computation of this formula in words, subtract $\mu_{..}$ from each measurement in the population, square the difference, and then divide by the total number of measurements.

If we make an additional assumption, that errors are random across measurements (i.e., vary in a nonsystematic way), we can prove that the variance of the measurements in the population equals the sum of the variance of the true scores plus the variance of the errors:

$$\sigma_X^2 = \sigma_T^2 + \sigma_e^2. \tag{6.5}$$

Based on Equation 6.5, the **reliability** of a population of measurements is equal to *the proportion of the variance of the measurements represented by the variance of the true scores:*

$$\rho_{XT}^2 = \frac{\sigma_T^2}{\sigma_X^2} = 1 - \frac{\sigma_e^2}{\sigma_X^2}. \tag{6.6}$$

The Greek lowercase letter rho, ρ, is often used to refer to a correlation in a population, so the symbol ρ_{XT}^2 for the reliability indicates that it represents the squared population correlation between the measurements and true scores on an indicator. Equation 6.6 also suggests that reliability has to do with how much of the variance of measurements is not due to error variance. This equation provides the basis for all computational formulas used to estimate reliability in a sample.

In the rest of this section I explore the implications of Equation 6.6 further. The first thing to note is that variances cannot be negative because they involve squaring, so the smallest possible value for the reliability of a population of measurements is 0. In practice, some formulas used to compute a sample estimate of reliability can actually take on negative values, but that would suggest that something is seriously wrong with your data. This might occur if there is something very odd about the sample, if the measurements are not really measuring a consistent characteristic, or—most likely—if the data were entered incorrectly. Also, because Equation 6.5 indicates $\sigma_T^2 \leq \sigma_X^2$, the largest possible value for reliability is 1.0.

Table 6.2 gives an example of what the data would have to look like for reliability to equal 0. There is variability in the scores across items, but there is no variability in the true scores: Each participant in the sample demonstrates the same total score across items (20). In this case, all variability in the measurements has to do with error variance, with variability in the measurements within individuals.

Table 6.3 demonstrates the opposite extreme, when there is no error variance. In this case, each individual generated exactly the same score on every item, so there is no variability within individuals. All the vari-

TABLE 6.2

Sample Data In Which Reliability = 0

Person	1	2	3	4	5	...	20	21	M	Score
						Item				
1	1	2	1	0	0		1	2	0.95	20
2	2	1	0	1	1		0	1	0.95	20
3	2	2	1	1	0		2	1	0.95	20
...										
100	1	0	2	0	0		2	2	0.95	20
M	1.04	0.92	0.76	0.81	0.35		0.91	1.01	**0.95**	20

Note. The value in boldface type (0.95) is the mean of the 21 item means and the mean of the 100 target means. In this case, there is no variability in the target means: All 100 sample members have a mean item score of 0.95.

ability in the measurements is accounted for by variability in the true scores. In this case, the reliability would equal 1.0.

Of course, the real world is always messier than the ideal one. There is usually variability both within the rows and in the column means, as in Table 6.1. The reliability of the measurements as a whole is a function of the degree to which the total variability in the measurements consists of variability between the targets.

ESTIMATING RELIABILITY

Lord and Novick (1968) found that the most accurate sample estimate of reliability occurs when the measurements result from **parallel tests**. Two indicators, X and X', or "tests," are parallel when *for each target the true score on indicator X equals the true score on indicator X' and the variance of the*

TABLE 6.3

Sample Data in Which Reliability = 1.0

Person	1	2	3	4	5	...	20	21	M	Score
						Item				
1	1	1	1	1	1		1	1	1.00	21
2	2	2	2	2	2		2	2	2.00	42
3	0	0	0	0	0		0	0	0.00	0
...										
100	1	1	1	1	1		1	1	1.00	21
M	1.40	1.40	1.40	1.40	1.40		1.40	1.40	**1.40**	29.4

Note. The value in boldface type (1.40) is the mean of all 21 item means and the mean of all 100 target means. In this case, there is no variability in the item means: All 21 items have a mean item score of 1.40.

errors for the two indicators are equal. If people are administered two parallel tests, then the population reliability can be defined as the correlation between the two tests, $\rho^{XX'}$ (notice that this symbol is not squared, as in the case of ρ^2_{XT}, but these quantities will be equal if the indicators are parallel).

Although the concept of parallel tests was important in the development of true-score theory, parallel tests rarely if ever exist in practice. The more typical case in psychology is that the multiple measurements used to estimate reliability are **congeneric tests,** *two tests that attempt to measure the same attribute but without assuming either equal true scores or equal error variances.*[1] One consequence of using congeneric tests is that sample estimates of reliability tend to underestimate the true population reliability.

With these concepts in hand I now turn to the description of how to estimate reliability in practice. Several approaches are common.

Internal Reliability

Internal reliability, or *test reliability*, is used *when the multiple items of an indicator are used as the repeated measurements of some true score for purposes of estimating reliability.* Given the popularity of multi-item indicators in psychology, it is not surprising to find that internal reliability is probably the most commonly reported form of reliability. Of course, this really makes sense only if all the items are on the same scale: If an indicator has some items on a 1-to-5 scale, whereas other items are ranked on a 0-to-3 scale, it makes no sense to combine them for purposes of estimating reliability.

Internal reliability increases to the extent to which the person responds in a similar manner to the different items that comprise the indicator. Statistics for the estimation of internal and other forms of reliability may be found in Table 6.4. As the table indicates, coefficient alpha is the dominant statistic used for estimation of internal reliability.[2]

Test–Retest Reliability

A second approach to estimating reliability involves administering the same indicator multiple times to the same individuals. The total score at

---

[1]In terms of characterizing the degree of similarity between indicators, two other categories have been described that fall between parallel and congeneric tests, called **tau equivalent** (*equal true scores, unequal error variances*) and **essentially tau equivalent tests** (*true scores differ by a constant, unequal error variances*). In practice, however, indicators are almost always congeneric.

[2]One practical aspect of computing internal reliability is worth mentioning. If some items are key-reversed before the indicator is scored (e.g., on a 1–5 scale 1 is supposed to be converted to 5, 2 to 4, etc.), those items should be reversed before test reliability is computed. When students tell me they found poor reliability for an established indicator in their research, the number one culprit I find is forgetting to key-reverse.

TABLE 6.4

Common Reliability Statistics

Reliability statistic	Description
Internal reliability	Relevant when an indicator consisting of multiple items is administered once.
Split–half reliability	Items are split in half to create two indicators and the correlation between the two halves is used to estimate reliability. This correlation is corrected for the greater length of the full indicator because longer scores are more reliable than shorter scales. The problem with this method is that different sorts of the items into two groups can produce different reliability estimates.
Rulon method	Sometimes also called the *Guttman method*. An alternate split–half method that uses the variance of differences between the total scores from the two halves as an estimate of error variance. This method has the same problem as split–half reliability.
Kuder–Richardson formulas	Kuder and Richardson (1937) offered simplified formulas for estimating reliability when the items are dichotomous (e.g., true–false items). KR-20 is generally applicable to dichotomous items; KR-21 is a simpler formula that can be used only if the distributions of the items are all the same (which they never are), for example, if the proportion answering false is always the same.
Coefficient alpha	Also called *Cronbach's alpha* (Cronbach, 1951). This formula has essentially supplanted all the previous statistics. If Rulon reliabilities were computed for every possible split of the items, the mean of those eliabilities would equal coefficient alpha. If items are dichotomous, KR-20 and alpha are equal. For congeneric scales, this represents the lower bound estimate of reliability.
Test–retest reliability	Relevant when an indicator is administered multiple times, or alternate forms are administered.
Pearson correlation coefficient	Traditionally the most commonly used statistic for test–retest reliability. Becomes cumbersome when the indicator is administered more than twice, because the correlation can handle only two administrations at a time.
Intraclass correlation coefficient (ICC)	Increasingly popular for this purpose. See following section on ICCs.
Interrater reliability	Relevant when an indicator involves judgments.
Percent agreement	Has been used as a measure of interrater reliability when judges place targets into two or more categories. However, this is *not* a true measure of reliability and is not recommended.
Kappa coefficient	Also called *Cohen's kappa* (Cohen, 1960; see also Fleiss, 1971). This is the most commonly used statistic when judges place targets into two or more categories. When there are more than two categories, **weighted kappa** may be used to gauge differing degrees of disagreement between judges (Cohen, 1968).
Intraclass correlation coefficient	The dominant choice when judgments are on a dimensional scale. See section on ICCs, next.

(continued)

TABLE 6.4 (*Continued*)

Common Reliability Statistics

Reliability statistic	Description
Intraclass correlation coefficients (ICCs)	Not a type of reliability but a set of related statistics increasingly used for estimating reliability. The ICC differs from Pearson correlations in that the latter addresses the linear relationship between the observations whereas the ICC also considers mean differences between observations (absolute agreement). The ICC is applicable whether observations are dichotomous or dimensional and can be computed regardless of the number of administrations or judges. Weighted kappa and coefficient alpha are special cases of ICCs. The ICC is computed differently depending on the context. The ICCs listed in the next several rows of this table are the most common variants (Shrout & Fleiss, 1979). The first value in parentheses has to do with the sources of the measurements, the second value with how many sources will be used in subsequent ratings. These are described in the context of interrater reliability as is traditional in this literature.
ICC(1,1)	Also called *one-way random-effect model, single measures.* This is the appropriate formula when 1) each target is rated by a different set of judges and 1) in the future each target will be rated by a single judge.
ICC(1,k)	Also called *one-way random-effect model, average measures.* This is the appropriate formula when 1) each target is rated by a different set of judges and k) in the future each target will be rated by the same number of judges and ratings will be averaged. ICC(1,k) should be > ICC(1,1), because continued use of multiple judges should enhance reliability.
ICC(2,1)	Also called *two-way random-effects model, single measures.* This is the appropriate formula when 2) all targets are rated by the same judges, drawn from a larger population of judges, and 1) in the future each target will be rated by a single judge.
ICC(2,k)	Also called *two-way random-effects model, average measures.* This is the appropriate formula when 2) all targets are rated by the same judges, drawn from a larger population of judges, and k) in the future each target will be rated by the same number of judges and ratings will be averaged.
ICC(3,1)	Also called *two-way mixed-effects model, single measures.* This is the appropriate formula when 3) all targets are rated by the same set of judges, and these judges represent the entire population of judges of interest, and 1) in the future each target will be rated by a single judge. This formula is also generally a good choice for test–retest reliability, in which the "judges" are the two or more administrations of the test and in the future the test will be administered only once.
ICC(3,k)	Also called *two-way mixed-effects model, average measures.* This is the appropriate formula when 3) all targets are rated by the same set of judges, and these judges represent the entire population of judges of interest, and k) in the future each target will be rated by the same number of judges and ratings will be averaged. This formula is equivalent to coefficient alpha, where the "judges" are the indicator items, and in the future all items will be administered to all targets.

(*continued*)

TABLE 6.4 (Continued)

Common Reliability Statistics

Reliability statistic	Description
Standard error of measurement (σ_e)	This statistic is related to reliability and represents the standard deviation of the sampling distribution of the measurements around the true score. The larger the σ_e, the more variability is expected from one administration of the indicator to the next, so smaller values are desirable. For example, if a person receives a score of 107 on an intelligence test with a standard error of 3.25, the 95% confidence interval for that score is [100.63, 113.37]. If the standard error is instead 15.3, that interval increases to [77.01, 136.99], which does not encourage much faith in the results. As you might anticipate, σ_e increases as reliability decreases.

Note. Statistics were included in this table for their popularity, not necessarily because they are always the best options. Some even involve conflicting assumptions about reliability and the nature of indicators.

each administration then serves as a measurement. This is what Balzac did when he weighed himself multiple times. External, or **test–retest reliability**, occurs *when multiple administrations of the same indicator are used as the repeated measurements of some true score for purposes of estimating reliability.*

Test–retest reliability can be a problematic undertaking. Remember that one of the conditions for estimating reliability is that the attribute being measured is consistent across measurements. Suppose the BDI is administered twice to the same individual to estimate reliability. If the interval between the two administrations is too long, the person's level of depression may change; if it is too short, the memory of the first administration may affect the person's responses the second time.

If we could be assured that one administration of the indicator would not influence the next, then shorter test–retest intervals would be acceptable. This led some test developers to try to develop alternate parallel forms of tests so they were independent. However, this option faded in popularity as psychologists realized that the alternate forms never met the criteria for parallel tests.

So, how long an interval should pass between administrations of the same indicator when one is estimating test–retest reliability? Common periods include 1 week, 1 month, and 6 months, but it is troubling to find that the interval is often chosen arbitrarily or on purely practical grounds. There is no one right answer to this issue of the appropriate interval; the best answer is to set the interval to the longest period over which the attribute being measured can be expected to remain constant. For example, if level of depression commonly remains stable for at least 3 months then this would be an optimal interval between administrations. This judgment is complicated by the possibility that distinct items in a multi-item indicator such as the BDI could fluctuate over different time intervals (McGrath, 2005), for example, if affective components of depression change more quickly than behavioral components. Finally, for state variables (variables reflecting a person's current state, e.g., "How anxious are you *right now?*") test–retest reliability may not be an appropriate standard for reliability at all.

Interrater Reliability

A third basis for estimating reliability is relevant only when multiple raters or judges independently observe the target. For example, in a study comparing two school-based treatments intended to reduce the frequency of aggressive behaviors in the classroom, the researcher has to be concerned about what raters observing the target consider an aggressive behavior. If the rater for Classroom A counts verbal threats as aggression but the rater for Classroom B does not, the frequency of aggressive behaviors will be higher in A than B even if the treatments used in the two classrooms are equally effective. One can address this issue by using multiple strategies. In well-controlled studies, raters receive extensive training in how to make the ratings. They must also demonstrate competency in the rating guidelines before they begin rating targets in the study. Finally, some or all of the targets are rated by two or more raters, and the reliability of the raters is computed. *When multiple raters using the same indicator are used as the repeated observations of some true score for purposes of estimating reliability*, this is referred to as **interrater reliability**.

BENCHMARKS FOR RELIABILITY

A common question about reliability is how much is enough. I will first respond to this question by indicating something that is not an acceptable benchmark for reliability. Significance tests are available for all the commonly used reliability statistics, and I have occasionally seen studies in which the authors offered a significant outcome on such a test as evidence of adequate reliability. Do not be fooled: This is insufficient evidence of reliability. A sample reliability of .30 can easily produce a significant test result, but this value indicates that the variance of the true scores is only 30% of the total variance, whereas 70% is error variance. No one would consider this an acceptable degree of consistency in observations of the same attribute.

Psychologists who have addressed the question of "how much is enough" have offered various benchmarks for acceptable and desirable levels of reliability (Fleiss, 1981; Landis & Koch, 1977; Shrout, 1998). The general consensus is that a reliability of .60 or higher is minimally acceptable, but a reliability of .80 or higher is desirable. Nunnally and Bernstein (1994) considered these standards acceptable when an instrument is being used for research purposes and the results will be averaged across many individuals. When the results will be used for applied purposes to learn and make decisions about a single individual, though, they recommended a minimum reliability of .90 and considered a reliability of .95 desirable. This is a standard that far too few psychological indicators achieve.

If the internal reliability of a new indicator proves to be less than .80, the test developer should seriously consider modifying the indicator until the results are more consistent with expectations. Major statistical software packages provide item statistics that can be used to identify particularly problematic items. One of the most useful is the reliability statistic that excludes a certain item. For example, you may find that the reliability of a certain indicator is only .53, but the reliability increases to .65 when a certain item is removed. Inspection of that item might reveal a wording problem or inconsistency with the rest of the items on the test. The developer may choose to modify the item—in which case a new estimate of reliability will need to be computed—or even eliminate it.

ISSUES IN TRUE-SCORE THEORY

Like null hypothesis significance testing, true-score theory provides a clever and popular approach to the mathematical modeling of error. There is no doubt that psychologists should avoid the use of indicators that demonstrate inadequate reliability, and good research articles provide reliability statistics for each indicator used in the study. However, true-score theory can be criticized on several grounds.

Assumption of True-Score Invariance

The measurement of reliability requires consistency in the true score across observations. This condition is reasonable for physical measurements, such as weights taken within a brief period of time. It is far less credible in the case of indicators that reflect attitudes or beliefs. The act of responding to an item about level of self-esteem or political opinion is likely to begin a process for respondents of clarifying and modifying what they actually believe about themselves (Knowles, Coker, Scott, Cook, & Neville, 1996; Schwarz, 1999). Similar concerns have been raised about the assumed random distribution of errors (Knowles, 1988). Note that this problem is inherent to the estimation of measurement error for psychological variables and is not specific to true-score theory.

Mathematical Definition of Reliability

True-score theory can be faulted for its definition of *reliability*. I began this chapter with a description of the commonsense notion of reliability: If

Balzac finds that his weight varies substantially from one measurement to the next, then his bathroom scale is unreliable. The commonsense notion requires only one target, Balzac. To create a quantitative model of reliability, however, the concept has been defined in terms of the proportion of total variability in a population that is represented by variability between targets. In basing the mathematical definition on a collection of targets, reliability becomes susceptible to the influence of factors that do not enter into the commonsense notion of reliability:

- The reliability of a set of measurements increases as the number of measurements per target increases. So, 10 measurements will generate a higher reliability estimate than five measurements, all other factors being equal, and an indicator that comprises 20 items will be more reliable than one that comprises 10. The extent of this increase can be predicted using something called the **Spearman–Brown prophecy formula**. This characteristic of reliability formulas means that increasing the number of items in an indicator can increase internal reliability, although it is hard to see why this should increase reliability from a common-sense perspective. Increasing the number of raters should also improve interrater reliability, and increasing the number of administrations should improve test–retest reliability, but these tend to be more costly options and so are rarely used.

- An indicator consisting of several very distinct subsets of items, each of which contains items that correlate well with each other, will tend to demonstrate adequate reliability even if the subsets do not correlate well with each other. Imagine an indicator on which some items measure intellectual ability, some items measure paranoid thinking, and some measure weight. It would seem meaningless to consider these items as converging on a single true score, but the reliability estimate for the resulting scale could still be acceptable, especially if the number of items associated with each subset is fairly large.

- The variance between targets' true scores is central to the mathematical model of reliability even though it has little to do with the commonsense notion of reliability. Mathematically, any factor that reduces the variance of the targets tends to reduce reliability. This means that the reliability of an indicator will generally be lower when administered in a homogeneous population (a population that does not show much variability on the attribute of interest) than when administered in a more heterogeneous population. For example, the reliability of a test of academic achievement should be lower in a sample of children with cognitive impairment than in the general population. For this reason it is inappropriate to refer to the reliability of an indicator, although psychologists have an unfortunate habit of doing so; it is more accurate to refer to the reliability of an indicator in *this* population.

This last characteristic of reliability has resulted in recent criticism of a common practice in psychological research articles: the use of reliability statistics from some optimal sample instead of the study sample. It is not unusual in a study in which the BDI was used to see the researchers cite reliability statistics from the BDI manual, for example. This *reliance on reliability data from another source* has been referred to as **reliability induction** (Vacha-Haase, Kogan, & Thompson, 2000), and it is now considered an undesirable practice. In particular, the manual statistics are often based on much more diverse samples than is true of individual studies, so there is reason to suspect that the reliability statistics reported in the manual overestimate the reliability appropriate for the current sample. Journal editors increasingly expect researchers to report reliability statistics for their own participants and raters. This issue has interesting implications for the common practice in applied settings of using the standard error of measurement (see Table 6.4) provided in the test manual to estimate the degree of error in the scores of individual test users.

The role of true-score variance in reliability also causes problems for the estimation of reliability in the case of dichotomous ratings. When ratings of targets are made on a dichotomous scale (e.g., improved–not improved, suicidal–not suicidal) the kappa coefficient is the most popular choice (see Table 6.4). It is often the case for dichotomous variables that one option is chosen far more frequently by the raters than the other option. It would not be surprising, for example, to find that raters classify only 10% of teenagers as at risk for committing violence and 90% as at no risk. The variance of a dichotomous variable shrinks as the imbalance in the relative frequency of the choices becomes more extreme. This shrinkage reduces true variance more than it reduces error variance, so the kappa coefficient can be quite poor (e.g., McGrath et al., 2005).

An extreme imbalance in ratings so seriously reduces the reliability of dichotomous variables that several statistics have been developed that are intended to be resistant to the distribution of the ratings (Brennan & Prediger, 1981; Rogers, Schmitt, & Mullins, 2002). These alternatives have their own problems (Hsu & Field, 2003). Shrout, Spitzer, and Fleiss (1987) noted that this problem is inherent to the definition of reliability as the proportion of total variance due to true score variance; that is, this problem is a consequence not of the kappa coefficient but of the definition of reliability that emerges from the true-score model.

An Integrated Approach to Reliability

One final criticism that can be leveled against true-score theory is the relative independence of the different forms of reliability. One study can

TABLE 6.5

A Multifaceted Study of Attention-Seeking Behavior

	Setting and behavior											
	School						Home					
	Aggressive		Dependent		Tantrums		Aggressive		Dependent		Tantrums	
Child	Rater 1	Rater 2	Rater 1	Rater 2	Rater 1	Rater 2	Rater 1	Rater 2	Rater 1	Rater 2	Rater 1	Rater 2
1	7	6	5	9	5	6	2	1	8	3	4	4
2	3	1	1	0	5	5	3	3	3	4	5	6
3	3	3	5	9	2	4	7	6	8	8	9	7
. . .												
50	4	3	3	2	0	2	3	3	6	9	7	8

Note. This hypothetical study involves multiple raters rating multiple behaviors in multiple settings for multiple children. For example, Rater 2 recorded six aggressive behaviors for Child 1 at school, whereas Rater 1 recorded three dependent behaviors for Child 2 at home.

incorporate multiple forms of repeated measurements. Imagine a study in which two raters evaluate the frequency of three attention-seeking behaviors in each of two settings—classroom and home—in a sample of 50 children. This study, which would involve multiple sources of repeated measurements, is mapped in Table 6.5.

Cronbach, Gleser, Nanda, and Rajaratnam (1972) developed **generalizability theory,** *a generalization of true-score theory that allows the estimation of multiple forms of reliability in a single analysis,* to address this problem. Generalizability theory allows the researcher to compare the relative impact of each of the three sources of multiple measurements, or *facets,* in the study described. It also offers methods for estimating the improvement in reliability that would result from increasing the number of measurements associated with each facet. This is basically a generalization of the Spearman–Brown prophecy formula to any source of multiple measurements. It is a fairly sophisticated statistical analysis, so it has become popular in only some areas of research. However, it is a useful option in any setting where there are multiple facets of measurement including items, settings, raters, and so on.

Validity Theory

For more than 100 years (Titchener & Major, 1895), psychologists have been using the term **validity** to refer to *the degree to which outcomes on an indicator accurately reflect the attribute of interest.* This is the issue exemplified with Balzac's second bathroom scale: Although the measurements were reliable, there was systematic error in them.

An important turning point in psychologists' understanding of validity was provided by Cronbach and Meehl (1995). Until the 1950s, psychologists generally equated the term *validity* with the degree to which indicators correlated with other variables of interest, for example, the degree to which a measure of intelligence correlated with other observed variables that should be associated with level of intelligence (Geisinger, 1992). By the late 1940s, however, a different conception of validity started to emerge, reflected in terms such as *factorial validity* (Guilford, 1946; Gulliksen, 1950), that dealt with the relationship between an indicator and a construct.

This trend was ultimately formalized by Cronbach and Meehl (1995) in their discussion of **construct validity**, which refers to *the degree to which an indicator accurately reflects a latent or unobserved attribute.* Central to their argument is the proposition that because the attribute of interest by definition cannot be directly observed, only indirect methods are available for assuring the validity of an indicator. A course of research to examine the validity of the indicator from multiple perspectives is therefore necessary before psychologists should feel comfortable using a particular indicator to represent a particular construct. All forms of evidence that attempt to validate an indicator contribute to the evaluation of an indicator's construct validity.

Construct validation is therefore not a single event or study; it is an ongoing process across the life span of an indicator. Construct validity also cannot be reduced to a single statistic; it is the sum product of all attempts made to evaluate the degree to which the indicator behaves in a manner consistent with the latent attribute it is intended to represent.

All subsequent discussion of test validity in the psychological literature has been informed by the concept of construct validity. In this section, I describe several types of validating evidence, including face validity, content validity, criterion-related validity, and convergent and discriminant validity. Another form of validity evidence, called *factorial validity*, must be understood in the context of factor analysis, and so I will defer my discussion of that to Chapter 7.

FACE VALIDITY

The term **face validity** has been used to refer to *an informal approach to evaluating validity in which the consumer judges whether the content of the measurement device seems appropriate to the attribute of interest.* Anyone who looks at the statements that form the items of the BDI—for example, "I am sad" or "I would like to kill myself"—would readily agree that this is a measure related to the measurement of the latent variable depression. The face validity of an instrument is easy to evaluate, but face validity is not considered a formal approach to the study of validity. Although it ensures that the contents of the measurement device are *relevant*, it does not ensure they are *comprehensive*. For example, there may be important elements of depression not addressed by the BDI items. Because of this concern, a better alternative is the evaluation of the measure's content validity.

CONTENT VALIDITY

Content validity is a more formal variant of face validity and has to do with *the extent to which an indicator reflects the universe of contents of interest according to some model of the attribute*. The development of a content-valid scale requires more than just combining a set of items that are relevant to the latent variable. First, a model of the latent variable must be proposed that identifies the various components of the construct. Second, items are developed to reflect each of those components. In this way, the indicator is likely to be comprehensive, at least according to the model on which the indicator was based. The BDI items were chosen because the author identified 21 key features of depression and created one item reflective of each. Content validity is a more formal process than face validity, although it is usually not an empirical or quantitative one. Of course, the content validity of a measure is only as good as the model used to identify the universe of contents.

CRITERION-RELATED VALIDITY

Criterion-related validity refers to *evaluating the validity of an indicator on the basis of its demonstrated relationship with some criterion*. The term *criterion* is used here in the sense of a standard. For example, the use of the BDI to predict whether or not people will attempt to commit suicide within the next 3 months is an example of criterion-related validity, because the ability to predict suicidality is a standard that a measure of depression should meet. Criterion-related validity can be divided further in terms of whether *the criterion is measured at the same time that the indicator to be validated is administered* (**concurrent validity**) or whether *the criterion is measured at some later point than the indicator is administered* (**predictive validity**). The use of the BDI to predict subsequent suicide attempts is an example of predictive validity. Administering a new, brief intelligence test immediately before or after a well-established lengthier test to see how well they correspond with each other represents an example of concurrent validation.

Because correlations with criteria represent a particularly popular method of indicator validation, Cronbach and Meehl (1955) awarded it particular attention in their discussion of validity. They framed such correlations in terms of evaluating the degree to which the indicator is related to other variables in a manner consistent with the corresponding attribute. They introduced the concept of a **nomological net**, *the hypothesized pattern of relationships among the construct of interest, other constructs, and observable events.* For example, an indicator that attempts to measure the latent variable anxiety should correlate with other measures of anxiety. It should also correlate, but not as strongly, with measures of latent variables that should be related to anxiety, such as self-esteem, level of depression, or the occurrence of panic attacks. It should also correlate with physiological indicators that are theoretically related to anxiety, such as level of sweat production, heart rate increases, or the tendency to stammer under stress. Scores on the scale should also tend to correlate with level of stress, for example, increasing shortly before skydiving for the first time or during midterms and decreasing in response to relaxation exercises.

Whether someone attempts suicide is an example of an unusually compelling criterion because it is almost always clear when a suicide attempt has occurred. Potential criterion variables in psychology rarely demonstrate such clarity. Suppose that an indicator of the attribute conscientiousness is used to predict subsequent work evaluations by a supervisor. This criterion is fairly subjective, depending on the supervisor's impressions of the person, the supervisor's honesty, and other factors. If the indicator of conscientiousness correlates only .10 with this criterion, it would be unclear what to make of this finding: Perhaps the conscientiousness indicator demonstrates poor validity, perhaps the supervisor's ratings are not particularly accurate, or perhaps conscientiousness is not nearly as important to job performance in this setting as the researcher suspected. On the basis of these results alone there is no way to judge the extent to which each of these factors contributes to the disappointing results. *The inability to identify a clear criterion* is an unfortunately common phenomenon in social research and has been referred to as the **criterion problem**.

Notice that the previous paragraph implied a relationship between validity and reliability: Good interrater reliability for classifying an act as a suicide attempt was considered when evaluating the adequacy of the criterion. This relationship between validity and reliability can be stated more formally. It can be demonstrated that the criterion-related validity of an indicator is reduced to the extent that the indicator and the criterion are not perfectly reliable. For indicator X and criterion Y,

$$\rho_{XY} \leq \sqrt{\rho_{XX'}\rho_{YY'}} \, , \tag{6.7}$$

where ρ_{XY} is the population correlation between the indicator and criterion, and $\rho_{XX'}\rho_{YY'}$ is the product of their population reliabilities. The less reliable the indicators involved in an analysis, the less those indicators can correlate with each other. This relationship serves as the basis for *a method of correcting a correlation for unreliability in indicators* called the **correction for attenuation** (Spearman, 1904):

$$r_{T_X T_Y} = \frac{r_{XY}}{\sqrt{r_{XX'} \cdot r_{YY'}}}; \tag{6.8}$$

that is, it is possible to estimate the correlation between the true scores on X and Y in a sample using the sample estimate of the correlation between observed variables X and Y, the sample estimate of the reliability of X, and the sample estimate of the reliability of Y.

Suppose I am interested in testing the hypothesis that more supportive supervisors are associated with more satisfied employees, and I administer a self-report indicator of job satisfaction to employees while trained observers rate supportive behaviors in their supervisors. The two variables correlate .37, with an internal reliability of .73 for the job satisfaction indicator and an interrater reliability of .87 for the supervisor ratings. If the goal is to evaluate how well *this* indicator of supervisor supportiveness predicts *this* indicator of job satisfaction, the best answer is .37; however, if the goal is to evaluate how well *supervisor supportiveness* as a latent variable predicts *job satisfaction* as a latent variable, a better estimate might be

$$r_{T_X T_Y} = \frac{.37}{\sqrt{.73 \times .87}} = .58. \tag{6.9}$$

The lower the sample estimates of reliability, the more correction for attenuation increases the sample estimate of the X–Y correlation. If these two indicators were associated with .35 and .49 reliabilities, then the corrected correlation would be

$$r_{T_X T_Y} = \frac{.37}{\sqrt{.35 \times .49}} = .89. \tag{6.10}$$

It is often the case that the researcher is more interested in the relationship between the latent variables than the specific indicators being used. In particular, Hunter and Schmidt (2004) recommended correction for attenuation as a regular component of meta-analyses that attempt to estimate the population correlation between latent variables. One of the only exceptions to this situation occurs when a study is specifically testing the criterion-related validity of an indicator, in which case the level of correlation between *this* indicator and the criterion is exactly the issue of interest to the researcher. Even in this case, though, the researcher may be justified correcting for attenuation only in the criterion:

$$r_{T_X T_Y} = \frac{r_{XY}}{\sqrt{r_{YY'}}}. \tag{6.11}$$

Despite what seems to be a strong argument for correcting for attenuation whenever the researcher is more interested in the latent variable than its observed indicator, there are several reasons to use the attenuation correction sparingly. The first is that it combines two to three sample statistics, which means the estimate itself can vary substantially from sample to sample. Second, remember that because most measurements are congeneric, sample reliability statistics tend to underestimate the true reliability, which means that the correction for attenuation will tend to overestimate the true correlation. For these reasons, the correction is infrequently used in practice (although to be honest, lack of familiarity with the correction is also a factor).

CONVERGENT AND DISCRIMINANT VALIDITY

The concepts of convergent and discriminant validity emerged as an outgrowth of Cronbach and Meehl's (1955) speculations on how to demonstrate validity under circumstances in which there is no clear criterion, although Gulliksen (1950) anticipated the concept of discriminant validity. Campbell and Fiske (1959) described a general approach to using correlations between indicators for validity purposes by means of a tool they called the **multitrait–multimethod matrix** (MTMM), *a correlation matrix of variables representing both multiple latent variables and multiple measurement methods.*

To demonstrate the MTMM, imagine a study that involves six variables. Three of these variables are based on self-report indicators completed by children, and three are based on teacher ratings of the same children. One self-report indicator and one teacher rating have to do with the child's level of anxiety. Two more variables, one self-report and one teacher based, have to do with the child's popularity with peers. The final two indicators have to do with the teacher's and the child's perception of the child's academic performance. In other words, the study involves three constructs, or latent variables, which in Campbell and Fiske's (1959) terminology are referred to as *traits:* (a) anxiety, (b) popularity, and (c) achievement. It also involves two methods of measurement: (a) self-report and (b) teacher ratings.

It is possible to compute 15 correlations using these six variables (see Table 6.6). These correlations can be divided into three groups. The three correlations in boldface type in Table 6.6 represent correlations involving a shared trait but different measurement methods. Campbell and Fiske (1959) referred to these as *monotrait–heteromethod correlations.* The six shaded correlations each involves a different trait measured using the

TABLE 6.6

A Multitrait–Multimethod Matrix

Variable	1	2	3	4	5	6
1. S-R anxiety	—					
2. S-R popularity	.18	—				
3. S-R achievement	.25	.19	—			
4. T-R anxiety	**.53**	.23	.18	—		
5. T-R popularity	.15	**.48**	.26	.23	—	
6. T-R achievement	.11	.18	**.40**	.32	.15	—

Note. The values on the diagonal are usually either a dash, indicating 1.00 (indicating an indicator's correlation with itself), or an estimate of the indicator's reliability. Other values represent correlations between indicators. The three monotrait–heteromethod correlations (correlations of the same construct using different methods) are in boldface type. The six heterotrait–monomethod correlations (correlations of different constructs using the same method) are shaded. The remaining six correlations are heterotrait–heteromethod correlations. S-R = self-reported; T-R = teacher-rated.

same method. These are examples of *heterotrait–monomethod correlations.* The remaining six correlations share neither trait nor method and are *heterotrait–heteromethod correlations.*

Convergent validity can be defined as *the extent to which indicators of the same latent variable tend to converge.* Statistically, this is similar to criterion-related validity in that the analysis is based on the correlation between two variables representing similar constructs. However, there are two important conceptual distinctions. First, in the MTMM neither variable is considered the criterion for the other. For example, the correlation of .53 between the two anxiety indicators does not require a person to identify one as the indicator to be validated and the other as the criterion. Cronbach and Meehl's (1955) discussion of how to study indicator validity in circumstances in which there is no true criterion was clearly influencing the thinking here.

Second, in the context of the MTMM the correlation between the two anxiety indicators is particularly interesting because they are measured with different methods, in this case self-report and teacher ratings. The definition of criterion-related validity did not consider how different the two measurement methods were. The extent to which they converge despite differences in method is an important piece of information about construct validity. However, the value of convergent validity has been questioned because different methods tend to demonstrate limited convergence (e.g., McGrath & Carroll, in press).

Discriminant validity can be defined as *the extent to which indicators of different constructs tend to diverge.* The two most important patterns in the matrix for evaluating discriminant validity are the following:

1. Monotrait–heteromethod correlations in general should be larger than heterotrait–monomethod correlations. In other words, a shared trait should produce stronger relationships than a shared method of measurement.

2. Monotrait–heteromethod correlations should be larger than heterotrait–heteromethod correlations. In fact, the latter should be the smallest in the matrix.

The MTMM approach to validation is interesting in at least two ways. First, it suggests that the nomological net will sometimes suggest that certain correlations will be relatively large, when the latent variables underlying the two indicators are expected to be strongly related. In other cases the nomological net will suggest that certain correlations should be small, when the latent variables underlying the indicators are relatively distinct.[3] Second, the focus on multiple measurement methods allows the researcher to compare the extent to which indicators correlate based on shared constructs versus shared measurement methods. *Correlation between variables resulting from a shared measurement method* is referred to as **method bias** and represents a possible source of invalidity in indicators.

The approach described by Campbell and Fiske (1959) has certain limitations. There is no real standard for determining when an indicator demonstrates sufficient convergent validity or sufficient discriminant validity. Neither is it clear how to interpret the results when some correlations in the matrix follow the patterns established by Campbell and Fiske but others do not. In response to these concerns, various statistical approaches have been suggested for analyzing the MTMM in a way that makes the interpretation simpler (see Sawilowsky, 2002; Westen & Rosenthal, 2003), some of which rely on the factor models I discuss in Chapter 7, but none has emerged as a standard. Finally, it is unclear how different measurement methods need to be before it is reasonable to treat them as distinct. Some MTMM studies treat different self-report indicators as different methods, although the original implication was that the method of administration should be quite distinct. Despite the problems, the concepts of convergent and discriminant validity and method bias continue to play an important role in the construct validation of psychological indicators.

THE MODERN PERSPECTIVE ON VALIDITY

One final topic on the concept of validity merits mention. The understanding of validity continues to evolve. In recent years it has become

---

[3]Notice that *small* here means "close to zero." An indicator of job satisfaction should correlate strongly and negatively with an indicator of likelihood of changing jobs. Even so, this correlation reflects the convergent validity of these indicators, because the two constructs are thought to be closely related to each other.

standard practice to associate validity not with the indicator but with the inferences derived from that indicator (Cronbach, 1971; Kane, 1992). This is a subtle but important distinction. It suggests that instead of considering whether an indicator is "valid" or "invalid," one should consider what sorts of conclusions can be validly derived from scores on that indicator. Just as it is considered inaccurate to refer to *the* reliability of an indicator, the common practice of referring to *the* validity of psychological indicators is also questionable (although psychologists often do so; Cizek, Rosenberg, & Koons, 2008). The American Educational Research Association, American Psychological Association, & National Council on Measurement in Education (1999) accepted the redefinition of validity as a characteristic of inferences rather than of indicators.

Conclusion

The random error and reliability of psychological indicators is an important consideration. True-score theory was developed as a mathematical approach to estimating reliability. In a population consisting of multiple measurements of multiple individuals, reliability is defined as the proportion of the total variance due to variance between the individuals, the variance not due to random error. Various reliability statistics have been developed on the basis of this definition.

True-score theory has been criticized on various grounds. Many of these criticisms have to do with whether the theory's basic conditions are generally relevant to the behavioral sciences and with disparities between the mathematical model and the commonsense notion of reliability. Despite these problems, true-score theory offers the standard classical framework used for evaluating the consistency to be expected from a psychological indicator. It is not the only game in town (I consider alternatives in Chapter 7, this volume), but it remains a popular one.

The true score is defined as the mean of a population of measurements. It tells us nothing about the accuracy of those measurements. Accuracy is examined in studies of validity. There are strong relationships between reliability and validity, between random error and systematic error in indicators. However, the concept of indicator validity is associated with a specific set of statistical and methodological tools distinct from those of reliability. In this chapter, I have summarized the various methodologies associated with validity in testing, as well as (briefly) described the evolution of the meaning of validity itself over time.

Latent-Variable Models 7

I n Chapter 6, I introduced the concept of validity as having to do with the relationships between indicators and the latent variables they represent. In Chapter 7, I focus on various methods that have been developed for using indicators to learn about the nature of the latent variables themselves. I use the term **latent-variable models** to refer to *statistical methods for modeling relationships between scores on observed indicators and latent variables.* A variety of statistical techniques have been developed with the intent of modeling such relationships. Accordingly, this chapter provides far too brief an introduction to these techniques. It is intended merely to familiarize you with basic concepts and provide you with tools for understanding how these techniques work.

The first section focuses on **factor analysis**, *a family of analyses primarily intended to detect dimensional latent variables from dimensional observed variables.* The second section focuses on **structural equation models**, which are *analyses for estimating relationships between latent variables detected using factor analytic techniques.* The third section focuses on **item response theory** (IRT), *a family of analyses primarily intended to detect dimensional latent variables from categorical observed variables.* The fourth and final section focuses on **latent categorical models**, *analyses that are relevant in circumstances involving categorical* *latent variables.* A summary of latent variable statistical methods is provided in Table 7.1.

The statistics that have been developed for the study of latent-variable models have certain commonalities. First, they are often quite complicated. The output of a confirmatory factor analysis or structural equation model in particular can be very difficult to interpret. In contrast to the relatively straightforward reject–retain decision associated with null hypothesis significance testing, latent-variable models may estimate dozens of parameters, and there can be significance tests for each estimate as well as for the model as a whole. Also, there is only one way to compute a correlation coefficient or analysis of variance between two variables. In contrast, there are multiple versions of factor analysis, cluster analysis, and structural equation modeling. Two different methods of factor analysis can give you different answers about a data set, and it is even possible in some cases for two software programs that supposedly conduct the same analysis to give you different answers. This is analysis not for the naive.

Because the statistical analysis of latent-variable models is such a broad and complex topic, and because many psychologists need only a general understanding of these methods, the format of this chapter is different from those of the other chapters. Whereas in the previous chapters I provided in-depth descriptions of a few topics, this chapter is a survey of a number of topics. I will attempt to alert you to some of the pitfalls of each method, but do not expect the same level of detail you have received until now. Instead, I will recommend readings that are more detailed, although also still intelligible.

TABLE 7.1

Latent-Variable Modeling Techniques

Analysis	Description
Cluster analysis	Using some measure of distance or similarity between cases on dimensional variables, cluster analysis can identify subgroups of cases on a latent categorical variable. It can also be used to identify latent subgroups of variables.
Confirmatory factor analysis (CFA)	In circumstances in which there is a preexisting model suggesting the number of latent factors, the association of variables with those factors, and whether factors are correlated, CFA can evaluate the fit of the model and provide estimates of parameters. CFA is used with dimensional observed variables to detect latent variables assumed to be dimensional.

(continued)

TABLE 7.1 (*Continued*)

Latent-Variable Modeling Techniques

Analysis	Description
Exploratory factor analysis (EFA)	In circumstances in which no preexisting model exists for the latent factors underlying a set of indicators, EFA can offer guidance. EFA is used primarily with dimensional observed variables to detect latent variables assumed to be dimensional.
Item response theory	Decomposes observed item scores into components reflecting the latent trait and the item difficulty. A variety of versions are available to allow for items with two or more options and models of varying complexity.
Finite mixture modeling	Decomposes dimensional variables into a mixture of groups from a latent categorical variable. Associated statistics can be used to evaluate whether the latent variable is dimensional or categorical and, if categorical, the number of groups. **Latent class analysis** is finite mixture modeling in which participants are classified into latent classes. **Latent profile analysis** is latent class analysis with dimensional indicators.
Multidimensional scaling	Identifies latent dimensions underlying a set of observed variables. This is a flexible method that can use various types of information to identify latent dimensions, so it can act like a cluster analysis or a factor analysis.
Perceptual mapping	Estimates the number of latent dimensions needed to explain how people group objects.
Principal components analysis (PCA)	An analytic strategy closely related to EFA. Whereas factor analysis assumes that there are preexisting latent factors that account for the correlations between observed variables, PCA instead creates components as a means of simplifying the data (referring to PCA as a "latent-variable model" is therefore not completely accurate). One advantage is that for any data set there is one unique principal components solution. Depending on the methods used, factor analysis allows for multiple equally justified solutions.
Structural equation modeling	A flexible method that can evaluate a variety of relationships between latent variables. Special software is available for this method that is also commonly used for CFA.
Taxometric analysis	Using a variety of statistical techniques, these methods were developed to determine whether a latent variable is inherently taxonic, consisting of two subgroups, or dimensional.
Trajectory analysis	Distinct from other methods in that the data are multiple observations of the same variables over time. Individuals are divided into subgroups in terms of similarities in their patterns of scores. For example, the analysis might identify a group of individuals whose scores are consistently low over time, another group with consistently high scores, and a third group whose members' scores increase over time.

Note. Statistics in boldface type are listed in the Index, to help you find brief descriptions of statistics in the future when reading research.

Factor Analysis

There are two main types of factor analysis: (a) exploratory factor analysis and (b) confirmatory factor analysis.

EXPLORATORY FACTOR ANALYSIS

Factor analysis was the first latent-variable analysis that became popular in psychology. Historically, factor analysis emerged out of efforts to understand the nature of intelligence. Early studies of intelligence treated it as a single latent variable that has come to be called *general intelligence*. However, Spearman (1904) noted that tests of different intellectual abilities, such as verbal ability, mathematical ability, or reaction time to visual stimuli, often did not correlate well with each other. To oversimplify matters, two explanations were possible for this finding. One would suggest that intellectual abilities are relatively independent of each other, that there are specific types of intelligence. If so, by chance there would be some people who do well on a variety of tasks and others who do poorly, and those extreme cases would be the source of the belief in general intelligence. Alternatively, there could be a general intelligence that influences performance on all these intellectual tasks, but any one task demonstrates substantial error as an indicator of the general intelligence latent variable. This could occur if, for example, one type of task required specific information that would be available only to people with a fair amount of formal education, whereas another task required some sensory skill that varies in the population.

Factor analysis was developed to test these sorts of questions about the nature of latent variables under circumstances in which the latent variables are assumed to be dimensional variables. Most factor analytic methods are also intended for use with dimensional indicators, although variants are available for dichotomous or categorical variables. The method I am about to describe here was originally referred to simply as *factor analysis*, but in recent years it has come to be called *exploratory factor analysis* (EFA) for reasons that will become clearer shortly.

To demonstrate EFA, consider a study my colleagues and I conducted in which 612 college students completed five scales associated with general self-concept (a description of the sample and methodology from that study may be found in McGrath, Rashid, Park, & Peterson, 2010). One was an indicator of emotional instability, one was an indicator of self-evaluation, one was an indicator of internal locus of control (i.e., the sense that one is in control of one's life), one was an indicator of self-efficacy (i.e., the ability to be effective), and one was an indicator of self-esteem. All scales except the first are scored so higher scores indicate a more positive self-concept. Students completed each scale twice, once

TABLE 7.2

Correlation Matrix Used to Demonstrate Factor Analysis

Variable	1	2	3	4	5	6	7	8	9	10
1. EIS-S	.88									
2. EIS-O	.36	.89								
3. CSE-S	−.61	−.30	.82							
4. CSE-O	−.31	−.67	.38	.87						
5. LOC-S	−.25	−.13	.55	.23	.58					
6. LOC-O	−.12	−.31	.19	.57	.34	.65				
7. GSE-S	−.50	−.24	.76	.33	.56	.20	.84			
8. GSE-O	−.28	−.56	.39	.80	.28	.62	.46	.88		
9. SE-S	−.55	−.25	.76	.33	.48	.14	.77	.37	.88	
10. SE-O	−.26	−.56	.35	.79	.21	.53	.32	.83	.37	.90

Note. EIS = emotional instability scale; CSE = Core Self-Evaluation Scale 1; LOC = internal locus of control scale; GSE = Global Self-Efficacy Scale 2; SE = self-esteem scale; -S = self-report; -O = description of other. All scales except EIS are keyed so higher scores represent a more positive description. Values in the diagonal are internal reliabilities based on the scale items.

with the instruction "Rate yourself" and once with the instruction "Rate someone with whom you have a close relationship."

One might consider various possibilities here. Do self-report and other-description really represent a single latent variable, either because we are attracted to people similar to ourselves or because we tend to assume others are like us? Do they instead reflect distinct latent variables? Is emotional instability something distinct from other aspects of self-concept? Is locus of control distinct? Factor analysis can address these sorts of questions.

The correlation matrix for this study is depicted in Table 7.2. As expected, all are positive except the correlations of the instability scales with other measures. Some of the correlations are quite small, in particular when ratings of self are correlated with ratings of others. This is not always the case, however; some correlations between self and other ratings exceeded .30.

On the basis of these correlations, we conducted a factor analysis (McGrath et al., 2010). The mechanics of factor analysis are not important here. What is important is that the results suggested the presence of two factors, or latent variables. In other words, the results of the factor analysis suggested that the correlations between the variables could be understood as resulting from the presence of two latent variables. What is known as the *factor matrix* is provided in Table 7.3. This matrix is similar to a correlation matrix; think of these numbers as the correlations between the two latent factors and each of the observed variables. Because these have to do with the relationship between an observed variable and a hypothetical variable estimated from the analysis, they are

TABLE 7.3

The Factor Matrix

	Factor 1	Factor 2
EIS-S	−.19	**−.58**
EIS-O	**−.61**	−.19
CSE-S	.19	**.89**
CSE-O	**.90**	.21
LOC-S	.16	**.55**
LOC-O	**.61**	.10
GSE-S	.19	**.85**
GSE-O	**.88**	.27
SE-S	.17	**.85**
SE-O	**.85**	.20

Note. This table provides the set of loadings for each factor on each scale. All loadings ≥ .40 or ≤ −.40 are in boldface type. EIS = emotional instability scale; CSE = Core Self-Evaluation Scale 1; LOC = internal locus of control scale; GSE = Global Self-Efficacy Scale 2; SE = self-esteem scale; -S = self-report; -O = description of other.

not exactly correlations, so the word *loading* is used instead. Despite the difference in terminology, loadings such as correlations fall in the interval [−1.0, 1.0], with values closer to 0 suggesting a weaker relationship.

These loadings are used to interpret the factors. In this case, all of the ratings of another person load strongly on the first factor and all of the self-ratings load strongly on the second factor. Notice that the emotional instability scale loads negatively, which again makes sense. As with regular correlations, it is the absolute distance from 0 that matters. This pattern tells us that the first factor can be thought of as ratings of others, and the second factor comprises ratings of self; that is, the results do not support the hypothesis that ratings of self and other represent a single common factor. They do support concluding that these five scales tap a single common dimension.

Notice that this interpretation of the factors requires one to draw some conclusions about which indicators were strongly related to each of the factors. This is the sort of yes–no decision that significance testing was designed to assist, but there is no significance test to tell you when the loading is large enough to use that scale to help interpret the factor. Instead, a convention has emerged whereby loadings ≥ .40 or ≤ −.40 are considered "meaningful" or "salient." This standard is as arbitrary as the .05 standard for alpha, however.[1]

---

[1]Like a correlation, a loading is an effect size estimate. Accordingly, it is increasingly recognized that loadings should be interpreted in the context of a confidence interval, although many researchers fail to do so.

The specifics of factor analysis are quite complicated. Various methods have been developed for deciding how many factors there are, easing interpretation of the factors, and generating estimated true scores on the factor. A summary of key concepts in factor analysis is presented in Table 7.4. The table covers most of the terms you are likely to see in research articles that summarize a factor analysis, and if you ever

TABLE 7.4

Concepts in Exploratory Factor Analysis

Term	Description
Global statistics	The most basic statistics generated in a factor analysis
Communalities (h^2)	Computed for each variable, it is the proportion of a variable's variance explained by the factors; h^2 = the sum of the squared factor loadings for that variable. $1 - h^2$ is called the *unique variance*, the variance unexplained by the factors, a combination of variance not accounted for by the factors and random error.
Eigenvalue	Computed for each factor, it is the variance of the factor. The eigenvalue for the first factor will always be the largest, with decreasing values indicating that each subsequent factor accounts for less of the variance of the variables.
% Total variance	Computed for each factor, it is the percentage of the total variable variance accounted for by the factor. It can be computed by dividing the eigenvalue by the number of variables.
% Common variance	Computed for each factor, it is smaller than the percentage of total variance to the extent that h^2 values are small.
Factor retention	The first task in a factor analysis involves deciding how many factors to retain. It is possible for the number of factors to equal the number of variables in the analysis, but in most situations the true number is much less than that. A number of techniques exist for deciding how many factors to retain; the following are only the most popular.
Kaiser criterion	This method involves conducting an initial analysis and retaining any factor with an eigenvalue > 1.0. Although popular at one time it is now recognized that the method retains far too many factors; do not trust the results.
Scree plot	This method involves retaining factors until differences in the remaining eigenvalues become small. It has been criticized because the best stopping point is sometimes difficult to determine.
Parallel analysis	This method has become very popular in recent years. It involves conducting factor analyses with random data and retaining factors so long as the eigenvalue from the real data is larger than that for the corresponding factor based on random data.
Factor extraction	Statistical methods that generate the factor analysis. There are many factor extraction methods available; only the primary ones are listed here.

(continued)

TABLE 7.4 (*Continued*)

Concepts in Exploratory Factor Analysis

Term	Description
Principal components analysis (PCA)	Distinct from factor analysis, PCA is intended as a practical method of reducing data rather than a method of detecting true latent variables. It attempts to account for all variability in the observed variables, so communalities = 1 and the two percentage-of-variance statistics are equal. Although results tend to be similar to those from factor analysis, PCA is unusual for a latent-variable analysis in that only one solution is possible. PCA should be used in analyses intended to determine the number of factors to retain even if subsequent techniques use factor analysis.
Principal axis factor analysis	Currently the most popular variant of true factor analysis. It is an iterative approach, meaning that it involves multiple attempts at estimating the key parameters, in this case the communalities.
Maximum likelihood	Described in Chapter 5; generates parameter estimates most likely to produce the original correlation matrix. Its usefulness is hampered by its requiring the normality assumption.
Alpha factoring	Attempts to generate factors with relatively high reliability.
Unweighted or generalized least squares	Attempt to minimize error in estimation of the original correlation matrix.
Factor rotation methods	Factors can be thought of as axes in a multidimensional space in which the number of dimensions equals the number of factors. Those axes can be shifted, or *rotated,* in various ways intended to enhance interpretation of the factors. Several rotation methods are available, of which the following are the most commonly used.
Varimax rotation	Maintains the axes at 90° angles, keeping them uncorrelated, or *orthogonal.* It also exaggerates differences in loadings between those variables that are salient and not salient, often simplifying the interpretation of the factors. Probably the most popular method.
Quartimax rotation	Another orthogonal rotation that tends to produce a first factor with many salient loadings and additional factors with few salient loadings. Not very popular.
Equimax rotation	A compromise between varimax and quartimax methods. Also not very popular.
Direct oblimin rotation	Allows factors to become correlated, or *oblique.* Doing so allows factors to account for a larger percentage of variance but complicates interpretation. An estimate of the size of the correlation between each pair of factors is generated.
Promax rotation	An alternative oblique rotation recommended only for very large data sets
Primary results	The tables of statistics used to evaluate the results of the factor analysis
Factor matrix	This table contains the factor loadings. No. columns = no. factors retained; no. rows = no. variables. As with correlations, values range from −1.0 to 1.0.

(*continued*)

TABLE 7.4	(*Continued*)

Concepts in Exploratory Factor Analysis

Term	Description
Rotated factor matrix	The factor matrix after rotation. If the rotation method is oblique, this matrix is replaced by two others. The factor structure matrix is the set of correlations between items and factors. Those correlations are affected by the degree to which both the item and the factor are correlated with other factors. The factor pattern matrix provides those correlations after correcting for the other factors, thereby estimating the direct effect of the factor on the item.[a] These matrices are equivalent if the factors are orthogonal (uncorrelated with each other). Warning: I have seen both the factor structure and factor pattern matrix referred to as *tables of loadings*. When dealing with an oblique rotation, make sure you know which is intended.
Residual matrix	As indicated in the description of factor extraction methods, factor analysis can generate an estimate of the correlation matrix based on the results. The extent to which the estimated correlation matrix matches the actual correlation matrix is an index of the accuracy of the model. This matrix contains differences between estimated and actual correlations; smaller values are desirable. No. rows and columns = no. variables.
Factor scores	It is possible for factor analysis to generate estimates of each person's score on each of the retained factors.
Factor score coefficient matrix	No. columns = no. factors retained; no. rows = no. variables. For example, to generate Person 1's score on Factor 1, that person's variable scores are multiplied by the corresponding values in Column 1, then summed.
Factor score matrix	The matrix of scores on each factor for each case. No. columns = no. factors retained; no. rows = no. cases. This is a new set of variables representing estimated scores on the factors. There are several methods for computing factor scores, with a regression-based method generally serving as the default.

Note. Some of these descriptions assume that variables are standardized with a mean of 0 and standard deviation of 1, which is typical in factor analysis. Some of these terms are also relevant to confirmatory factor analysis.
[a]The issue here is very similar to what in Chapter 9 I refer to as a *spurious relationship*.

participate in the conduct of a factor analysis the information in the table should help to get you started.

CONFIRMATORY FACTOR ANALYSIS

As I mentioned earlier, the type of factor analysis described so far is sometimes referred to as an **exploratory factor analysis,** *a factor analysis in which the latent-variable model emerges from the correlational statistics.* As the preceding discussion and Table 7.4 demonstrate, it is the factor analytic results that help you decide how many factors to retain, which variables are saliently loaded on which factors, and so forth. More recently, a new form of factor analysis has been developed called **confirmatory factor analysis** (CFA; Jöreskog, 1969), *a factor analysis in which correlational statistics are used to test preexisting latent-variable models.* The goal is to confirm a model, not to hunt for one. EFA was more useful in the early days of social science, when there were few models of latent psychological phenomena. As the understanding of various latent variables has progressed, the focus has shifted to testing models.

One such model for a hypothetical 10-item self-esteem indicator is depicted in Figure 7.1. In this diagram, the ovals refer to latent variables and the rectangles to observed variables, which in this case consist of items from the indicator. The "e" circles represent unique variance (see the description of communalities in Table 7.4), the variance of the items not accounted for by the latent factors. If this model is correct and you conducted an EFA in this situation, you would probably find evidence of three factors, evidence of salient loadings in those cases in which an arrow connects an item with a factor, and evidence of correlation among the factors if you conducted an oblique rotation (see Table 7.4).

FIGURE 7.1

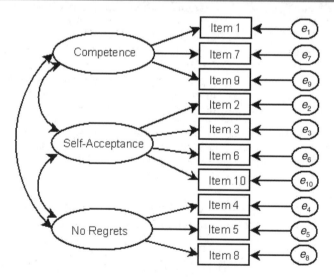

This model is based on the hypothesis that a 10-item self-esteem indicator reflects three latent variables. The two-headed arrows indicate an expectation that the latent variables are correlated (oblique).

CFA takes a different approach. In CFA, you would instruct the software to use the model in Figure 7.1. The software then estimates the parameters of that model (e.g., the item loadings and the strength of the relationships between the latent variables) based on that model and evaluates how well the model fits your data. It also allows you to compare different models. For example, is the fit of the model improved when a general self-esteem factor is added to the three specific factors? How much does the fit of the model deteriorate if the latent variables are treated as uncorrelated? CFA even permits you to evaluate whether the fit of the model differs across populations of individuals. This is the kind of statistical firepower that can make a statistician giddy!

The process of CFA can be outlined briefly. First, covariances are computed between each pair of items. The **covariance** is the *unstandardized correlation coefficient;* that is, it is not restricted to the range [–1, 1]. Sometimes correlations are used instead, but covariances are preferred for CFA. Second, the software uses an estimation procedure, usually maximum likelihood (see Chapter 5, this volume), to identify an optimal set of estimates for the model parameters. The software also computes estimates of the population covariances between the items based on the estimated model parameters. For example, the model in Figure 7.1 would suggest that the estimated covariance between Items 1 and 7 should be larger than that between Items 1 and 6, all other things being equal, because 1 and 6 are more distantly related in the model.

Although CFA often involves estimating dozens of model parameters, in the end researchers are often interested in answering two simple yes–no questions: (a) "Is Model A good enough?" (the goodness-of-fit question) and (b) "Is Model A better than Model B?" (the relative-fit question). Notice that these are almost the same questions addressed by significance testing ("Is the null hypothesis true?") and null hypothesis significance testing ("Is the alternative hypothesis more likely to be true than the null hypothesis?").

In general, goodness of fit and relative fit are evaluated by comparing the estimated values for the covariances with the actual observed covariances in the sample. For example, if the observed covariance in the sample between Items 1 and 6 is actually larger than that for Items 1 and 7, that finding would tend to lower the fit of the model in Figure 7.1. More than 20 statistics have been developed for gauging the fit of a latent-variable model, including both significance tests and dimensional indicators of fit. One of the most basic is a chi-square test that evaluates whether the matrix of observed covariances and the matrix of covariances estimated from the model are significantly different. A significant difference would theoretically suggest poor fit. I use the word *theoretically* because in fact the large sample sizes required for CFA result in a chi-square test that is so powerful it is rarely not significant. One interesting feature of this chi-square test is that the difference between the chi-square values for two models is itself the basis for a chi-square test of the two models' relative fit.[2]

The dimensional indicators of fit gauge the degree of discrepancy between the two covariance matrices, many on a 0-to-1 scale. Depending on how they are computed, higher values (e.g., the Tucker–Lewis Index or comparative fix index) or lower (e.g., the standardized root-mean-square residual or root-mean-square error of approximation) values may indicate better fit. Still others are meaningful only in the context of relative fit, so that the model with the lower value is the better fitting model (e.g., the Akaike Information Criterion or Bayesian Information Criterion). There are many options available for deciding the goodness-of-fit and relative-fit questions in the context of CFA.

USES OF FACTOR ANALYSIS

Factor analysis has been used in a number of ways to address questions about latent variables. Five examples follow, but there are many others.

1. The example I used for EFA in which college students rated both themselves and someone else demonstrates its use to study convergent and discriminant validity. The identification of two distinct factors suggests that the two sets of instructions are distinct methods. At the same time, within self-rating and other-rating scales there is clear evidence of convergence, suggesting that these scales to some extent measure the same trait.

2. Factor analysis is relevant to construct validation. In particular, it can be used to evaluate the **factorial validity** of an indicator, or *the degree to which the latent factors revealed by factor analysis are consistent with the conceptual understanding of the construct underlying the indicator*. If the latent factors in Figure 7.1 are consistent with a reasonable conceptual model of self-esteem, then finding that this model offers a good fit to the data provides support for the factorial validity of this indicator.

   However, it is important to realize that the factor model may not correspond perfectly with any a priori conceptual model of the construct. This is because the results of the factor analysis depend on the correlations between variables, not on conceptual distinctions. For example, if I analyzed variables reflecting height and weight in a factor analysis they would collapse into a single factor, which I might call "Volume," because height and weight are strongly correlated in the general population. This does not mean

---

[2]Most CFA statistics available for comparisons of models require that one model be *nested* within the other. Before using CFA to compare models it is important to ensure that this condition is met (Bentler & Satorra, 2010).

that conceptual distinctions between height and weight do not matter. Factor analysis cannot substitute for conceptual analysis.

3. Factor analysis offers an alternative approach to reliability analysis. Factor scores (see Table 7.4) can be thought of as true scores and the loadings as estimates of relationships between observed scores and true scores. This is the same thing as reliability (remember that one symbol for reliability was ρ^2_{XT}, or the squared correlation between true and observed scores). Whereas true-score theory assumes that indicator items are multiple measurements of a single true score, factor analysis considers the possibility that the items represent several latent variables, each with its own true or factor score. For example, although the internal reliability of the BDI tends to be quite high (Beck, Steer, & Brown, 1996), and there is evidence the BDI items are affected by a general depression factor, there is also evidence that somatic and cognitive aspects of depression are distinct latent variables (Ward, 2006). It is also possible for more than one factor to load strongly on a single item, suggesting that responses to that item are influenced by several latent variables. Thus, factor analysis offers a more nuanced model of indicator reliability than is possible with true-score theory. Jöreskog (1971) described how to use CFA to generate estimates of reliability that are potentially more accurate than the commonly used statistics listed in Table 6.4, because they incorporate the possibility of multiple latent variables.

4. Factor analysis has been used to suggest subscales for multidimensional scales. For example, Zebrack, Ganz, Bernaards, Petersen, and Abraham (2006) conducted factor analyses of 70 items relevant to long-term cancer survivors and concluded that they reflected 10 underlying constructs, such as health worries and a negative life outlook. The items that were most strongly related to each latent variable became the items for each of 10 subscales.

5. A form of factor analysis called *Q factor analysis* can be used to identify subgroups of people rather than items or indicators. In Q analysis, factors load on members of the sample, and the size of the loadings is used to divide members of a sample into subgroups based on latent dimensions.

ISSUES IN FACTOR ANALYSIS

Behavioral researchers originally had high hopes for factor analysis and, later, for CFA, believing these methods would offer deep insights into the structure of latent variables. Some of that initial enthusiasm has waned, however, for a variety of good reasons:

- Factor analysis is only as good as the data entered into the analysis. A self-esteem questionnaire that includes a set of items having to do with feelings of competence is likely to produce a "Feelings of Competence" factor; one that does not include more than one or two such items probably will not. The results of the factor analysis usually say more about the variables used for the analysis than anything about the "true" nature of the latent variables.

- A variety of decisions must be made in the course of a factor analysis: how many factors to retain, whether to treat the factors as oblique or orthogonal, how large a loading indicates a salient relationship between items and factors, which of the many factor analytic methods to use, and even which software to use. Each of these decisions can change the results, sometimes slightly and sometimes substantially.
- CFA can be particularly problematic. Sometimes arbitrary decisions about the model have to be made just to get the software to run correctly.
- The multiplicity of fit indicators is a great source of confusion. In a very influential article, Hu and Bentler (1999) suggested cutoff values for a variety of fit statistics to determine whether the evidence supports a given model. For example, they suggested that a comparative fit index value ≥ .93 indicated good fit, as did a standardized root-mean-square residual ≤ .08. Unfortunately, as with any yes–no judgment, the cutoffs are arbitrary, and in this case the cutoffs have been widely criticized (e.g., Marsh, Hau, & Wen, 2004). Complicating matters further are the following four facts: (a) Fit statistics in CFA are sensitive to all sorts of factors that should be trivial to fit, such as sample size and the number of model parameters, and can produce conflicting results; (b) different researchers tend to use different fit statistics, so results across studies may not be strictly comparable; (c) many researchers do not report confidence intervals for the fit statistics, so the possibility that small differences in the statistics are due to sampling error is often ignored; and (d) it is possible for very different models to produce equally acceptable values for fit statistics. There is simply no gold standard for concluding that a model is good or that one model is better than another. This is an important issue for you to realize because CFA studies regularly select a "best" model, and they do so by ignoring serious problems with the methods available for making such judgments.
- CFA also offers a set of statistics called *modification indices* that identify which additional changes in a model would most improve its fit. Modifying the model on the basis of these statistics is tempting but should be done cautiously, if at all, because it represents an example of a fishing expedition or capitalization on chance (see Chapter 2, this volume).

- Although general statistical software packages such as SPSS/PASW and SAS offer EFA, specialized software is needed to conduct CFAs. Leading options include LISREL, EQS, AMOS, OpenMx (which has the advantage of being free for download), and Mplus. This last program has the advantage of being capable of analyzing just about any sort of latent-variable model you can imagine, and many you cannot.

Despite these concerns, factor analysis in its various forms is an essential tool for the study of latent variables. Readable introductions to factor analysis have been provided by T. A. Brown (2006) and P. Kline (1993).

Structural Equation Modeling

CFA is conducted using **structural equation modeling** (SEM), *a class of statistics capable of estimating both a measurement and structural model for latent variables*. Factor analysis is an example of a measurement model. If you look at Figure 7.1 you will see that the focus is on the relationship between the latent variables and the items that are used to measure those variables. SEM software can estimate this type of measurement model; it can also estimate the structural model between the latent variables. The measurement model in Figure 7.2 is the same as that in Figure 7.1, but there are now explicit hypotheses included about the relationships among the latent variables; specifically, it is suggested that self-acceptance and absence of regrets are both a product of competence, whereas absence of regrets is also a result of self-acceptance. I will not discuss structural modeling further at this point, especially because it requires an understanding of certain concepts, such as direct effects, indirect effects, and suppressor relationships, that I do not explore until Chapter 9. A good introduction to the topic was provided by Schumacker and Lomax (2010). I will, however, leave you with a few comments about SEM:

- Although CFA is conceptually a special case of factor analysis, statistically (i.e., in terms of the statistical methods used) it is a special case of SEM. All of the concerns listed earlier about CFA—the problems with fit indices, the lure of modification indices, and the problems with some of the software—apply equally well to SEM.
- Sometimes you may want to define a circle among the latent variables. For example, if you thought a lack of regrets helps people act more competently, you would draw the arrow in Figure 7.2 from No Regrets to Competence instead of the other way, which would create a circle from Competence, to Self-Acceptance, to No Regrets, to Competence. Similarly, you might believe that competence and

FIGURE 7.2

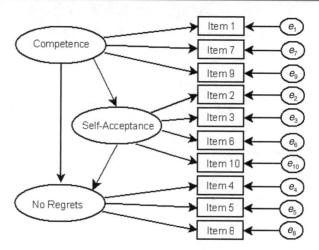

This model matches that in Figure 7.1 except the nature of the relationships between the latent variables is modeled more explicitly.

self-acceptance each enhances the other, which implies an arrow from Competence to Self-Acceptance and another from Self-Acceptance to Competence. These are examples of **nonrecursive models**, *models in which the arrows make a circle.* In some instances the software will simply refuse to compute the results. This is an example of an important general principle with SEM, which is that the software is not always able to test what you would consider the best model.

- SEM can tell you whether there is reason to believe a relationship exists between two latent variables but cannot tell you whether the direction of the relationship you hypothesize is correct. If the three arrows between the latent variables were all reversed in Figure 7.2, so that No Regrets were affecting the other two and Self-Acceptance were affecting Competence, the results would look equally good. Directions of relationships must be based on a sound conceptual justification, not on SEM results.

Item Response Theory

I introduced factor analysis by discussing some observations Spearman (1904) made about the possible existence of both general intelligence and specific intelligences. This debate has continued into modern times, with

EXHIBIT 7.1

A Hypothetical History Test With Four-Alternative Multiple-Choice Items That Are Converted to Pass–Fail Form Before Scoring

Item No.	1	2	3	4	...	23	24	25
John's answers	A	C	B	B		D	A	A
Answer key	A	C	C	B		D	C	B
Outcome	P	P	F	P		P	F	F
Point value	1	1	0	1		1	0	0

the general consensus being that both general and specific intelligences exist (e.g., Carroll, 1993).

Factor analysis uses correlational statistics to address these sorts of issues, which makes sense given its relevance to dimensional variables. IRT is another alternative for understanding relationships between latent and observed variables. I start with the simplest form of IRT, called *Rasch modeling* (Rasch, 1960) or *one-parameter IRT*.[3] I also focus on tests consisting of dichotomous items. Items on many abilities tests are scaled as dichotomous variables even if they are presented to the test-taker as multiple-choice items. For example, Exhibit 7.1 depicts how, on a history test consisting of four-alternative multiple-choice items, the items are converted to pass–fail form before they are scored. The last row of the exhibit indicates that John received 1 point for every item passed and 0 points for every item failed. The representation of success as 1 and failure as 0 is standard in IRT modeling of dichotomous items. In this way *variables with more than two categories* (**polytomous variables**) can often be converted to dichotomous variables.

Suppose that intelligence does represent a single general ability. How then does one account for differences in performance on the different items? Classical test theory attributes this finding to random error. Rasch models instead attribute this finding to error plus differences in item difficulty, how hard the item is; specifically, Rasch modeling attempts to estimate the *odds* of person *i* getting item *j* correct. The odds ratio is an odd statistic: It is the ratio of the probability of getting the item correct over the probability of getting the item incorrect:

$$odds\left(Y_{ij} = 1\right) = \frac{p\left(Y_{ij} = 1\right)}{1 - p\left(Y_{ij} = 1\right)}. \tag{7.1}$$

---

[3] The terminology of IRT can be confusing here. One-parameter IRT actually encompasses two procedures. In addition to Rasch modeling, there is the *one-parameter logistic model*, which models scores as normally distributed. Complicating matters is that scores generated by the two approaches differ by a constant of 1.7. Be forewarned.

In the context of Rasch modeling, this odds ratio is estimated from the following formula:

$$log\text{-}odds\left(Y_{ij} = 1\right) = \ln\left(\theta_{i.} - b_{.j}\right). \qquad (7.2)$$

Notice that the mathematics of the Rasch model is computed in logarithmic values because parameters are estimated using maximum likelihood (see Chapter 5, this volume). What this formula suggests is that the log-odds, or *logit*, that person *i* will get item *j* correct is a function of person *i*'s intellectual ability, symbolized by $\theta_{i.}$ (the Greek lowercase letter theta), and the difficulty of the item, $b_{.j}$.

The latent trait $\theta_{i.}$ is conceptually very much like the latent factor I described when discussing factor analysis. Equation 7.2 introduces a new parameter not discussed in factor analysis, the item difficulty. This is an important difference between IRT and traditional models of measurement. Whereas traditional models treat the observed score as the best estimate of the latent variable, IRT indicates that the difficulty of the items must first be accounted for. To offer just one example here of how this approach can inform testing, imagine two intelligence tests that differ dramatically in how hard the items are. From the perspective of traditional test theory these two tests would be associated with very different true scores, because test-takers would on average probably get much lower scores on the more difficult test. In theory, IRT would subtract out differences in item difficulty and so would allow an estimate of underlying intelligence from each test that is independent of the average item difficulties; that is, IRT offers an approach to gauging latent variables independent of the specific set of items used. This is a very important feature of IRT.

So Rasch modeling produces an estimate of the latent ability variable $\theta_{i.}$ for each person in the sample and an estimate of the latent difficulty parameter b_j for each item. To understand how this estimation task is accomplished, a little more information about the relationship between theta and item difficulty is needed.

In the case of Rasch modeling with dichotomous variables, **item difficulty** can be defined as *the value of theta at which 50% of individuals in the population pass the item*. This definition is illustrated in Figure 7.3. Remember that at the moment the discussion is focusing on the hypothetical population level, not on a sample. The value on the x-axis in Figure 7.3 is θ, which is location on the latent variable. The value of θ is estimated on a standardized scale, so a value of 1.0 is 1 standard deviation above the population mean, whereas a score of −1.3 is 1.3 standard deviations below the mean. The value on the y-axis is the probability of passing the item at a given value for θ.

FIGURE 7.3

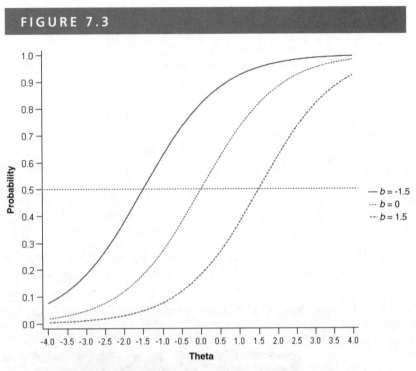

Three item characteristic curves are presented. The *x*-axis is theta (location on the latent trait), while the *y*-axis is the probability of a correct response at a given value for theta. The three curves indicate items with a difficulty (*b*) of −1.5, 0, and 1.5.

The three curves in the figure represent three examples of item characteristic curves. In the context of Rasch modeling, an **item characteristic curve** is *a graphic representation of the probability of success on an item as a function of a latent trait*. All three curves are similar in that people with a very low value on θ have a low probability of getting the item correct. As a person's θ value (ability) increases, the probability of getting the item correct also increases.

What differs for the three items is their level of difficulty. The solid curve is associated with an item difficulty (*b*) of −1.5. This means that 50% of test-takers with a θ value 1.5 standard deviations below the mean get the item correct, which suggests a relatively easy item. Among people with a θ of 0 or greater almost 100% get the item correct. In contrast, an item with *b* = 0 (the dotted curve) indicates that the average person, the person with a θ value of 0, has only a .50 probability of getting the item correct. An item difficulty of 1.5 (the dashed line in Figure 7.3) indicates a fairly difficult item. For this item, only 90% of people with θ values 4 standard deviations above the mean get the item correct. The item characteristic curve provides a simple way to compare items in terms of difficulty: The farther to the right on the x-axis the curve for that item appears, the more difficult it is.

I have indicated several times that Rasch modeling is not the only form of IRT. There are also two-parameter and three-parameter versions that estimate more complex models of item responding. The two-parameter model allows items to differ not only in terms of difficulty but also in slope, so there are now two parameters per item:

$$\frac{p\left(Y_{ij}=1\right)}{1-p\left(Y_{ij}=1\right)} = a_{.j}\left(\theta_{i.}-b_{.j}\right). \tag{7.3}$$

Notice that if the slope $a_j = 1.0$, the model reduces to the Rasch model. The three curves in Figure 7.3 had the same slope, 1.0, but different item difficulties. In Figure 7.4, three item characteristic curves are depicted that have the same item difficulty, 0, but different slopes. Notice

FIGURE 7.4

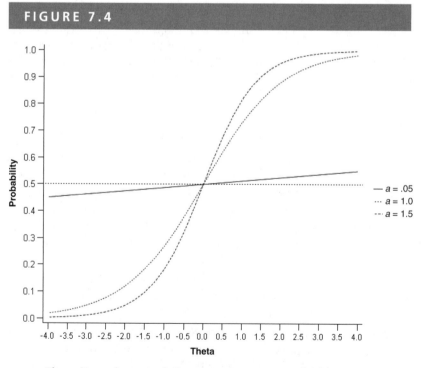

Three item characteristic curves are presented. The three items have an item difficulty (b) of 0, but differ in slope (a).

that when $a = .05$, which is close to a slope of 0, the curve is pretty close to a straight horizontal line. When the slope equals 0, the item characteristic curve is a horizontal line and performance on the item has no relationship with latent ability (a sign of a very bad item). As the slope increases, the curve becomes steeper. With $a = 1.5$ (the dashed line), most of the improvement in pass rate occurs among individuals with θ values between −1.0 and 1.0. The item with slope $a = 1.0$ (the dotted line) demonstrates a more gradual rate of increase. Although the Rasch model is popular, it is often argued that the two-parameter model is more generally useful.

The three-parameter model goes even further, adding a correction for guessing on each item. If there is reason to expect guessing is occurring, then the three-parameter model will presumably be more accurate than the two- or one-parameter model. Estimating more parameters requires more participants if the results are to be reliable, however. This is a common problem in latent structure analyses, including both IRT and factor analysis, and has been discussed extensively in the literature on the use of these methods.

For all three models—the one-, two-, and three-parameter IRT models—there are also variants available for studying polytomous items without first converting them to dichotomous items. Examples include the *partial credit model* and the *graded response model*. In the case of dichotomous items, you can think of the item difficulty as an indication of the probability of getting a 1 (pass the item) versus a 0 (fail the item) at different levels of the underlying trait. The polytomous BDI items each have four options, with 0 representing the lowest level and 3 the highest. IRT treats these items as categorical and computes an item difficulty for the probability of getting a 1 versus a 0, a 2 versus a 1, or a 3 versus a 2. Again, this requires estimating more parameters than in the case of dichotomous items.

There has been a great deal of discussion about the potential for IRT. Like factor analysis, IRT offers a much more sophisticated approach to modeling test responding than is possible with true-score theory. In practice, latent variable estimates generated using IRT will tend to correlate highly with scores resulting from simple summation of the items, so criterion-related validity is unlikely to change much. On the other hand, differences between scores on the estimated latent variable θ are at least theoretically a more accurate representation of the distance between people than differences between observed scores (T. G. Bond & Fox, 2001).

IRT has historically been particularly useful for the evaluation of latent ability variables, such as intelligence. Some have questioned IRT's relevance for studying variables that have to do with attitudes or self-perceptions, for which the concept of item difficulty seems less relevant. For example, consider two items, "I am depressed" and "I am suicidal," both coded 1 for a response of "false" and 2 for a response of "true." The second item would likely be found more difficult than the first: Respondents on average need to be at a higher level on θ (depression) to answer "true" to the suicide item than to the depression item. The difficulty of the item is directly related to the severity of the symptom addressed by the item; however, difficulty is not necessarily related to severity when θ is an attribute of a person.

Despite this concern, the use of IRT with self-reported variables is increasing. Although I have been describing IRT primarily in terms of its use as a method for estimating latent variables, this growing popularity of IRT stems in part from its ability to estimate item difficulties. In Chapter 6, I suggested in the context of true-score theory that items can be evaluated in terms of the degree to which they reduce the reliability of an indicator. Item difficulty offers an alternative basis for evaluating items. For example, Gray-Little, Williams, and Hancock (1997) found that the items of the most popular self-report measure of self-esteem are better at discriminating between individuals with low levels of self-esteem than those with high levels (i.e., too many items were of low difficulty).

Second, the computation of item difficulties makes it possible to generate systems for **computerized adaptive testing** (CAT), *testing in which subsequent items are determined by responses to earlier items*. In CAT, items of moderate difficulty (items with b values of approximately 0) are administered first. Respondents who achieve high scores on the moderate items are then administered more difficult items because it is reasonable to expect that they would achieve a high score on low-difficulty items as well. By the same logic, respondents with low scores on the moderate items are then administered items of lower difficulty. In this way it is possible to zero in on the person's location on the latent trait with just a few items. Although it involves computerized administration of the indicator, the efficiency of CAT is rapidly revolutionizing testing practice. The Graduate Record Exam is one of many indicators that uses CAT (for an example outside the area of abilities testing, see Reeve et al., 2007).

Like CFA, at this point IRT must be conducted with specialized software. Popular packages include WINSTEPS, BILOG, and MULTILOG, and Mplus has some IRT functionality. A relatively readable introduction to IRT is provided by Embretson and Reise (2000).

Categorical Latent-Variable Models

I now turn to a discussion of the fourth type of latent-variable models, categorical latent-variable models.

CLUSTER ANALYSIS

The methods described so far generally assume that latent variables are dimensional. Factor analysis allows for multiple latent variables, whereas IRT generally assumes a single latent variable. **Cluster analysis** is *a statistical method that groups cases on the basis of similarity.* Cluster analysis is based on the assumption that some qualitative difference exists among the observed cases on a single latent categorical variable, and it attempts to categorize cases into groups on the basis of that difference. Although other methods exist for dividing individuals into groups (e.g., latent class analysis), cluster analysis is the most popular method for doing so. It can also be used to divide variables into groups.

A particularly interesting example of the usefulness of cluster analysis was provided by Salvador et al. (2005), who used functional magnetic resonance imaging to examine co-occurrence of brain activity over time in 90 brain regions among 12 healthy adults. They concluded on the basis of cluster analysis that the brain could be categorized into six sets of functionally related regions. One set comprised 22 regions primarily devoted to motor and spatial functions; another comprised 22 regions that had to do with planning and self-control; a third set comprised 14 regions that specialized in visual processing; a fourth comprised 12 regions that had to do with hearing and speech; a fifth comprised 10 regions devoted primarily to memory and emotion; and a sixth set comprised 10 regions devoted to more evolutionarily primitive functions, such as reward, smell, and sleep.

Conducting a cluster analysis requires three key decisions. The first is the **distance metric**, *the statistic that is used in a cluster analysis to gauge similarity or distance.* The second is the selection of a clustering method. The final issue is how many clusters to retain. This is similar to the issue of the number of factors to retain in factor analysis, although in that case the decision had to do with the number of latent variables whereas in cluster analysis the decision has to do with the number of groups comprising a single latent categorical variable.

The Distance Metric

Suppose I administer five questionnaires measuring risk factors for heart disease to a sample of individuals and want to cluster them in terms of risk group. Exhibit 7.2 lists the scores for three members of the sample. Which two questionnaires are more likely to be clustered? The answer depends on the distance metric you choose. The most popular such metric is the **squared Euclidean distance**,[4] which is *the sum of the squared*

---

[4]When variables are on very different scales, an alternative called *Mahalanobis distances* is often recommended instead.

EXHIBIT 7.2

Hypothetical Clustering of Questionnaire Respondents

Variable	John	James	Patrice
1	7	12	21
2	23	16	27
3	16	17	25
4	8	12	21
5	9	19	23

differences between two cases. In Exhibit 7.2, for John and James, this would equal

$$(7 - 12)^2 + (23 - 16)^2 + (16 - 17)^2 + (8 - 12)^2 + (9 - 19)^2 = 191. \quad (7.4)$$

We could also compute correlations for each pair as an index of similarity. The complete set of Euclidean distances and correlations is as follows:

	Correlations	Distances
John and James	.39	191
John and Patrice	.97	658
James and Patrice	.60	363

Distance is a measure of dissimilarity, so smaller distances are better, whereas the correlation is a measure of similarity, so larger values are better. Euclidean distances would lead us to start by combining John and James into a cluster because they are the least distant from one another, but correlations would lead us to conclude that John and Patrice are most alike. I will leave it to the motivated student to examine the data and figure out why this difference occurred. The point is that it does occur, and the choice of a distance metric can result in dramatic differences in the results of a cluster analysis.

Clustering Methods

There are two primary methods of cluster analysis: (a) hierarchical or agglomerative hierarchical clustering and (b) iterative partitioning. The former begins by setting each case as a cluster, so the number of clusters equals the number of cases. Then the two cases with the smallest distance are combined so there are $N - 1$ clusters. This process repeats until there is only one cluster left that contains everybody. Various statistics are available for comparing the results across steps to suggest the optimal number of clusters (which I discuss in the next section). The best-known variant of agglomerative hierarchical clustering is called *Ward's method.*

Iterative partitioning, of which the most popular variant is called k-*means cluster analysis*, requires that one set the number of clusters first. The software randomly sorts cases into that many clusters of approximately equal size. A **centroid**, *the mean of all scores for all cases in the cluster*, is then computed for each cluster. Suppose at this point Alfonse is in Cluster Y but is closer to the centroid for Cluster X than the centroid for Cluster Y. Alfonse is shifted from X to Y, and centroids are recomputed. This is done repetitively until no more shifts occur.

Unfortunately, it has been demonstrated that the results of k-means clustering can vary depending on the original random sort. Even so, evidence suggests that if the number of clusters is accurate then it will give you the most accurate grouping of cases. For this reason, common practice now is to start with a hierarchical cluster analysis, usually Ward's method. The results of this analysis are then used to decide on the number of clusters for a k-means cluster analysis.

Cluster Retention

Finally, the researcher must decide on a method for choosing the number of clusters to retain based on the hierarchical clustering. A number of methods have been suggested for this task (see Steinley, 2006). Although none has ever emerged as a standard, several statistics suggested by Milligan and Cooper (1985) as particularly effective, called the *pseudo*-F *statistic* and the *cubic clustering criterion*, are probably the most popular. I must admit that in my own research I have been underwhelmed by the effectiveness of these statistics, however. For one thing, it is not unusual for these statistics to suggest several conclusions. What to do when the results suggest there may be three, four, or seven clusters is not quite clear.

SUMMARY OF CLUSTER ANALYSIS

For a brief, readable introduction to cluster analysis, I recommend Aldenderfer and Blashfield's (1984) book, but I will briefly summarize here standard practice in the cluster analysis method. It requires making choices about a distance metric, a method of analysis, and a method for setting the number of clusters to retain. In practice, the first is usually the squared Euclidean distance, although there are important advantages to the Mahalanobis distance. Most researchers start with Ward's method to generate hierarchical results and then apply the cubic clustering criterion and pseudo-F to decide on the number of clusters to retain. Once the number of clusters is determined, they repeat the analysis using k-means clustering to produce a better subgrouping of cases. Although the results may be interesting, there are random elements to the analysis, and often there are multiple reasonable solutions.

DECIDING ON THE TYPE OF MODEL

Now that the possibility of both dimensional and categorical latent variables has been raised,[5] I must address one final issue in latent-variable modeling: Which model should one pursue? The methods described so far simply assume that one or the other is true. Factor analysis and IRT will produce results that look like a dimensional latent variable even if that variable is categorical, and the opposite is true of cluster analysis.

Several other statistics are particularly useful for evaluating what type of latent variable is present. For example, *finite mixture modeling* is a family of statistical analyses that attempt to decompose observed distributions into mixtures of different groups, so-called mixture models (see Table 7.1). The methodology therefore assumes the presence of a latent categorical variable. However, associated with finite mixture modeling are several significance tests and fit indices that can evaluate whether a two-category model is superior to a one-category model. If it is not, the results support a dimensional model because a dimensional variable can be thought of as a one-category variable. Similarly, some of the statistics Milligan and Cooper (1985) described for cluster analysis will evaluate the fit of a one-cluster (dimensional) model. These methods also have the ability, if a categorical model is indicated, to provide an estimate of the correct number of categories.

Another option, called *taxometric analysis* (Ruscio, Haslam, & Ruscio, 2006), was originally developed to distinguish between dimensional and dichotomous latent structure. Even so, taxometric analysis has become a very popular statistical choice in recent years, in particular for the study of personality and psychopathology, because it produces a particularly large set of statistics relevant to the type of latent variable that is present. More recent work has suggested that it can be used more generally to distinguish between dimensional and categorical latent structures (e.g., McGrath & Walters, 2010).

Conclusion

I know this has been a tough chapter. My guess is that the information here is not really going to become concrete for you unless you are specifically interested in working with or reading a study that used one of these methods. If you find yourself in that situation, I recommend you return

---

[5]In the literature these are more frequently referred to as *continuous* and *discrete* latent variables (e.g., Haertel, 1990), but I prefer *dimensional* and *categorical,* for reasons I discuss in Chapter 8.

to this chapter and reread the relevant sections. My hope is that once you relate it to real-world examples you will find the information more helpful. At least, that is my hope.

For now, more than anything else my intention is to provide you with some intuitive sense not only of the potential value of latent-variable modeling but also of its complexity. Many of the most important psychological variables are difficult if not impossible to observe directly; this is one of the great burdens of psychological science. Even so, it is important to try to understand the nature of those variables, and that is the goal of latent-variable modeling.

In this chapter, I have provided a brief survey of the most important these methods, including factor analysis (EFA and CFA), SEM, IRT, and cluster analysis. Factor analysis attempts to identify one or more latent dimensional variables that account for relationships, usually between dimensional observed variables. EFA is optimal when no preexisting hypothesis exists about the nature of those latent variables other than that they are dimensional, whereas CFA is optimal when there is a basis for a model of the latent variables. SEM extends factor analysis to allow for testing various relationships between latent variables. IRT instead generally assumes a single latent dimensional variable is at work, but observed items are treated as a categorical combination of that latent variable plus item difficulty. Cluster analysis differs from the others in that it assumes a single underlying categorical variable.

It should come as no surprise that all attempts to relate observed and unobserved variables are open to a great deal of error. Even so, it is really the latent variables that interest us, not any one indicator of those variables, so latent-variable modeling will play an increasingly important role in trying to understand psychological phenomena.

STRUCTURAL MODELING

Preliminary Concepts in Structural Modeling

8

An intermittent theme of this book has been the distinction between invented models that are used as tools of inference and the modeling of psychological reality. Null hypothesis significance testing is an invented model that incorporates principles from logic and probability theory to provide a useful tool for drawing inferences about populations from samples; it compares two models of psychological reality, one in which an effect exists and one in which it does not. True-score theory is more of an invention, latent-variable modeling an attempt at modeling reality.

Chapters 8 and 9 of this volume focus exclusively on the second type of modeling. They have to do with how psychologists use quantitative methods to understand psychological variables. When a researcher conducts a study concerning, for example, variables X and Y, several types of relationships can exist between two variables, and the options increase further when we discuss relationships that involve three or more variables. The researcher's guess about the relationship between X and Y will then determine which statistics are appropriate for studying these variables.

The choice of statistics for a particular type of model also depends on the types of variables one is studying. To provide some background to the issue of how to model relationships between variables or distributions of individual variables (which is the topic of Chapter 9), I first provide this brief introduction to the issue of classifying variables.

Formal Classification of Variables

Consider a study in which a researcher collects information about ethnicity on a scale that ranges from 1 to 5 (*Caucasian* = 1, *African American* = 2, etc.), information about attitudes about political affiliation on a scale that ranges from 1 to 5 (1 = *strongly Democratic*, 2 = *leaning toward Democratic*, 3 = *neutral*, 4 = *leaning toward Republican*, 5 = *strongly Republican*), and age in years. Even though the first two variables are on the same 1-to-5 scale, the relationship between the values of the variables differs. Whereas there is a difference in *degree* associated with the political affiliation question, so that higher scores mean more Republican, there is a difference in *kind* for ethnicity. Values of age demonstrate a more complex relationship in that the difference between being 20 and 25 is equal to the difference between being 25 and 30. To say there are different types of variables is to say there are differences in the types of relationships that hold among the values of variables, and so the variable values mean different things.

Since the end of the 19th century, mathematicians and mathematically sophisticated scientists have been actively struggling with how to characterize measured variables. Most statistics texts limit their discussion of the types of variables to Stevens's (1946) measurement model, which was an attempt to define a mathematical model for measurement in psychology. In that article, he focused on the following four qualities of true numbers:

1. Different numbers can indicate a *difference:* Saying Faustus is 2 ft (0.6 m) tall and Gwendolyn is 4 ft (1.2 m) tall indicates that there is a difference in their heights.
2. Different numbers can indicate *relative amount:* Saying Faustus is 2 ft (0.6 m) tall and Gwendolyn is 4 ft (1.2 m) tall indicates that Gwendolyn is taller than Faustus.
3. Equal intervals between numbers can indicate *equal differences:* Saying Faustus is 2 ft (0.6 m) tall, Gwendolyn is 4 ft (1.2 m) tall, and Arturo is 6 ft (1.8 m) tall indicates that the difference in height between Faustus and Gwendolyn (2 ft [0.6 m]) is equal to the difference in height between Gwendolyn and Arturo (also 2 ft [0.6 m]).

4. Ratios of numbers can indicate *proportional amounts:* Saying Faustus is 2 ft (0.6 m) tall and Gwendolyn is 4 ft (1.2 m) tall indicates that Gwendolyn is twice as tall as Faustus.

Stevens (1946) distinguished among four types of variables on the basis of how many of these qualities applied to the values of that variable. His four variable types are hierarchical in that each includes all the mathematical qualities of the preceding category plus an additional feature.

Nominal variables are *variables for which different values indicate only some difference in the characteristic being measured.* Male–female is an example of a nominal variable with two possible values. Researchers often use numbers to represent the values of a nominal variable, for example, using a 1 for females and a 2 for males when recording data, but these numbers are arbitrary and demonstrate nothing more than a difference in terms of the construct gender. Any two numbers could have filled the purpose just as well.

Ordinal variables are *variables for which different values indicate a difference in relative amount of the characteristic being measured.* Any rank ordering is ordinal. If John's rank on a statistics test is 1, Phillipe's is 2, and Rhonda's is 3, the numbering indicates their relative performance on the test. However, these numbers do not indicate the distance between John, Phillipe, and Rhonda.

Interval variables are *variables for which equal intervals between variable values indicate equal differences in the amount of the characteristic being measured.* The Fahrenheit temperature scale is an interval variable. The amount of heat associated with a 3°F temperature change is always the same, so whether the temperature increases from 25°F to 28°F, or from 50°F to 53°F, the increase in heat is equivalent. Another example of an interval variable is years on the calendar. The same number of years passed between the years 1492 and 1497 as passed between 2000 and 2005.

Ratio variables are *variables for which ratios of variable values indicate proportional amounts of the characteristic being measured.* Height is an example of a ratio variable because concepts such as "twice as tall" are meaningful. Achieving meaningful proportions typically requires the presence of an absolute zero point, a value that represents the absence of the quality being measured. The division of 6 ft (1.8 m) by 3 ft (0.9 m) produces a meaningful value because there is an absolute zero point on the scale of height: The value 0 inches is associated with the absence of height. This is not true of the Fahrenheit scale of temperature because the value 0°F is not an absolute zero point. In contrast, 0° on the Kelvin scale of temperature refers to the point at which heat is absent. An object heated to 200°K is therefore twice as hot as an object heated to 100°K.

A particularly influential component of this model was Stevens's (1946) assertion of a relationship between the mathematical qualities of a variable and the choice of statistics applicable to that variable. For example, because nominal and ordinal variables allow meaningful addition of values, he asserted that statistics that require summing scores, such as the mean or multiple regression, should be used only with interval or ratio variables. This assertion instigated a lengthy debate on the relationship between the mathematical qualities of psychological variables and the types of statistics relevant to those variables (e.g., Boneau, 1961; Lord, 1953).

As a mathematical model of measurement, the Stevens model is seriously flawed. First, it was unclear whether this four-category model exhausted the universe of mathematical possibilities for the assignment of numerals to events or objects. In fact, Stevens (1959) himself later added a fifth category, the log-interval variable, although by then his original four-category model had been incorporated into psychological lore.

In addition, the model ignores other mathematical concepts associated with measurement. One example is the mathematical distinction between continuous and discrete variables. A **continuous variable** is *a variable for which gradations in values are infinitely small.* Distance is an example of a continuous variable: No matter how precisely the distance between two points is measured, even if distance is measured to millionths or billionths of an inch, it is theoretically possible to measure distance even more precisely. As a result, practical measurement of continuous variables always involves rounding. A **discrete variable** is *a variable for which clear boundaries exist between values.* Variables based on counting something always represent discrete variables, because only integer values such as 12 or 13 are possible.

Third, Stevens (1946, 1959) never provided much detail on how to classify variables. The result, as Cliff (1992) noted, was that psychologists assumed no formal criteria existed for identifying variable type. As a result, you can find arguments in the literature about whether the variables generated from psychological indicators such as personality tests are ordinal or interval, because they seem to have features of both. An even more troubling consequence is that psychologists often act as though the determination of the type of variable is up to them.

Finally, Stevens's (1946) model ignores more sophisticated work on the mathematical qualities of measurement scales that preceded his own. Interest in the mathematical qualities of scales also did not end with Stevens, and over the years a much more sophisticated perspective on measurement, usually called *representational* or *axiomatic measurement theory* (AMT; Krantz, Luce, Suppes, & Tversky, 1971), has emerged.[1]

---

[1]Given space constraints I can provide here only the briefest introduction to AMT. This is unfortunate because AMT represents a distinct model of measurement from those presented in the chapters of Part II of this book. It also probably represents the most mathematically sophisticated work ever involving psychologists. It has resulted in profound contributions to mathematical topics as basic as the addition of variable values, and it is an achievement of which we as members of the discipline should be proud.

I will now grossly oversimplify AMT. AMT is concerned with issues such as identifying the necessary and sufficient mathematical conditions, or axioms, for concluding that a variable meets criteria for a mathematical quality such as ordinal, quantitative, or continuous structure. For example, imagine we are measuring the lengths of steel rods. On the basis of prior experience we tend to have an intuition that measurements of length are at least ordinal. In contrast to Stevens's (1946) model, mathematicians have described a number of different types of ordinal relationships. One of the most familiar is called *weak order*, symbolized mathematically by ≥.

Roberts (1979) demonstrated that the rod lengths must meet two conditions for the weak order relationship to apply to measurement of those lengths:

1. If Rod A is as long as or longer than Rod B, and Rod B is as long as or longer than Rod C, then Rod A must be as long as or longer than Rod C. If this condition is met, then the relationship "as long as or longer than" is *transitive*.
2. Either Rod A is "as long as or longer than" Rod B, or Rod B is as long as or longer than Rod A, or both. If so, then the relationship is *complete*.

If the relationship "as long as or longer than" between rod lengths is transitive and complete, then the relationship meets the conditions for the mathematical property weak order, and the symbol ≥ can be applied to pairs of values on that scale. An important issue here is that the conditions apply to any subset of rods taken from the sample.

Now I apply this example to variables in psychology. This is a rational basis for concluding that variables such as age or the frequency of aggressive behaviors are at least ordinal (in fact, these are ratio variables). However, perhaps the most common type of variable in the psychosocial sciences is the multi-item scale, on which the total score is computed by summing across a series of items. There are serious difficulties involved in demonstrating that such scores comply with the axioms required for simple order. For example, assuring that scores on the Beck Depression Inventory (BDI; Beck, Steer, & Brown, 1996) are transitive would require demonstrating that any individual who achieves a score of 25 on the BDI is more depressed than any individual assigned a score of 24 and less depressed than any individual with a score of 26. Even in the absence of measurement error, the nature of the BDI makes such a demonstration impossible. BDI scores are derived by summing outcomes across 21 items scored on a 0-to-3 scale, each of which reflects a different aspect of depression. Given that there may be thousands of combinations of item outcomes that would produce scores of 24, 25, or 26 in practice, there is no reasonable rationale for concluding that these scores represent a consistent order; that is, the total score does not have a consistent meaning concerning location on the latent variable of depression (Michell, 2009).

From the perspective of AMT, the presence of an order relationship is a particularly important mathematical quality to demonstrate, because order turns out to be a precondition for meeting the axiomatic requirements for many other mathematical properties, including continuous measurement, additivity, and ratio scaling. Accordingly, AMT raises serious questions about whether the majority of psychological scales are demonstrably ordinal, ratio, or continuous, or accurately represented by any more complex mathematical property.

What are we to make of the fact that we cannot be sure even that our scales meet the criteria for representation by an ordinal structure, no less ratio or continuous, yet statistics that were developed specifically for use with variables whose values can be meaningfully added together, such as the mean and the analysis of variance (ANOVA), still produce information that is meaningful, sensible, and useful? The answer lies in recognizing that the conditions a set of scores must meet to produce meaningful statistical information can be less restrictive than the conditions needed for a mathematical quality; specifically, if there is no basis for saying any *individual* with a score of 25 on the BDI is more depressed than any individual with a score of 24, even when there is no error, then from the AMT perspective the scores cannot be considered ordinal. On the other hand, if it is reasonable to say that *on average* individuals with a score of 25 on the BDI are more depressed than individuals with a score of 24, then statistics that aggregate these scores across many people can still produce results with meaning; that is, the axiomatic approach looks for universal relationships, whereas the statistical approach requires only aggregate relationships over an entire sample. This analysis suggests that psychological scales are a good choice when the goal is to detect general patterns in a population. However, their meaning is more difficult to determine in the individual case (McGrath, 2005).

One important implication of this analysis is that attempts to conclude that a psychological variable is ordinal or interval will often prove inconclusive and unsatisfying. The more important question is what statistical techniques produce useful information when applied to that variable. For example, statistical software will compute an ANOVA using a nominal scale, such as marital status as the dependent variable, so long as the values of the variable are represented by numbers. However, the results have a good chance of being nonsense because ANOVA requires that there be a dimensional quality to the dependent variable, at least on average.

Practical Classification
of Variables

To summarize the key points discussed so far, many psychological variables cannot be formally classified, but formal classification does not necessarily matter to generating meaningful statistical results. Instead, I propose a classification of variables based on the practical issue of which statistical methods tend to produce meaningful information. In Chapter 1, I introduced three types of variables that provide the basis for a practical classification system for variables: (a) categorical, (b) dimensional, and (c) dichotomous. To these I now add a fourth, called *ranked variables*. I will warn you now that some of what follows is idiosyncratic to this book, but this is my attempt to provide practical advice in light of the problems with the formal classification of variables.

CATEGORICAL VARIABLES

The values of a categorical variable (also called a *class variable*) imply nothing more than a difference. Important examples of categorical variables include ethnic or cultural status and the treatment condition to which a person is assigned in a study. Comparing this concept with that of a nominal variable, discussed earlier in this chapter, will help clarify the distinction between the axiomatic and pragmatic approaches. Nominal variables were defined as variables for which different values only indicate a qualitative difference in the characteristic being measured; it is a characteristic of the scale, not of how it is used in a statistical analysis. For purposes of a statistical analysis, a researcher could take even a ratio variable and treat the different values of the variable as if they were only an indication of a difference. For example, if you conduct a study in which you measure age in years in a group of elementary school children, you could conduct analyses in which you look for simple group differences between 6-year-olds, 7-year-olds, and so forth. In this case, age is a ratio variable but it is being used as a categorical variable.

As with nominal variables, numbers are often used to represent the values of a categorical variable, but these numbers indicate nothing more than that the objects assigned those numbers differ in some way. Using numbers to represent values of a categorical variable does create one risk for the naive user of statistics in that he or she may inadvertently conduct statistics that assume the variable is dimensional. For example, I have seen students do things like compute a correlation, which should not be computed for categorical variables, between marital status and intelligence test score. An important reason for understanding the types of variables you are using is to ensure you use only those statistical methods that are appropriate to your variables.

DIMENSIONAL VARIABLES

A dimensional variable was defined earlier as one that implies some ordering of cases. This is a much more liberal standard than that required for a formal ordinal scale. It is a broad category; examples of dimensional variables include responses to a five-choice item that range from *strongly disagree* to *strongly agree;* a total score on a multi-item indicator such as an intelligence test or the BDI; frequency counts; clearly ordered variables, such as age or income; or any variable for which increasing values imply something about relative location on some dimension.

DICHOTOMOUS VARIABLES

Many statistics require that at least one of the variables used consist of only two values. Given their relevance to many statistical methods, it is appropriate for practical purposes to treat dichotomous variables as a distinct class of variables. Most dichotomous variables are categorical variables with only two values, such as male–female; however, it is possible for a dichotomous variable to be dimensional. The most common example of this occurs when *scores on a quantitative variable are used to divide participants into high and low groups,* a process called **dichotomization**. The division is often based on a median split, so that approximately half of the sample falls in each group. It can also be based on an optimal cut score, as when a score of 70 on an intelligence test is used to determine the presence or absence of intellectual impairment.

I am referencing dichotomization here only because it is a common practice; I do not recommend it. Dichotomizing variables makes them less reliable, and statistical analyses of dichotomized variables can be substantially less powerful as a result (MacCallum, Zhang, Preacher, & Rucker, 2002). There are also significant problems associated with identifying an optimal cut score (Dwyer, 1996). Dichotomization should be used only when there is a compelling justification for doing so. The best reason I know to dichotomize is when the purpose of the research is to study the use of dimensional scores from psychological indicators as the basis for dichotomous decisions in applied situations, such as hiring employees (DeCoster, Iselin, & Gallucci, 2009).

RANKED VARIABLES

Ranked variables represent *a special case of dimensional variables in which distances between levels of the variable are explicitly ignored.* Just as I compared the categorical variable with the nominal variable, the ranked variable parallels the ordinal variable. Whereas a reference to ordinal structure refers to an inherent characteristic of the variable, a variable can be considered ranked whenever the researcher decides to ignore information about distances.

THE CONCEPT OF GROUPING

A variable that is categorical, whether dichotomous or polytomous (i.e., having more than two values), can also be thought of as a variable that defines two or more groups. For this reason many of the statistics intended for use with categorical variables are discussed in terms of group differences. ANOVA was developed to identify relationships between categorical and dimensional variables, for example. Finding a significant result suggests that in the population the mean of the dimensional variable varies across the subpopulations represented by the groups of the categorical variable.

A categorical variable can consist of dependent or independent groups and can represent a fixed effect or a random effect. **Dependent groups** occur when *each observation in one group is linked with one unique observation in every other group*. This may be because of a matching procedure, as when the participants with the three highest scores on an intelligence test are randomly assigned to three different teaching interventions, then the next three highest are assigned, and so forth. It also occurs when the study involves repeated measures, for example, if the same participants complete some measure at three different points in treatment. **Independent groups** occur when *no such linkage exists, when participants in Group A are not associated with any particular participant in Group B.*

The concepts of fixed and random effects were introduced earlier in connection with meta-analysis. In the context of variables, a variable represents a **fixed effect** if *the findings generalize only to the values of the variable included in the study.* Suppose a researcher chooses to compare a high and low dose of a medication. The results are intended to represent the only difference between those two treatments. In contrast, suppose patients are randomly assigned a level of the drug across the entire range of possible dosages, so that some randomly receive 10 mg, others 12 mg, and still others 17 mg. The dose variable could then be treated as a **random effect**, *one that allows the researcher to generalize across all possible values of the variable.*

If you want a deeper understanding of these concepts, I encourage you to consider the similarities between the use of the terms here and in meta-analysis. I also note that most of the categorical variables you think about when designing studies are fixed effects (e.g., treatment group, gender), but random effects are more common than you might think. The participants in your sample usually represent a random effects categorical variable because the sample is generally assumed to be a random selection from a larger population to which you would like to generalize. Similarly, in reliability studies the raters are often assumed to be a selection from a larger population of possible raters to which you would like to generalize; see the "ICC(2,1)" and "ICC(2, k)" rows in Table 6.4. For practical purposes, though, all you need to know is the meaning of the terms and that the types of variables you are using affect the mathematics of statistics.

Exploratory Versus Confirmatory Modeling

Imagine that a public health agency has collected a large database that includes variables such as rates of various forms of cancer, cigarette smoking, socioeconomic status, education, and dozens of others. A researcher with access to this database might focus on those relationships for which he or she has a clear hypothesis. For example, the researcher could look at the relationship between cigarette smoking or pollutants and cancer rates across communities. Alternatively, he or she could focus on questions for which there is no prior expectation: Does the relationship between cigarette smoking and cancer vary depending on pet ownership; do levels of various compounds in the drinking water predict cancer rate? Finally, the researcher could simply conduct analyses in a scattershot manner and look to see whether certain patterns emerge that were completely unanticipated.

These represent steps on a dimension from purely confirmatory to purely exploratory research, from deductive to inductive research, from research in which the goals of the analyses are well defined ahead of time to research in which the outcomes could be completely unexpected. Many studies combine elements of the two. For example, in Chapter 7, I noted that although confirmatory factor analysis can be used to confirm or disconfirm a proposed model for the relationships between latent and observed variables, the software also generates a set of statistics called *modification indices*. These statistics help identify elements of the model that if changed, would most improve the model's fit to the data. In studies involving ANOVA the researcher may conduct some significance tests that emerge from the hypotheses and others that are simply generated as part of the procedure. Researchers who work with the aforementioned hypothetical public health database may look at some predictors of cancer risk because they are reasonable and others simply because they are part of the database.

Thanks to the legacy of Sir Ronald Fisher and his emphasis on predefining null hypotheses, psychologists have always been skeptical of exploratory research. There are some good reasons for this skepticism. Using the data to decide what analyses to conduct can easily lead to what I described in Chapter 2 as a fishing expedition, with an excessive number of Type I errors. Those attitudes started to change when the well-respected statistician John Tukey (1977) argued that psychologists focus excessively on confirmatory research and developed new tools for data exploration. It is reasonable to expect that exploratory analyses are more likely to provide reliable information when samples are large, when variables are well specified (i.e., clearly ordinal or ratio variables instead of the uncertain sorts of scales that result from multi-item indicators), and when the exploratory results make intuitive sense.

Conclusion

For the practical purpose of selecting a statistical analysis, I have suggested that there are four types of variables. In this instance I am not referring to the inherent character of a variable, which is what AMT is about; instead, I am referring to how a variable will be used in a statistical analysis to generate meaningful aggregated information. *Categorical variables* are treated as consisting of multiple groups. A categorical variable can define dependent groups (if each case in one group is matched in some way with one case in every other group) or independent groups (groups that are completely unrelated). It can also represent a random effect (if the researcher wants to generalize the results to other possible values of the variable) or a fixed effect (if the researcher wants to generalize only to the set of values included in the study). A *dimensional variable* is one for which different values imply a difference in level. A *ranked variable* is a special case of a dimensional variable in which distances between values are explicitly ignored, and a *dichotomous variable* is one with two values. In Chapter 9, I combine this information with information about the types of patterns and relationships one may find in psychological variables, to provide guidance on the selection of statistics for modeling those variables.

Modeling Psychological Phenomena 9

With the background I provided in Chapter 8 it is now possible to discuss the various types of quantitative models that are available for understanding psychological phenomena and the statistical procedures available for evaluating those models. In this chapter, I introduce the various options for modeling variables using statistics. To help guide you through the process, I offer Table 9.1 as a road map to this chapter. Many of the statistical methods reviewed in this chapter were developed with the expectation that they will test a certain model for a variable distribution or a relationship between variables via significance tests. However, effect sizes can be identified for most of these statistical methods, usually involving some variant of d, r, or the odds ratio. Velicer et al. (2008) argued that models are more rigorously tested by computing effect size statistics and corresponding confidence intervals because this approach requires that one evaluate not just whether a relationship exists but whether it is of the size that would be expected on theoretical grounds.

TABLE 9.1

Outline of Options for Modeling Real-World Phenomena

No. of variables	Types of models	Notes
One	Variable distribution	For example, mean of a dimensional variable or the set of frequencies for a categorical variable
Two	Correspondence relationship	A relationship between two variables in which the two variables are treated equally
	Contingent relationship ▪ Linear ▪ Quadratic ▪ Cubic	A relationship between two variables in which one is treated as a function of the other
More than two	Additive relationship	Two predictors of Y (X_1 and X_2) are combined to improve prediction of Y.
	Suppressor relationship	A predictor of Y (X_1) and a predictor of X_1 (X_2) are combined to improve prediction of Y.
	Mediating relationship	The effect of X_1 on Y occurs through X_2.
	Spurious relationship	The effect of X_1 on Y occurs because both are affected by X_2.
	Moderator relationship	The relationship between X_1 and Y changes across values of X_2.
	Nested relationship	Some values of X_2 only appear in combination with a certain value of X_1.

Modeling Variable Distributions

Many statistical methods have been developed for the purpose of evaluating the pattern or distribution of data for a single variable. Examples of attempts to model a variable distribution would include determining how many members of a sample chose each option on a 1-to-5 scale reflecting the importance of gun control, or the mean age in a population, or testing the null hypothesis that a population distribution is normally distributed. Although the first example is a descriptive statistic for a sample, the second is a parameter estimate, and the third is a significance test, in each case the analysis attempts to reveal something about a single variable. Sample demographics, or descriptive statistics for variables used in a study, usually involve analyses of one variable at a time. Survey research also relies heavily on reporting responses to single variables, such as the proportion of eligible voters who support a certain candidate. The hypothetical study I described in

TABLE 9.2

Examples of Statistical Methods Appropriate to Modeling Variable Distributions

Type of variable	Options
Dichotomous	Graphical: The **histogram** presents the frequency of each group. Descriptive: The **frequency** or **percentage** in each group is often used. Inferential: The **binomial test** or the **chi-square goodness-of-fit test** evaluates a null hypothesis about the percentage of the population in each group. If the distribution involves repeated measurement of the same variable over time (longitudinally), the **Wald–Wolfowitz runs test** can be useful.
Categorical	Graphical: The **histogram** presents the frequency of each group. Descriptive: A **frequency distribution** is relevant, as is the **mode**. Inferential: The **chi-square goodness-of-fit test** tests a null hypothesis about the percentage of the population in each category.
Ranked	Patterns in a single ranked variable are rarely analyzed because the transformation to ranks creates a rectangular distribution (all values are equally frequent).
Dimensional	Graphical: **Box-and-whisker plots, frequency polygons, histograms,** or **stem-and-leaf plots** are particularly popular. The **Q–Q plot** can be used to compare a sample distribution with some hypothetical distribution shape, such as the normal distribution. Descriptive: The **frequency distribution** is relevant, as are all measures of central tendency (**mean, median,** and **mode**), variability (**standard deviation, range, variance,** and **coefficient of variation**), **skew,** and **kurtosis.** Inferential: The **one-group z test** and **one-group t test** can each be used to test hypotheses about the population mean. The **Lilliefors test** can test the null hypothesis that a population distribution is normal. A more general alternative is the **Kolmogorov–Smirnov test,** which can test the null hypothesis that a population distribution matches whatever distribution shape the researcher chooses, including the normal distribution. The **chi-square test of a variance** can evaluate hypotheses about the size of the population variance. If the distribution involves repeated measurement of the same variable over time (longitudinally), various forms of **time series analysis** called **ARIMA** (autoregressive integrated moving average) and **spectral analysis** can be of interest.

Note. Statistics in boldface type are listed in the Index, to help you find brief descriptions of statistics in the future when reading research.

Chapter 1 having to do with the mean intelligence among people who completed a nutritional supplement treatment is an example of a situation in which the researcher was interested in an aspect of the variable distribution in the population. Examples of statistics relevant to the modeling of some component of the distribution for a single variable may be found in Table 9.2.

Modeling Two-Variable Relationships

A much more common scenario in psychological research involves modeling the relationship between two variables in some way. A relationship can be said to exist between two variables when information about one variable, X, provides additional information about the other variable, Y. Knowing that the mean score on a particular intelligence test is 100 among adult citizens of the United States, the best estimate of any person's score would be 100. If it turns out that that person is a physician, however, it would make sense to guess something higher, perhaps 120, because the categorical variable "occupation" and the dimensional variable "intelligence test score" are related to each other, and the physician group on the categorical variable occupation has a relatively high mean intelligence test score compared with other occupational groups. Of course, relationships between empirical variables are probabilistic, so these predictions are rarely perfect. If knowing information about one variable *on average* improves prediction of location on the other variable, no matter how small that improvement, then there is a nonzero relationship between those variables; using terminology from Chapter 3, there is an effect.

When conceptualizing a two-variable relationship and choosing the statistical methods used to model it, two issues must be considered. The first has to do with whether the relationship is best conceptualized in terms of a contingency or simple correspondence. The second has to do with the type of function to be modeled.

CONTINGENCY VERSUS CORRESPONDENCE

I use the term **contingent relationship** here to refer to *relationships involving two variables in which one is treated as a function of the other*.[1] Many statistical methods in science—and mathematical methods in general—model one variable as a function of another variable. The following is a list of circumstances in which researchers tend to be interested in modeling one variable as contingent on the other.

- *When one variable is thought to be caused or influenced by the other variable.* Consider a hypothetical study in which college students rate the intelligence of other students on the basis of only their photo-

---

[1] Some statisticians have attempted to develop definitions for contingency that do not require treating one variable as a function of the other, including the Rev. Thomas Bayes. You do not need to worry about these technical issues.

graphs to test the hypothesis that estimates of intelligence tend to be higher for more attractive individuals, that is, that attractiveness influences perceptions of intelligence. Another example would be an experiment in which different regions of the amygdala are stimulated in rats to see which produces a fear reaction.

- *When one variable will be used to predict another variable.* Psychological tests are often used for predictive purposes. For example, several studies have found that a single item ("How many times in the past year have you had X or more drinks in a day?" where X was 5 for men and 4 for women, and a response > 1 was considered positive) successfully predicted unhealthy alcohol use or an alcohol-related disorder (e.g., P. C. Smith, Schmidt, Allensworth-Davies, & Saitz, 2009), and Nock and Banaji (2007) were able to predict current and future suicidal ideation using a brief performance-based indicator.

- *When one variable is thought to be a precursor of future events.* Hokanson, Rubert, Welker, Hollander, and Hedeen (1989) found that social problems at the beginning of college predicted whether or not a student would become depressed over the ensuing months. This finding does not imply that social problems are a cause of depression, but it does provide useful probabilistic information about risk for the future.

In mathematics, the contingent relationship is symbolized by $Y = f(X)$, which means "Y is a function of X." Y is referred to as the **dependent variable**, and X is referred to as the **independent variable**.[2]

Still other statistics do not require that one consider one variable as a function of the other; instead, *the statistic implies only that the values of one variable in some way correspond with values on the other variable.* Such statistics suggest what can be called a **correspondence relationship**. I suggested earlier that a relationship exists between two variables when information about X provides additional information about Y. In the case of a correspondence relationship it is equally appropriate to say that Y provides additional information about X. A researcher may be interested in whether children with social problems also tend to demonstrate greater aggression. There is no implication here that social problems cause aggression, or vice versa, or that one has precedence in some way over

---

[2]Various other terms are associated with contingent relationships. You may see references to Y being *dependent* or *conditional* on X. In certain statistical contexts, X is referred to as the *exogenous variable* or as the *predictor*, whereas Y is referred to as the *endogenous variable* or the *criterion*. Also, it is worth noting that the term *independent variable* has a more restricted meaning in the context of research methods, where it refers specifically to a variable manipulated by the researcher, such as an intervention versus a placebo. The way I am using the term, to refer to any variable used to predict or estimate another variable, is more consistent with how the term is used in mathematics.

the other; the goal is simply to see whether a relationship exists. If one finds a relationship between aggression and social problems, then finding that Martin is a relatively aggressive child would lead you to expect that he has more social problems than average, whereas finding that Martin has a fair number of social problems would lead you to expect that he is also relatively aggressive. Compare this with the case of contingency: It is not particularly interesting to use the presence of problem drinking to predict how that person will respond to the single item in P. C. Smith et al.'s (2009) study, or to use response to treatment to predict which treatment the person received. There is something symmetrical in the correspondence relationship that is not true of the contingency relationship.

Another way to symbolize the contingent relationship is: $X \rightarrow Y$, for example, attractiveness $\rightarrow$ perceived intelligence, or amygdala stimulation $\rightarrow$ fear response. In contrast, the correspondence relationship can be symbolized by $X \leftrightarrow Y$, for example, social problems $\leftrightarrow$ aggression.

Various statistics were developed with contingent or correspondence relationships in mind. For example, regression and the correlation coefficient are closely related statistical methods mathematically (Cohen, Cohen, West, & Aiken, 2003), yet regression was developed assuming a contingent relationship (Y is a function of X), and the correlation coefficient assumes no precedence in the variables.[3] Regression has some advantages over correlation as a method for modeling Y as a function of X. That being said, there is no inherent problem with using a statistic that assumes a contingent relationship for a correspondent relationship, although doing so requires arbitrarily setting one variable as the independent variable and one as the dependent variable. There is similarly no problem with using a statistic that assumes a correspondent relationship for a contingent relationship, although the statistic ignores the asymmetrical nature of the relationship.

TYPE OF FUNCTION

Once you decide to model the relationship between X and Y as a contingent relationship, the next step is to decide what *type* of function exists between X and Y. Technically, there is an infinite set of functions available for modeling the relationship between two variables, but there are only a couple of options that are commonly used in psychological research.

---

[3]Some statistics textbooks attempt to capture this difference with the phrase "Correlation does not imply causality," but a close reader of the argument here will recognize that the issues are far more complex than this. For one thing, causality is only one of the reasons why a contingency model might be preferred.

Various possibilities in terms of a contingent relationship involving two variables are depicted in Figure 9.1. Imagine a study in which participants' change in heart rate in response to a loud noise is measured after ingesting one of four levels of caffeine: 6 mg per kg of body weight, 4 mg, 2 mg, or 0 mg of caffeine (the placebo condition). Figure 9.1A depicts the case in which a relationship between the two variables does not exist, where the mean heart rate change is no different across independent variable groups. Figures 9.1B through 9.1D represent examples of contingent relationships, relationships that would allow one to make a prediction about a person's heart rate change based on that person's group. For example, the line marked "Positive linear relationship" in Figure 9.1B would lead you to predict that the increase in heart rate for a person in the 6-mg group would be 5 beats per minute, whereas the increase for someone in the 2-mg group would be 3 beats per minute.

Figure 9.1B illustrates an example of **linear relationships**, *contingent relationships in which the dependent variable consistently increases (or decreases) as the independent variable increases.* Figure 9.1C provides examples of **quadratic relationships**, *contingent relationships in which there is a bend or curve in the line that relates the two variable.* The researcher in our example might hypothesize a quadratic relationship if he or she believes that caffeine increases heart rate until 4 mg, at which point the effect levels off (as in Quadratic Relationship 1) or even declines (as in Quadratic Relationship 2). Alternatively, a researcher might think the effectiveness increases to a certain dosage, then levels off, and then actually declines as doses get higher. This would suggest *a line with two bends*, or a **cubic relationship**, as in Figure 9.1D. *Functions used to represent linear, quadratic, cubic, or higher order relationships between two variables* are examples of **polynomial functions**.

Note that these are all hypothetical *models* the researcher might hypothesize for the relationship between X and Y. If the researcher hypothesizes a linear relationship between the two variables there is bound to be error when looking for that relationship in real-world data. Whereas the theoretical positive linear relationship in Figure 9.1B is associated with group means of 2, 3, 4, and 5, the true means might be 2.7, 2.9, 4.6, and 5.1.[4] Even so, significance testing can provide evidence to support the hypothesis of a linear pattern in the population. Furthermore, we can expect some variability within the groups, so predictions based on the group means would not be perfect either.

More complicated options are possible. In fact, the number of relationship patterns you can test for is 1 less than the number of values on

---

[4]You may see the term **monotonic function** used when there is *a linear trend in the data without perfect linearity.*

FIGURE 9.1

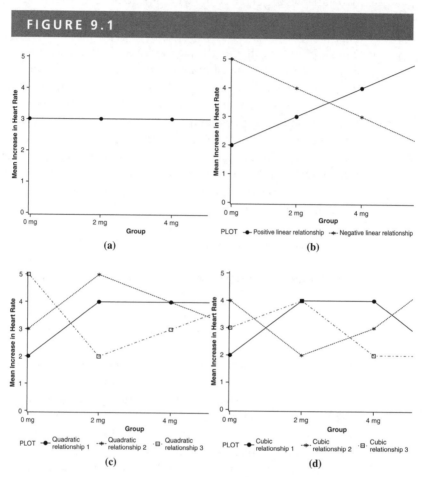

For two variables, these are examples of (a) the absence of a contingent relationship. (b–d) Various contingent relationships. (b) Positive (as *X* increases *Y* increases) and negative (as *X* increases *Y* decreases) linear relationships. (c) Quadratic relationships, where 1 indicates a positive relationship to a certain level, then no relationship; 2 indicates a positive relationship to a certain level, then a negative relationship; and 3 indicates a negative relationship to a certain level, then a positive relationship. (d) Cubic relationships, where 1 indicates a positive, then zero, then a negative relationship; 2 indicates a positive, then negative, then zero relationship; and 3 indicates a negative, then positive, then a stronger positive relationship.

the X variable. With a four-level X variable you can test for three relationships: (a) linear, (b) quadratic, and (c) cubic. In the case in which the X variable is Beck Depression Inventory (Beck, Steer, & Brown, 1996) score, and there are 64 possible scores, it is technically possible to test for 63 different relationships defined by increasing numbers of bends in the line. How does one choose among the different possible functions?

The answer has both conceptual and practical components. Conceptually, the answer depends on what you believe is true. If there is good reason to expect two bends in the line relating the two variables, then that should be the hypothesis you propose. However, there are practical limitations to consider. First, the more bends in the line you hope to test, the more data you need to test it. Second, after one or two bends it starts to become difficult to develop a reasonable rationale for the model. Finally, when X is a dimensional variable, such as a score on the Beck Depression Inventory, it is unusual for psychologists to find consistent evidence even for quadratic or cubic relationships. I suspect one reason for this phenomenon is that because psychological scales do not comply with axiomatic measurement (see Chapter 8, this volume), nonlinear relationships are difficult to detect. Even though the number of possible options is overwhelming, in practice psychologists infrequently look beyond linear relationships when X is a dimensional variable and almost never look beyond a quadratic or cubic relationship.

The situation is somewhat different when X is a categorical variable. Suppose marital status is coded 1 for married, 2 for single, 3 for divorced, and so on, and Y is self-rated happiness. There is no ordinal quality to the values of X, so there is no basis to expect a consistent direction for changes in Y across the groups. For this reason, when X is a categorical variable it makes sense to use statistics that are sensitive to any contingent relationship between X and Y. For example, the analysis of variance (ANOVA) was designed for X to be a categorical variable, and it is sensitive to any of the $k - 1$ possible relationships between X and Y, where k is the number of levels of X. Table 9.3 provides a number of examples of statistics relevant to modeling relationships between two variables.

Modeling Relationships With Three or More Variables

Now things get even more complicated! There are various cases in which a researcher believes three variables are required to understand some psychological phenomenon. In general, this occurs because a Y variable is seen as a function of two or more X variables. These include additive relationships, spurious relationships, suppressor relationships,

TABLE 9.3

Examples of Statistical Methods for Modeling Two-Variable Relationships

Types of variables	Options
Two dichotomous	Descriptive (correspondence): If the study is about the reliability of raters dividing targets into two groups, **agreement** (but see Table 6.4) and the **kappa coefficient** are relevant. Options in other circumstances include the **Pearson correlation coefficient** (sometimes called the *phi coefficient* for two dichotomous variables), **Yule's Q**, the **tetrachoric correlation coefficient**, and the **binomial effect size display**.
	Descriptive (contingency): Common choices in medicine include the **odds ratio, risk ratio,** and **number needed to treat.** If the goal is to evaluate prediction accuracy, **diagnostic efficiency statistics** are often used. **Goodman–Kruskal's lambda** and the **contingency coefficient** are less popular options.
	Inferential: The **chi-square test of independence** or **Fisher's exact test** can evaluate correspondence. **McNemar's test for symmetry** is available to test for contingency when X consists of two dependent groups.
One dichotomous, one categorical	Descriptive: Choices include **Cramer's V** (correspondence), **Goodman–Kruskal's lambda,** and the **contingency coefficient** (contingency).
	Inferential: The **chi-square** test of independence is probably the most common effect size measure in these circumstances.
One dichotomous, one ranked	Inferential (contingency): The **Wilcoxon T test** or the **sign test** is available when X consists of two dependent groups, the **Mann–Whitney U test** or **Cochran's test of linear trend** applies to independent groups.
One dichotomous, one dimensional	Graphical: **Box-and-whisker plots** can be compared for the two groups.
	Descriptive (correspondence): The **Pearson correlation coefficient** (sometimes called the **point-biserial correlation** in this situation) and **biserial correlation** are also available.
	Descriptive (contingency): The most popular effect size is *d.* **Signal detection analysis** can be used when the dimensional variable is used to predict the dichotomous variable.
	Inferential: Many choices are available, including the *t* **test** or *z* **test** and the **one-way analysis of variance** for evaluating mean differences between groups. If instead of a single dimensional variable the data include multiple dimensional variables thought to represent a single latent variable, Hotelling's *T* (**multivariate analysis of variance**) is available. **Survival analysis** is an analysis in which the dimensional variable is time and the dichotomous variable is whether or not the person has experienced a certain event. If the dimensional variable is measured longitudinally, **interrupted time series analysis** may be of interest. The **Kolmogorov–Smirnov test** allows one to evaluate whether the shape of the dimensional frequency distribution varies in the two populations represented by the dichotomous variable, and the *F* **test** or **Levene test** can be used to evaluate whether the variance is the same in the two populations. The **reliable change index** is a relatively recent innovation that allows evaluation of change from before to after treatment in individual cases.

(continued)

TABLE 9.3 (*Continued*)

Examples of Statistical Methods for Modeling Two-Variable Relationships

Types of variables	Options
Two categorical	Descriptive (correspondence): If the study is about the reliability of raters' dividing targets into categories, **agreement** and the **kappa coefficient** are relevant. Choices in other situations include **Cramer's V.** Descriptive (correspondence): The **contingency coefficient** is relevant. Inferential: The **chi-square test of independence** is the most common choice whether the researcher is interested in contingency or correspondence.
One categorical, one ranked	Graphical: **Box-and-whisker plots** can be generated for each of the groups and placed next to each other. Inferential: The **Kruskal–Wallis *H* test** is available for independent groups, the **Friedman test** can be used if they are dependent.
One categorical, one dimensional	Graphical: **Box-and-whisker plots** can be generated for each of the two groups and placed next to each other. Descriptive: *d* is often used to evaluate each pair of groups defined by the categorical variable. **Omega hat squared** and **eta squared** can evaluate the strength of relationship between the two variables. Inferential: The **one-way analysis of variance** is available whether groups are dependent or independent, and **multivariate profile analysis** is available if the groups are dependent. Related to analysis of variance is a variety of **multiple comparison procedures** that typically allow tests involving subsets of the groups. For example, the **Tukey test** and the **Newman–Keuls test** allow comparison of each pair of groups on the dimensional variable. If instead of a single dimensional variable the data include a set of dimensional variables thought to represent a single latent construct, **multivariate analysis of variance** is available.
Two ranked	Descriptive (correspondence): If the study is about reliability, the weighted **kappa coefficient** can be relevant. In other circumstances, **Spearman's rho**, the **polychoric correlation, Goodman–Kruskal's gamma, Kendall's tau-b**, and **Stuart's tau-c** are available. Inferential: The **rank randomization test** can be used, in particular in combination with Spearman's rho.
One ranked, one dimensional	This situation is usually treated as if both were dimensional.
Two dimensional	Graphical: The most common choice is the **scatterplot** to evaluate whether two variables are related. The **Q–Q plot** can be used to evaluate the degree to which the distributions of two variables match. Descriptive (correspondence): If the study is about reliability, some version of the **intraclass correlation coefficient** is relevant. The **correlation coefficient** is the most common choice in other circumstances. Inferential (correspondence): The *t* test and *z* test for the correlation **coefficient** are relevant. Inferential (contingency): If the dimensional variables are measured longitudinally, **two-process time series** may be applicable. If the values of one variable are equidistant—for example, participants are administered 5, 10, 15, or 20 milligrams of a drug—a variant of **analysis of variance** called *trend analysis* can be used. **Simple regression** also is relevant.

Note.   Statistics in boldface type are listed in the Index, to help you find brief descriptions of statistics in the future when reading research.

mediating relationships, moderator relationships, and nested relationships. If you understand these concepts you will have gone a long way toward understanding how researchers convert empirical phenomena into quantitative models. To simplify the discussion from here on I refer only to contingent relationships.

ADDITIVE RELATIONSHIPS

An analysis has to do with an **additive relationship** when *two or more independent variables that each predicts the dependent variable are combined to improve the prediction of the dependent variable.* This can be symbolized by $X_1 + X_2 \rightarrow Y$.

If the researcher believes that social problems and intellectual abilities both predict how aggressive a child will be in the classroom, the researcher may hypothesize that the combination of the two would improve the prediction of classroom aggression: social problems + intellectual abilities $\rightarrow$ aggression.

In this case, it is reasonable to hypothesize that social problems will contribute in a positive direction to classroom aggression (the more social problems, the more aggression), whereas intellectual abilities will contribute negatively (the greater the intellectual ability, the less aggression). *The extent to which each independent variable improves prediction over the other independent variable in an additive relationship* is known as the independent variable's **incremental validity**.

Another way you will see additive relationships represented pictorially is presented in Figure 9.2. The use of the double-headed arrow between X_1 and X_2 in the figure implies that there may be a correspondence relationship between X_1 and X_2, but the study will not focus on that relationship. Examples of statistics relevant to investigating additive relationships can be found in Table 9.4. From this point forward, tables are organized around statistics rather than types of variables.

FIGURE 9.2

An additive relationship.

TABLE 9.4

Examples of Statistical Methods for Modeling Additive Relationships

Statistical method	Description
Canonical correlation	Relevant when there is a set of independent variables and a set of dependent variables, all of which are dimensional.
Conjoint analysis	Can be used when there are one or more dichotomous or categorical independent variables and one or more dimensional dependent variables; popular only in certain fields of research.
Discriminant function analysis	Sometimes used when there are one or more dimensional independent variables and one categorical dependent variable. The analysis looks for additive relationships among the independent variables for the prediction of group membership.
Logistic, logit, and probit regression	Has become a popular in circumstances in which there is one or more independent variables (usually dimensional, sometimes dichotomous, rarely polytomous) and one dependent variable (usually dichotomous, sometimes polytomous). The analysis is similar to multiple regression for categorical dependent variables.
Multiple regression	Often the first choice when there are one or more independent variables of any type and one dimensional outcome variable. If the independent variables are all dichotomous or categorical, the results are equivalent to analysis of variance without an interaction term (see Table 9.8). Various correlational statistics are also available for looking at one independent variable after partialing out another, including the **partial correlation** and **semipartial correlation.**
Path analysis	Can be used when there are multiple dimensional independent and dependent variables and the goal of the analysis is to evaluate whether a certain model fits the relationships among them. Path analysis allows for different types of relationships (additive, spurious, mediated, or suppressor, but not moderator) within a single model. It is similar to the structural model in structural equation modeling.
Set correlation	Can be used when there is one or more sets of independent variables, all of which are dimensional, and one set of dependent variables, all of which are dimensional. It is not often seen in the literature.
Structural equation modeling	A very popular choice when there are multiple independent and dependent constructs, some or all of which are represented by a set of observed dimensional variables, and the goal of the analysis is to evaluate whether a certain model fits the relationships among the constructs. Structural equation modeling allows for different types of relationships (additive, spurious, mediated, or suppressor) within a single model.

Note. All of these methods produce a combination of descriptive and inferential statistics appropriate to the hypothesis. Statistics in boldface type are listed in the Index, to help you find brief descriptions of statistics in the future when reading research.

How do you tell when your data provide evidence of an additive relationship? I will delay addressing that question until I have finished introducing the next three relationships. As you will see, there are some important similarities in the statistics used to look for additive, suppressor, mediating, and spurious relationships, but there are also important differences in terms of their implications for statistical outcomes.

SUPPRESSOR RELATIONSHIPS

Another three-variable relationship similar to the additive relationship is the **suppressor relationship**, which occurs when *an independent variable and a predictor of the independent variable are combined to improve the prediction of the dependent variable*. In the case of suppression, this improvement in the prediction of the dependent variable occurs not because of the relationship between each *X* variable and *Y* but because of the relationship among the *X* variables.

For example, a researcher might hypothesize that college students' anxiety levels affect their academic performance, so students who are more anxious do more poorly in school. The researcher uses an indicator on which students indicate how anxious they generally feel. However, these scores are also influenced by how willing students are to admit to feelings of anxiety. The tendency for students to describe themselves in a more positive manner than is accurate is referred to as *socially desirable responding*. If this model is accurate, whether a student tends to respond to questionnaires in a socially desirable manner might have little relationship to academic performance but should correlate well with scores on the anxiety indicator. In this case, socially desirable responding should reduce the strength of the relationship between anxiety indicator scores and academic performance because the score on the anxiety indicator reflects two latent variables: (a) how anxious the student is (which should predict academic performance, according to the hypothesis) and (b) how much the student tends to respond in a socially desirable way (which probably has little to do with actual academic performance).

Fortunately, there are indicators available that attempt to measure the tendency to respond to other scales in a socially desirable way. The Marlowe–Crowne Social Desirability Scale (Crowne & Marlowe, 1960) includes a series of items that involve denying normal social flaws (e.g., responding "false" to "I sometimes feel resentful when I don't get my own way") or claiming superior morals (e.g., responding "true" to "I am always polite, even to people who are disagreeable"). A higher than average score on the Marlowe–Crowne is thought to suggest someone who tends to deny personal faults.

On the basis of the preceding discussion, it is reasonable to expect a relationship between the anxiety indicator and academic performance, and a relationship between scores on the social desirability indicator and the anxiety indicator, but no (or minimal) relationship between the social desirability indicator and academic performance. Yet it is still possible that combining the anxiety and social desirability indicators as independent variables will improve the prediction of academic performance because certain statistical analyses in a sense can subtract, or *partial out*, or *control for*, the influence of social desirability on the anxiety score. After controlling for social desirability, what is left of the anxiety score should then be a purer indicator of anxiety. This complex relationship can be symbolized as $X_1 \cdot X_2 \rightarrow Y$. The dot in this expression suggests that the analysis examines the relationship between X_1 and Y after controlling for X_2. Whereas X_1 is the independent variable, X_2 can be referred to as the **suppressor variable**.

Including a possible suppressor variable such as social desirability is worth considering any time you think your substantive X variable is tapping into more than one latent variable and one or more of those latent variables is irrelevant to predicting the dependent variable. If a paper-and-pencil test of management skills could reflect both management skills and reading ability, or raters' estimates of job candidates' competence are affected by candidates' physical attractiveness, addressing these hypotheses by including possible suppressor variables can potentially enhance the strength of the relationship with Y. For a more detailed discussion of suppressors, see Cohen et al. (2003). Some statistics appropriate to examining suppressor relationships are listed in Table 9.5.

MEDIATING RELATIONSHIPS

In the discussion of two-variable relationships I suggested that one situation in which it is reasonable to model one variable as a function of another is when the independent variable is thought to have an influence or effect on the dependent variable. Although this may be true, it is often the case that the effect is indirect. For example, research suggests that antipsychotic medication reduces the severity of paranoid thinking, but it is commonly believed that this relationship is indirect. The medication has a direct effect on certain physiological systems, which in turn are thought to have a direct effect on the intensity of paranoia. It may even prove to be the case that several physiological effects occur in a chain between medication and paranoia. You can probably identify all sorts of similar examples of direct and indirect effects.

A **mediating relationship** is one in which *the effect of an independent variable on a dependent variable passes through a third variable:* $X_1 \rightarrow X_2 \rightarrow Y$, for example, medication $\rightarrow$ physiological changes $\rightarrow$ paranoid thinking. In such cases, X_2 is often referred to as the mediating variable. It can also be said that X_1 has an indirect effect on paranoia, whereas X_2 has a direct effect.

TABLE 9.5

Examples of Statistical Methods for Modeling Suppressor Relationships

Statistical method	Description
Analysis of covariance	Popular when the substantive independent variable or variables, X_1, are categorical. The suppressor variable or variables, X_2, are usually dimensional but can be categorical. The one Y variable is dimensional. If Y consists of a set of dimensional variables thought to represent a common latent variable instead of a single dimensional variable, **multivariate analysis of covariance** can be used instead.
Multiple regression	Often the first choice when there are one or more substantive independent variables, X_1, of any type, though usually dimensional, as are the suppressor variable or variables, X_2. The one Y variable must be a nondichotomous dimensional variable. If the substantive independent variables are all categorical, the results are equivalent to analysis of covariance. Various correlational statistics are also available for looking at one independent variable after partialing out another, including the **partial correlation** and **semipartial correlation.**
Path analysis	Can be used when there are multiple dimensional independent and dependent variables and the goal of the analysis is to evaluate whether a certain model fits the relationships among them. Path analysis allows for different types of relationships (additive, spurious, mediated, or suppressor, but not moderator) within a single model. It is similar to the structural model in structural equation modeling.
Structural equation modeling	Allows for different types of relationships (additive, spurious, mediated, or suppressor, but not moderator) within a single model (see Chapter 7, this volume)

Note. All of these methods produce a combination of descriptive and inferential statistics appropriate to the hypothesis. Statistics in boldface type are listed in the Index, to help you find brief descriptions of statistics in the future when reading research.

The expression $X_1 \rightarrow X_2 \rightarrow Y$ suggests that the only reason for the relationship between X_1 and Y is the mediating effect of X_2. That is not necessarily the case in the real world, where it is possible for X_1 to have both a direct and an indirect effect on Y. For example, research suggests that gender has a small but reliable relationship with performance in mathematics, with females consistently receiving lower scores than males (McGraw, Lubienski, & Strutchens, 2006). One possibility is that a direct effect exists, suggesting that males have greater innate mathematical ability on average than females.[5] Alternatively, a variety of mediating factors

---

[5] I am using this example for illustration because I think it is an interesting one, but I should note that objections have been raised to the conclusion that there are genetic differences between males and females in mathematical abilities (e.g., Spelke, 2005).

have been considered, including research suggesting that teachers pay more attention to boys during mathematics instruction and more attention to girls during reading instruction (Leinhardt, Seewald, & Engel, 1979). If both were true, then there would be a direct effect of gender on mathematical skills as well as an indirect effect that is mediated by teachers' differential reinforcement of boys versus girls.

The study of mediating effects tends to follow a consistent course. The first studies are simply intended to demonstrate the existence of a relationship between the variables identified as X_1 and Y in $X_1 \rightarrow X_2 \rightarrow Y$. Once this relationship is firmly established, researchers' interests turn to why the relationship exists. Subsequent studies therefore focus on what occurs in between X_1 and Y that potentially accounts for the relationship.

Studies of mediating effects can be important for several reasons. In the case of antipsychotic medications, identifying the specific physiological mediators of the effect can suggest ways to develop more effective or safer drugs. Similarly, if it is found that gender differences in mathematics are mediated by teachers' differential reward of males, then teacher training can reduce those differences. Examples of statistics available for the test of mediating relationships can be found in Table 9.6.

SPURIOUS RELATIONSHIPS

A spurious relationship exists when the relationship between X_1 and Y exists only because both are related to a third variable, X_2. This third variable is referred to as a **confound** or a nuisance variable; in some statistical contexts it can also be referred to as a **covariate**. For example, suppose research finds that children sent to private schools perform better on standardized tests. This might lead one to hypothesize a contingent relationship between X_1 and Y as follows: type of school $\rightarrow$ academic achievement; however, socioeconomic status predicts whether parents place their children in private schools and has an indirect effect on academic performance in that wealthier parents provide their children with more educational opportunities.[6] Socioeconomic status (X_2) therefore may account for the relationship between X_1 and Y:

$$X_1 \swarrow \overset{X_2}{} \searrow Y \tag{9.1}$$

---

[6]It is worth acknowledging that you could develop a much more complex model here, including the relationship between socioeconomic status and the parents' level of academic achievement, which in turn has direct and indirect effects on the child's level of achievement, and so forth. This example is admittedly an oversimplification.

TABLE 9.6

Examples of Statistical Methods for Modeling Mediating and Spurious Relationships

Statistical method	Description
Multiple regression	Often the first choice when the initial independent variable, X_1, is often any type, though usually dimensional, as is the mediating variable, X_2. The Y variable is a nondichotomous dimensional variable. A variety of tests have been developed specifically for evaluating the presence of a mediating relationship based on a multiple regression (MacKinnon et al., 2002). Various correlational statistics are also available for looking at one independent variable after partialing out another, including the **partial correlation** and **semipartial correlation.**
Path analysis	Can be used when there are multiple dimensional independent and dependent variables and the goal of the analysis is to evaluate whether a certain model fits the relationships among them. Path analysis allows for different types of relationships (additive, spurious, mediated, or suppressor, but not moderator) within a single model. It is similar to the structural model in structural equation modeling.
Structural equation modeling	Allows for different types of relationships (additive, spurious, mediated, or suppressor, but not moderator) within a single model (see Chapter 7, this volume).
Two-stage least squares regression	A form of multiple regression involving one dimensional dependent variable and multiple independent variables (usually dimensional, sometimes dichotomous, rarely categorical), at least one of which is believed to mediate the relationship between other independent variables and the dependent variable.
Sobel test	The best known of a number of procedures that have been developed specifically for testing mediating relationships (MacKinnon et al., 2002). However, as noted in the text, a significant outcome on the Sobel or similar tests could also indicate a spurious relationship.

Note. All of these methods produce a combination of descriptive and inferential statistics appropriate to the hypothesis. Statistics in boldface type are listed in the Index, to help you find brief descriptions of statistics in the future when reading research.

In the present example,

$$\text{Type of school} \nwarrow \overset{\text{Socioeconomic status}}{} \searrow \text{Academic achievement} \qquad (9.2)$$

Notice that the arrow between X_1 and Y has disappeared: The relationship between type of school attended and academic achievement is spurious because it is completely accounted for by the parents' socioeconomic status.

Various strategies have been developed for controlling nuisance variables through the design of the study itself. Random assignment to groups and matched groups are the best known; however, when methodological options are not available (e.g., one cannot decide at random which students attend private school and which public), then statistical control is required instead.

There is a striking conceptual similarity between the mediating and spurious relationship that is often overlooked in the literature. If X_2 is moved right between X_1 and Y in Equation 9.1, it would look like this: $X_1 \leftarrow X_2 \rightarrow Y$.

The only difference between this and $X_1 \rightarrow X_2 \rightarrow Y$ is that in $X_1 \leftarrow X_2 \rightarrow Y$ the left arrow points from X_2 to X_1 but points the other way in $X_1 \rightarrow X_2 \rightarrow Y$. Any statistical analysis capable of identifying a spurious relationship could also be detecting a mediating relationship, and vice versa. The distinction is purely conceptual, not statistical, so the statistics in Table 9.6 can be applied to spurious as well as to mediating relationships. Although there has been extensive discussion in the literature about the most appropriate way to identify a mediating relationship (e.g., MacKinnon, Lockwood, Hoffman, West, & Sheets, 2002), the authors often fail to warn the reader that these tests are not specific to mediating relationships.

In the example I am using here, socioeconomic status could not be a mediating variable because that would require the following model: type of school $\rightarrow$ socioeconomic status $\rightarrow$ academic achievement.

Because the type of school to which parents send their children does not determine their socioeconomic status, this model makes no sense. For this reason, if we find that the relationship between type of school and academic achievement disappears when we partial out the socioeconomic status of the parents, that finding suggests a spurious rather than a mediating effect. Determining whether an effect is indirect or spurious is therefore largely a conceptual rather than a statistical issue.

ADDITIVE, SUPPRESSOR, MEDIATING, OR SPURIOUS?

Because of similarities among the three-variable relationships described so far, I have included Table 9.7, which summarizes their differences. The first two relationships have to do primarily with improving prediction of the dependent variable. In contrast, tests of mediating and spurious relationships are intended to learn more about why X_1 and Y are related to each other.

The column labeled "Necessary conditions" in Table 9.7 provides information about the two-variable relationships between the independent and dependent variables that would be needed before it even makes sense to look for a certain type of relationship. For example, an additive relationship cannot exist unless both X_1 and X_2 are related to Y to start

TABLE 9.7		

Distinguishing Among Additive, Suppressor, Mediating, or Spurious Relationships

Model	Goal	Necessary conditions	Results
Additive	Improve prediction of Y	1. X_1 and Y are related 2. X_2 and Y are related 3. X_1 and X_2 may be related	1. X_1 and X_2 together predict Y better than either alone. 2. If X_1 and X_2 are related, each alone is a poorer predictor of Y after partialing out the other.
Suppressor	Improve prediction of Y	1. X_1 and Y are related 2. X_2 and Y may be related 3. X_1 and X_2 are related	1. X_1 and X_2 together predict Y better than either alone. 2. X_1 is a better predictor of Y after partialing out X_2.
Mediating	Understand relationship between X_1 and Y	1. X_1 and Y are related 2. X_2 and Y are related 3. X_1 and X_2 are related	1. X_1 and X_2 together predict Y no better than X_2. 2. X_1 no longer predicts Y after partialing out X_2.[a]
Spurious	Understand relationship between X_1 and Y	1. X_1 and Y are related 2. X_2 and Y are related 3. X_1 and X_2 are related	1. X_1 and X_2 together predict Y no better than X_2. 2. X_1 no longer predicts Y after partialing out X_2.

Note. When working in the context of null hypothesis significance testing (NHST), each of these conditions can be verified by a significance test. For example, if the sample correlation between X_1 and Y is .17, but the significance test does not result in rejecting this null hypothesis, then according to the rules of NHST the necessary conditions are not met for any of these relationships. It is not a mistake that mediating and spurious relationships are so similar: They cannot be distinguished statistically.
[a]This description assumes that the relationship between X_1 and Y is only indirect. If X_1 also has a direct effect on Y then X_1 is a weaker predictor of Y after partialing out X_2.

with. The next step involves conducting an analysis to test whether (in the case of additive and suppressor effects) the combination of independent variables improves prediction of Y, or (in the case of mediating and spurious effects) if partialing out X_2 eliminates or at least substantially reduces the relationship between X_1 and Y.

MODERATOR RELATIONSHIPS

A **moderator relationship** exists *when the relationship between X_1 and Y changes depending on where a person is located on variable X_2*. A researcher may find, for example, that self-esteem has a strong positive relationship with academic performance in the early grades but becomes unimportant to or even correlates negatively with academic performance in later grades. Or, in an employee satisfaction study a researcher may find that individuals at lower intelligence levels report more satisfaction in settings in which jobs duties are clearly defined, whereas individuals at higher levels of intelligence are more satisfied with jobs that allow more flexibility and innovation on the part of the employee.

This is different from a simple additive effect. If intelligence and setting were additive predictors of satisfaction, then satisfaction would be higher if, say, intelligence is higher *and* a respondent is working in a certain setting. What the moderator relationship suggests is that the relationship between intelligence and satisfaction *changes* depending on setting and that the relationship between setting and satisfaction changes depending on intelligence. This possibility may be symbolized by $X_1 \times X_2 \rightarrow Y$; that is, the moderator term represents the product of the original independent variables.[7] In our two examples, self-esteem × grades → academic achievement, and setting × intelligence → job satisfaction.

Historically, there has been an unfortunate tendency for behavioral researchers to confuse the terms *mediator* and *moderator,* so do not be surprised if you sometimes find a published study that uses these terms incorrectly. Several articles have been devoted to helping psychological researchers distinguish between the two (Baron & Kenny, 1986; Frazier, Tix, & Barron, 2004). If you are having difficulties figuring out which type of model you are hypothesizing, I encourage you to read these very useful references.

One reason for this confusion may be that people seem to have a hard time grasping the concept of a moderator. I find one test very useful. If you are asked to describe the relationship between two variables, and you indicate that "it depends" on a third variable, the hypothesis has to do with a moderator.

Among behavioral researchers, the best-known statistical test of a moderator effect is the test of interactions in the ANOVA. However, as indicated in Table 9.8, there are many others. In particular, moderated multiple regression is often seen as *the* statistical strategy for investigating moderator relationships. Moderated regression permits both dimensional and categorical independent variables; in fact, ANOVA is mathematically equivalent to moderated regression with only categorical independent variables. Cohen et al. (2003) provided a detailed description of the method.

---

[7]Note that polynomial functions, although they involve only two variables, also involve multiplication; specifically, the quadratic relationship between X and Y involves treating Y as a function of X^2, or $X \times X$. I mention this because many of the issues described that make it difficult to detect moderator relationships (small size, problems with scaling) also apply to attempts to detect nonlinear relationships.

TABLE 9.8

Examples of Statistical Methods for Modeling Moderator Relationships

Statistical method	Description
Analysis of variance	Involves one or more dichotomous or categorical original independent variables and one dimensional dependent variable. Moderator terms are referred to as *interactions*. By extension, the same is true for independent variables used in similar statistical methods: **analysis of covariance, multivariate analysis of variance and covariance,** and **multivariate profile analysis.**
Hierarchical linear modeling	Looks for moderator effects involving nested independent variables (see Table 9.9).
Intensive design	A recent alternative to analysis of variance when the goal is to evaluate whether a moderator relationship exists between a categorical treatment variable and time, but the timing or number of measurements varies across participants.
Log-linear analysis	Used to evaluate whether the relationship between dichotomous or categorical variables differs as a function of other dichotomous or categorical variables. One of the few examples of a statistic for three or more variables that assumes a correspondence relationship.
Moderated multiple regression	A variant of multiple regression that includes a moderator term that is generated by multiplying two (or more) of the original independent variables. The analysis involves one or more independent variables of any type and one dimensional dependent variable. If independent variables are dimensional, current practice suggests subtracting the mean so they are centered at 0 (Cohen et al., 2003). If the input variables are all dichotomous or categorical, the results are equivalent to analysis of variance. This is often considered *the* method of choice for investigating moderator relationships (McClelland & Judd, 1993).
t test for dependent correlations	Used to evaluate whether the **correlation coefficient** between two variables differs as a function of a third dichotomous variable. This test is appropriate when the same sample generated both correlations.
z test for independent correlations	Used to evaluate whether the **correlation coefficient** between two variables differs as a function of a third dichotomous variable. This test is appropriate when the correlations were generated by different samples.

Note. Each of these methods produces a combination of descriptive and inferential statistics appropriate to the hypothesis. Statistics in boldface type are listed in the Index, to help you find brief descriptions of statistics in the future when reading research.

I need to make several points about testing moderator terms. Moderators are the most mathematically complicated of the relationships described here because they involve multiplication of the X variables. The moderator relationship is the only type of relationship not adequately covered by the practical model of variable classification introduced in Chapter 8; specifically, there is good evidence that tests of moderators cannot be trusted unless the dependent variable is at least interval scaled (Davison & Sharma, 1990; Embretson, 1996), although psychologists ignore this issue regularly.[8]

Another mathematical problem occurs because tests of moderator relationships require an analysis in which X_1, X_2, and their product are combined additively to predict Y. It should make intuitive sense that the product of X_1 and X_2 will tend to correlate highly with X_1, X_2, or both. *When predictors correlate highly with each other* (a condition referred to as **multicollinearity**), the results tend to be unreliable. Although some authors have suggested that mean-centering dimensional X variables (subtracting the mean from each score) can address this problem, there is no evidence to suggest this is the case (Kromrey & Foster-Johnson, 1998). The moral of this story is that you should be very hesitant about accepting the existence of a moderator effect until it has been successfully replicated.

It is also worth knowing that effect sizes for moderator relationships in psychological research tend to be quite small (Aguinis, Beaty, Boik, & Pierce, 2005). Often the improvement in the prediction of Y from adding a moderator term is less than 1%. This phenomenon occurs for computational reasons not worth discussing here (McClelland & Judd, 1993). However, the significance test for moderated regression tends to be fairly powerful, and the results are often significant even for very small increases. The point is that the size of a moderator effect should not be directly compared with the improvement in prediction of Y resulting from the other relationships discussed previously in this section.

My final point is that moderator relationships can work in combination with other relationships as the basis for models involving four or more variables. The best known of these is what could be called "moderated moderation," in which the moderated relationship between X_1 and X_2 varies depending on another independent variable, X_3. For example, S. Brown and Locker (2009) exposed college students to anti-alcohol images that varied in terms of the degree to which they were intended to cause an emotional reaction. They found that college students saw their risk as lower in response to the high-emotion images than to lower emotion images; that is, more extreme messages actually had the opposite result from what was intended. However, this was true only among individuals who had higher scores on an indicator of denial *and* were identified as being at greater risk for problems with alcohol. In ANOVA

---

[8]In Chapter 7, I suggested that "differences between scores on the estimated latent variable theta are at least theoretically a more accurate representation of the distance between people than differences between observed scores." Using terminology you have learned since then, this proposition suggests that θ estimates are on an interval scale and so would provide more useful values for testing moderator effects (Embretson, 1996). However, Michell (2008) argued on the basis of axiomatic measurement theory that the mathematical status of θ has not been established axiomatically.

terms this represents a three-way interaction among image type, level of denial, and personal risk as independent variables predicting estimates of personal risk from drinking alcohol.

It is also possible to model a moderated mediation or moderated suppression. For example, if X_2 is a mediator between X_1 and Y in one population but not another, then moderated mediation is occurring. Similarly, if social desirability suppresses the relationship between self-reported conscientiousness and supervisor ratings, but no longer does so when employees are told that some of the questions are intended to pick up inaccurate responding, then the variable "type of instructions" has moderated the suppressor relationship between social desirability and conscientiousness. Instead of making your head spin talking about situations you may never experience, I will stop here and just reiterate that moderation can be combined with other types of relationships to create even more complicated relationships with four or more variables.

NESTED RELATIONSHIPS

One more to go! The models I have discussed so far that involve two or more independent variables are examples of **crossed designs**, *designs in which there are cases that represent the entire range of possible combinations for the independent variables.* For example, in the hypothetical study examining the moderating effect of self-esteem on the relationship between grade level and academic achievement, all the possible combinations of the two independent variables should be present: There should be children in the lower grades with relatively poor self-esteem and relatively good self-esteem, and the same should be true in the later grades. The two independent variables are therefore referred to as *crossed*.

In contrast, a **nested design** occurs when *each value of one independent variable occurs only in combination with one value of another independent variable.* The classic example of nesting is found in educational research. Imagine an educational intervention in which students in Classrooms 1 and 2 receive Treatment A and students in Classrooms 3 and 4 receive Treatment B. In this case, the categorical variable classroom is *nested* within treatment, because certain combinations such as "Classroom 1–Treatment B" do not occur.

Nested designs are symbolized by $X_2(X_1) \rightarrow Y$, suggesting that X_2 (classroom) is nested within X_1 (treatment). More complex alternatives are available, such as nesting classroom within school within treatment (e.g., if classes in Schools A and B all receive Treatment 1 and classes in Schools C and D all receive Treatment 2).

Nested factors are relatively unusual as a focus in psychological research, with one exception. In studies that involve independent groups, the participants are essentially nested within the independent variable: Participant 1 is only in Group A, Participant 2 is only in Group B, and so forth. I mention this exception only because it plays an important role in the mathematics of many significance tests.

Researchers often ignore the issue of nesting even when it is clearly an element of the research design. For example, many treatment studies provide the treatments in groups; for example, the Monday and Tuesday evening groups receive Treatment A, whereas Wednesday and Thursday evening groups receive Treatment B. When analyzing the results it is common for researchers to ignore the nested factor, but they do so at their own peril. Baldwin, Murray, and Shadish (2005) reviewed 33 studies that reported a significant difference between the effectiveness of psychological treatments that were administered in nested groups. None of these studies considered the nested relationship in the statistical analysis. They estimated that if the nested variable had been considered, as many as six to 19 of the 33 studies would not have reported a significant effect, although this was only an estimate. Perhaps this is the sort of information researchers do not want to know!

With the growing popularity of a statistical analysis called *hierarchical linear modeling*, the issue of nesting has been receiving greater attention in recent years. The few popular statistical methods that specifically address nested models are described in Table 9.9.

TABLE 9.9

Examples of Statistical Methods for Modeling Nested Relationships

Statistical method	Description
Hierarchical analysis of variance	Involves at least one categorical independent variable, at least one categorical nested independent variable, and one dimensional dependent variable. This analysis treats the nested variable as a confound to be controlled.
Hierarchical linear modeling	Also known as *multilevel analysis,* this variant of multiple regression tests for moderator effects among independent variables that are nested within other independent variables. The dependent variable is dimensional. For example, within each classroom, dimensional student variables (e.g., time spent studying) can be used to predict grade outcomes. Within each school, dimensional classroom variables (e.g., size of class) can be used to see if they moderate the relationship between student input variables and outcomes. Within the school district, dimensional school variables (e.g., mean socioeconomic status) can be used to see if they moderate the relationship further.

Note. Both of these methods produce a combination of descriptive and inferential statistics appropriate to the hypothesis. Statistics in boldface type are listed in the Index, to help you find brief descriptions of statistics in the future when reading research.

Conclusion

I will not even try to summarize all the information in this chapter! Any summary would be too cursory to be helpful anyway. Instead, I will make some comments about the tables in this chapter. It is my hope that they will serve as a helpful resource to you. In fact, there is a possibility they will become more helpful to you over time, as you become more involved in reading and conducting research. That possibility is true for a number of tables in this book: Table 1.2, on the distinction between sample, sampling, and population distributions; Table 1.4, on some of the more common sampling distributions; Table 4.2, on selecting the smallest important effect size; Exhibit 4.1, on recommendations concerning significance tests; Table 5.1, on terminology in decision-making research; Table 6.4, on reliability statistics; Table 7.1, on statistics for latent-variable models; Table 7.4, on exploratory factor analysis; and all the tables in this chapter are intended to provide you with brief summaries of concepts that may require your review multiple times before you really understand them.

Even if you never look at this book again, though, I hope you have a better understanding of the complex process of quantitative modeling in psychology, using both invented and real-world models, than you did when you started. Psychologists will continue to lurch toward more accurate, or at least more useful, models of psychological phenomena. By their specificity and objectivity, quantitative methods will always play an essential role in that process.

References

Aguinis, H. (1995). Statistical power problems with moderated multiple regression in management research. *Journal of Management, 21*, 1141–1158.

Aguinis, H., Beaty, J. C., Boik, R. J., & Pierce, C. A. (2005). Effect size and power in assessing moderating effects of categorical variables using multiple regression: A 30-year review. *Journal of Applied Psychology, 90*, 94–107. doi:10.1037/0021-9010.90.1.94

Aiken, L. S., West, S. G., & Millsap, R. E. (2008). Doctoral training in statistics, measurement, and methodology in psychology: Replication and extension of Aiken, West, Sechrest, and Reno's (1990) survey of PhD programs in North America. *American Psychologist, 63*, 32–50. doi:10.1037/0003-066X.63.1.32

Aldenderfer, M. S., & Blashfield, R. K. (1984). *Cluster analysis.* Newbury Park, CA: Sage.

American Educational Research Association, American Psychological Association, & National Council on Measurement in Education. (1999). *Standards for educational and psychological testing.* Washington, DC: American Psychological Association.

American Psychiatric Association Committee on Electroconvulsive Therapy. (2001). *The practice of electroconvulsive therapy: Recommendations for treatment, training, and privileging* (2nd ed.). Washington, DC: American Psychiatric Association.

American Psychological Association. (2010). *Publication manual of the American Psychological Association* (6th ed.). Washington, DC: Author.

Baldwin, S. A., Murray, D. M., & Shadish, W. R. (2005). Empirically supported treatments or Type I errors? Problems with the analysis of data from group-administered treatments. *Journal of Consulting and Clinical Psychology, 73,* 924–935. doi:10.1037/0022-006X.73.5.924

Baron, R. M., & Kenny, D. A. (1986). The moderator–mediator variable distinction in social psychological research: Conceptual, strategic, and statistical considerations. *Journal of Personality and Social Psychology, 51,* 1173–1182. doi:10.1037/0022-3514.51.6.1173

Beck, A. T., Steer, R. A., & Brown, G. K. (1996). *Beck Depression Inventory manual* (2nd ed.). San Antonio, TX: Psychological Corporation.

Belia, S., Fidler, F., Williams, J., & Cumming, G. (2005). Researchers misunderstand confidence intervals and standard error bars. *Psychological Methods, 10,* 389–396. doi:10.1037/1082-989X.10.4.389

Benjamini, Y., & Hochberg, Y. (1995). Controlling the false discovery rate: A practical and powerful approach to multiple testing. *Journal of the Royal Statistical Society Series B: Methodological, 57,* 289–300.

Bentler, P. M., & Satorra, A. (2010). Testing model nesting and equivalence. *Psychological Methods, 15,* 111–123. doi:10.1037/a0019625

Bolstad, W. M. (2007). *Introduction to Bayesian statistics* (2nd ed.). Hoboken, NJ: Wiley. doi:10.1002/9780470181188

Bond, C. F., Jr., Wiitala, W. L., & Richard, F. D. (2003). Meta-analysis of raw mean differences. *Psychological Methods, 8,* 406–418. doi:10.1037/1082-989X.8.4.406

Bond, T. G., & Fox, C. M. (2001). *Applying the Rasch model: Fundamental measurement in the human sciences.* Mahwah, NJ: Erlbaum.

Boneau, C. (1961). A note on measurement scales and statistical tests. *American Psychologist, 16,* 260–261. doi:10.1037/h0038668

Bonett, D. G. (2008). Confidence intervals for standardized linear contrasts of means. *Psychological Methods, 13,* 99–109. doi:10.1037/1082-989X.13.2.99

Borenstein, M., Hedges, L. V., Higgins, J. P. T., & Rothstein, H. R. (2009). Introduction to meta-analysis. New York, NY: Wiley. doi:10.1002/9780470743386

Borges, J. L. (1999). *Collected fictions* (A. Hurley, Trans.). New York, NY: Penguin.

Bradley, J. V. (1980). Nonrobustness in Z, t, and F tests at large sample sizes. *Bulletin of the Psychonomic Society, 16,* 333–336.

Brennan, R. L., & Prediger, D. (1981). Coefficient kappa: Some uses, misuses, and alternatives. *Educational and Psychological Measurement, 41,* 687–699. doi:10.1177/001316448104100307

Brenner-Golomb, N. (1993). R. A. Fisher's philosophical approach to inductive inference. In G. Keren & C. Lewis (Eds.), *A handbook for data analysis in the behavioral sciences: Methodological issues* (pp. 283–307). Hillsdale, NJ: Erlbaum.

Brown, S., & Locker, E. (2009). Defensive responses to an emotive anti-alcohol message. *Psychology & Health, 24,* 517–528. doi:10.1080/08870440801911130

Brown, T. A. (2006). *Confirmatory factor analysis for applied research.* New York, NY: Guilford Press.

Campbell, D. T., & Fiske, D. W. (1959). Convergent and discriminant validation by the multitrait–multimethod matrix. *Psychological Bulletin, 56,* 81–105. doi:10.1037/h0046016

Carroll, J. B. (1993). *Human cognitive abilities: A survey of factor-analytic studies.* New York, NY: Cambridge University Press. doi:10.1017/CBO9780511571312

Cashen, L. H., & Geiger, S. W. (2004). Statistical power and the testing of null hypotheses: A review of contemporary management research and recommendations for future studies. *Organizational Research Methods, 7,* 151–167. doi:10.1177/1094428104263676

Chow, S. L. (1988). Significance test or effect size? *Psychological Bulletin, 103,* 105–110. doi:10.1037/0033-2909.103.1.105

Cizek, G. J., Rosenberg, S. L., & Koons, H. H. (2008). Sources of validity evidence for educational and psychological tests. *Educational and Psychological Measurement, 68,* 397–412. doi:10.1177/0013164407310130

Cliff, N. (1992). Abstract measurement theory and the revolution that never happened. *Psychological Science, 3,* 186–190. doi:10.1111/j.1467-9280.1992.tb00024.x

Cohen, J. (1960). A coefficient of agreement for nominal scales. *Educational and Psychological Measurement, 20,* 37–46. doi:10.1177/001316446002000104

Cohen, J. (1962). The statistical power of abnormal-social psychological research: A review. *Journal of Abnormal and Social Psychology, 65,* 145–153. doi:10.1037/h0045186

Cohen, J. (1968). Weighted kappa: Nominal scale agreement provision for scaled disagreement or partial credit. *Psychological Bulletin, 70,* 213–220. doi:10.1037/h0026256

Cohen, J. (1969). *Statistical power analysis for the behavioral sciences.* Hillsdale, NJ: Erlbaum.

Cohen, J. (1988). *Statistical power analysis for the behavioral sciences* (2nd ed.). Hillsdale, NJ: Erlbaum.

Cohen, J. (1994). The earth is round (*p* <. 05). *American Psychologist, 49,* 997–1003. doi:10.1037/0003-066X.49.12.997

Cohen, J., Cohen, P., West, S. G., & Aiken, L. S. (2003). *Applied multiple regression/correlation analysis for the behavioral sciences* (3rd ed.). Mahwah, NJ: Erlbaum.

Cooper, H. M. (2009). *Research synthesis and meta-analysis: A step-by-step approach* (4th ed.). Thousand Oaks, CA: Sage.

Creswell, J. W. (2006). *Qualitative inquiry and research design: Choosing among five approaches.* Thousand Oaks, CA: Sage.

Cronbach, L. J. (1951). Coefficient alpha and the internal structure of tests. *Psychometrika, 16,* 297–334. doi:10.1007/BF02310555

Cronbach, L. J. (1971). Test validation. In R. L. Thorndike (Ed.), *Educational measurement* (2nd ed., pp. 443–507). Washington, DC: American Council on Education.

Cronbach, L. J., Gleser, G. C., Nanda, H., & Rajaratnam, N. (1972). *The dependability of behavioral measurements: Theory of generalizability for scores and profiles.* New York, NY: Wiley.

Cronbach, L. J., & Meehl, P. E. (1955). Construct validity in psychological tests. *Psychological Bulletin, 52,* 281–302. doi:10.1037/h0040957

Crowne, D. P., & Marlowe, D. (1960). A new scale of social desirability independent of psychopathology. *Journal of Consulting Psychology, 24,* 349–354. doi:10.1037/h0047358

Cumming, G. (2008). Replication and *p* intervals: *p* values predict the future only vaguely, but confidence intervals do much better. *Perspectives on Psychological Science, 3,* 286–300. doi:10.1111/j.1745-6924.2008.00079.x

Cumming, G., Fidler, F., Leonard, M., Kalinowski, P., Christiansen, A., Kleinig, A., . . . Wilson, S. (2007). Statistical reform in psychology: Is anything changing? *Psychological Science, 18,* 230–232. doi:10.1111/j.1467-9280.2007.01881.x

Davison, M. L., & Sharma, A. R. (1990). Parametric statistics and levels of measurement: Factorial designs and multiple regression. *Psychological Bulletin, 107,* 394–400. doi:10.1037/0033-2909.107.3.394

DeCoster, J., Iselin, A. R., & Gallucci, M. (2009). A conceptual and empirical examination of justifications for dichotomization. *Psychological Methods, 14,* 349–366. doi:10.1037/a0016956

Dickersin, K. (2005). Publication bias: Recognizing the problem, understanding its origins and scope, and preventing harm. In H. R. Rothstein, A. J. Sutton, & M. Borenstein (Eds.), *Publication bias in meta analysis: Prevention, assessment and adjustments* (pp. 11–34). Chichester, England: Wiley.

Dwyer, C. A. (1996). Cut scores and testing: Statistics, judgment, truth, and error. *Psychological Assessment, 8,* 360–362. doi:10.1037/1040-3590.8.4.360

Efron, B., & Tibshirani, R. (1986). Bootstrap methods for standard errors, confidence intervals, and other measures of statistical accuracy. *Statistical Science, 1,* 54–75. doi:10.1214/ss/1177013815

Embretson, S. E. (1996). Item response theory models and spurious interaction effects in factorial ANOVA designs. *Applied Psychological Measurement, 20,* 201–212. doi:10.1177/014662169602000302

Embretson, S., & Reise, S. (2000). *Item response theory for psychologists.* Mahwah, NJ: Erlbaum.

Erceg-Hurn, D. M., & Mirosevich, V. M. (2008). Modern robust statistical methods: An easy way to maximize the accuracy and power of your research. *American Psychologist, 63*, 591–601. doi:10.1037/0003-066X. 63.7.591

Erdfelder, E., Faul, F., & Buchner, A. (1996). GPOWER: A general power analysis program. *Behavior Research Methods, Instruments, & Computers, 28*, 1–11.

Eysenck, H. J. (1965). The effects of psychotherapy. *International Journal of Psychiatry, 1*, 97–178.

Faraone, S. V., Spencer, T., Aleardi, M., Pagano, C., & Beiderman, J. (2004). Meta-analysis of the efficacy of methylphenidate for treating adult attention-deficit/hyperactivity disorder. *Journal of Clinical Psychopharmacology, 24*, 24–29. doi:10.1097/01.jcp.0000108984. 11879.95

Fidler, F., Thomason, N., Cumming, G., Finch, S., & Leeman, J. (2004). Editors can lead researchers to confidence intervals, but can't make them think: Statistical reform lessons from medicine. *Psychological Science, 15*, 119–126. doi:10.1111/j.0963-7214.2004.01502008.x

Fisher, R. A. (1922). On the mathematical foundations of theoretical statistics. *Philosophical Transactions of the Royal Society of London, 222A*, 309–368.

Fisher, R. A. (1925). *Statistical methods for research workers.* Edinburgh, Scotland: Oliver and Boyd. Retrieved from http://psychclassics.yorku. ca/Fisher/Methods

Fisher, R. A. (1955). Statistical methods and scientific induction. *Journal of the Royal Statistical Society Series A: General, 17B*, 69–78.

Fisher, R. A. (1971). *The design of experiments* (8th ed.). New York, NY: Hafner. (Original work published 1935)

Fisher, R. A. (1973). *Statistical methods and scientific inference* (3rd ed.). Edinburgh, Scotland: Oliver & Boyd. (Original work published 1956)

Fleiss, J. L. (1971). Measuring nominal scale agreement among many raters. *Psychological Bulletin, 76*, 378–382. doi:10.1037/h0031619

Fleiss, J. L. (1981). *Statistical methods for rates and proportions.* New York, NY: Wiley.

Fleiss, J. L. (1993). The statistical basis of meta-analysis. *Statistical Methods in Medical Research, 2*, 121–145. doi:10.1177/096228029300200202

Fletcher, R. H., & Fletcher, S. W. (1979). Clinical research in general medicine journals: A 30-year perspective. *The New England Journal of Medicine, 301*, 180–183. doi:10.1056/NEJM197907263010403

Frazier, P. A., Tix, A. P., & Barron, K. E. (2004). Testing moderator and mediator effects in counseling psychology research. *Journal of Counseling Psychology, 51*, 115–134. doi:10.1037/0022-0167.51.1.115

Frick, R. W. (1998). Interpreting statistical testing: Process and propensity, not population and random sampling. *Behavior Research Methods, Instruments, & Computers, 30,* 527–535.

Galton, F. (1879). Psychometric experiments. *Brain, 2,* 149–162. doi:10. 1093/brain/2.2.149

Garb, H. N., Florio, C. M., & Grove, W. M. (1998). The validity of the Rorschach and the Minnesota Multiphasic Personality Inventory: Results from meta-analyses. *Psychological Science, 9,* 402–404. doi:10. 1111/1467-9280.00075

Geisinger, K. F. (1992). The metamorphosis of test validation. *Educational Psychologist, 27,* 197–222. doi:10.1207/s15326985ep2702_5

Gigerenzer, G. (1993). The superego, the ego, and the id in statistical reasoning. In G. Keren & C. Lewis (Eds.), *A handbook for data analysis in the behavioral sciences: Methodological issues* (pp. 311–339). Hillsdale, NJ: Erlbaum.

Gigerenzer, G., Gaissmaier, W., Kurz-Milcke, E., Schwartz, L., & Woloshin, S. (2007). Helping doctors and patients make sense of health statistics. *Psychological Science in the Public Interest, 8,* 53–96.

Gigerenzer, G., & Murray, D. J. (1987). *Cognition as intuitive statistics.* Hillsdale, NJ: Erlbaum.

Gillispie, C. C., Grattan-Guinness, I., & Fox, R. (2000). *Pierre-Simon Laplace, 1749–1827.* Princeton, NJ: Princeton University Press.

Glass, G. V. (1976). Primary, secondary, and meta-analysis of research. *Educational Researcher, 5,* 3–8.

Gold, D. (1969). Statistical tests and substantive significance. *American Sociologist, 4,* 42–46.

Gray-Little, B., Williams, V. S. L., & Hancock, T. D. (1997). An item response theory analysis of the Rosenberg Self-Esteem Scale. *Personality and Social Psychology Bulletin, 23,* 443–451. doi:10.1177/ 0146167297235001

Guilford, J. P. (1946). New standards for test evaluation. *Educational and Psychological Measurement, 6,* 427–438.

Gulliksen, H. (1950). Intrinsic validity. *American Psychologist, 5,* 511–517. doi:10.1037/h0054604

Haertel, E. H. (1990). Continuous and discrete latent structure models for item response data. *Psychometrika, 55,* 477–494. doi:10.1007/ BF02294762

Hagen, R. L. (1997). In praise of the null hypothesis statistical test. *American Psychologist, 52,* 15–24. doi:10.1037/0003-066X.52.1.15

Harlow, L. L., Mulaik, S. A., & Steiger, J. H. (Eds.). (1997). *What if there were no significance tests?* Mahwah, NJ: Erlbaum.

Hemphill, J. F. (2003). Interpreting the magnitudes of correlation coefficients. *American Psychologist, 58,* 78–79. doi:10.1037/0003-066X. 58.1.78

Herrnstein, R., & Murray, C. (1994). *The bell curve: Intelligence and class structure in American life*. New York, NY: Free Press.

Hokanson, J. E., Rubert, M. P., Welker, R. A., Hollander, G. R., & Hedeen, C. (1989). Interpersonal concomitants and antecedents of depression among college students. *Journal of Abnormal Psychology, 98*, 209–217. doi:10.1037/0021-843X.98.3.209

Hsu, L. M., & Field, R. (2003). Interrater agreement measures: Comments on kappan, Cohen's kappa, Scott's π, and Aickin's α. *Understanding Statistics, 2*, 205–219. doi:10.1207/S15328031US0203_03

Hu, L., & Bentler, P. (1999). Cutoff criteria for fit indexes in covariance structure analysis: Conventional criteria versus new alternatives. *Structural Equation Modeling, 6*, 1–55. doi:10.1080/10705519909540118

Huberty, C. J. (1993). Historical origins of statistical testing practices: The treatment of Fisher versus Neyman–Pearson views in textbooks. *Journal of Experimental Education, 61*, 317–333.

Hunter, J. E., & Schmidt, F. L. (2004). *Methods of meta-analysis: Correcting error and bias in research findings* (2nd ed.). Thousand Oaks, CA: Sage.

Iversen, G. R. (1984). *Bayesian statistical inference*. Newbury Park, CA: Sage.

Jones, L. V., & Tukey, J. W. (2000). A sensible formulation of the significance test. *Psychological Methods, 5*, 411–414. doi:10.1037/1082-989X.5.4.411

Jöreskog, K. G. (1969). A general approach to confirmatory maximum likelihood factor analysis. *Psychometrika, 34*, 183–202. doi:10.1007/BF02289343

Jöreskog, K. G. (1971). Statistical analysis of sets of congeneric tests. *Psychometrika, 36*, 109–133. doi:10.1007/BF02291393

Kane, M. T. (1992). An argument-based approach to validity. *Psychological Bulletin, 112*, 527–535. doi:10.1037/0033-2909.112.3.527

Kazdin, A. E. (1986). Comparative outcome studies in psychotherapy: Methodological issues and strategies. *Journal of Consulting and Clinical Psychology, 54*, 95–105. doi:10.1037/0022-006X.54.1.95

Kazdin, A. E., & Bass, D. (1989). Power to detect differences between alternative treatments in comparative psychotherapy outcome research. *Journal of Consulting and Clinical Psychology, 57*, 138–147. doi:10.1037/0022-006X.57.1.138

Kirk, R. E. (1996). Practical significance: A concept whose time has come. *Educational and Psychological Measurement, 56*, 746–759. doi:10.1177/0013164496056005002

Kline, P. (1993). *An easy guide to factor analysis*. New York, NY: Routledge.

Kline, R. B. (2004). *Beyond significance testing: Reforming data analysis methods in behavioral research*. Washington, DC: American Psychological Association. doi:10.1037/10693-000

Knowles, E. S. (1988). Item context effects on personality scales: Measuring changes the measure. *Journal of Personality and Social Psychology, 55*, 312–320. doi:10.1037/0022-3514.55.2.312

Knowles, E. S., Coker, M. C., Scott, R. A., Cook, D. A., & Neville, J. W. (1996). Measurement induced improvement in anxiety: Mean shifts with repeated assessment. *Journal of Personality and Social Psychology, 71,* 352–363. doi:10.1037/0022-3514.71.2.352

Kraemer, H. C., Gardner, C., Brooks, J. O., III, & Yesavage, J. A. (1998). Advantages of excluding underpowered studies in meta-analysis: Inclusionist versus exclusionist viewpoints. *Psychological Methods, 3,* 23–31. doi:10.1037/1082-989X.3.1.23

Krantz, D. H., Luce, R. D., Suppes, P., & Tversky, A. (1971). *Foundations of measurement* (Vol. 1). New York, NY: Academic Press.

Kromrey, J. D., & Foster-Johnson, L. (1998). Mean centering in moderated multiple regression: Much ado about nothing. *Educational and Psychological Measurement, 58,* 42–67. doi:10.1177/0013164498058001005

Kuder, G. F., & Richardson, M. W. (1937). The theory of the estimation of test reliability. *Psychometrika, 2,* 151–160. doi:10.1007/BF02288391

Landis, J. R., & Koch, G. G. (1977). The measurement of observer agreement for categorical data. *Biometrics, 33,* 159–174. doi:10.2307/2529310

Lehmann, E. L. (1993). The Fisher, Neyman–Pearson theories of testing hypotheses: One theory or two? *Journal of the American Statistical Association, 88,* 1242–1249. doi:10.2307/2291263

Leinhardt, G., Seewald, A. M., & Engel, M. (1979). Learning what's taught: Sex differences in instruction. *Journal of Educational Psychology, 71,* 432–439. doi:10.1037/0022-0663.71.4.432

LeLorier, J., Grégoire, G., Benhaddad, A., Lapierre, J., & Derderian, F. (1997). Discrepancies between meta-analyses and subsequent large randomized, controlled trials. *The New England Journal of Medicine, 337,* 536–542. doi:10.1056/NEJM199708213370806

Lem, S. (1983). *His master's voice* (M. Kandel, Trans.). San Diego, CA: Harcourt Brace Jovanovich. (Original work published 1968)

Lipsey, M. W., & Wilson, D. B. (1993). The efficacy of psychological, educational, and behavioral treatment: Confirmation from meta-analysis. *American Psychologist, 48,* 1181–1209. doi:10.1037/0003-066X.48.12.1181

Lipsey, M. W., & Wilson, D. B. (2000). *Practical meta-analysis.* Thousand Oaks, CA: Sage.

Lopez, B. (2000). *Light action in the Caribbean: Stories.* New York, NY: Knopf.

Lord, F. M. (1953). On the statistical treatment of football numbers. *American Psychologist, 8,* 750–751. doi:10.1037/h0063675

Lord, F. M., & Novick, M. R. (1968). *Statistical theories of mental test scores.* Reading, MA: Addison-Wesley.

MacCallum, R. C., Zhang, S., Preacher, K. J., & Rucker, D. D. (2002). On the practice of dichotomization of quantitative variables. *Psychological Methods, 7,* 19–40. doi:10.1037/1082-989X.7.1.19

MacKinnon, D. P., Lockwood, C. M., Hoffman, J. M., West, S. G., & Sheets, V. (2002). A comparison of methods to test mediation and other intervening variable effects. *Psychological Methods, 7,* 83–104. doi:10.1037/1082-989X.7.1.83

Marsh, H. W., Hau, K. T., & Wen, Z. (2004). In search of golden rules: Comment on hypothesis-testing approaches to setting cutoff values for fit indexes and dangers in overgeneralizing Hu and Bentler's (1999) findings. *Structural Equation Modeling, 11,* 320–341. doi:10.1207/s15328007sem1103_2

Maxwell, S. E. (2004). The persistence of underpowered studies in psychological research: Causes, consequences, and remedies. *Psychological Methods, 9,* 147–163. doi:10.1037/1082-989X.9.2.147

Maxwell, S. E., Kelley, K., & Rausch, J. R. (2008). Sample size planning for statistical power and accuracy in parameter estimation. *Annual Review of Psychology, 59,* 537–563. doi:10.1146/annurev.psych.59.103006.093735

McClelland, G. H., & Judd, C. M. (1993). Statistical difficulties of detecting interactions and moderator effects. *Psychological Bulletin, 114,* 376–390. doi:10.1037/0033-2909.114.2.376

McDowell, M. A., Fryar, C. D., Ogden, C. L., & Flegal, K. M. (2008). *Anthropometric reference data for children and adults: United States, 2003–2006* (National Health Statistics Reports No. 10). Hyattsville, MD: National Center for Health Statistics.

McGrath, R. E. (1998). Significance testing: Is there something better? *American Psychologist, 53,* 796–797. doi:10.1037/h0092167

McGrath, R. E. (2005). Conceptual complexity and construct validity. *Journal of Personality Assessment, 85,* 112–124. doi:10.1207/s15327752jpa8502_02

McGrath, R. E., & Carroll, E. J. (in press). The current status of "projective" tests. In H. Cooper (Ed.), *The handbook of research methods in psychology.* Washington, DC: American Psychological Association.

McGrath, R. E., & Meyer, G. J. (2006). When effect sizes disagree: The case of *r* and *d. Psychological Methods, 11,* 386–401. doi:10.1037/1082-989X.11.4.386

McGrath, R. E., Pogge, D. L., Stokes, J. M., Cragnolino, A., Zaccario, M., Hayman, J., . . . Wayland-Smith, D. (2005). Field reliability of Comprehensive System scoring in an adolescent inpatient sample. *Assessment, 12,* 199–209. doi:10.1177/1073191104273384

McGrath, R. E., Rashid, T., Park, N., & Peterson, C. (2010). Is optimal functioning a distinct state? *The Humanistic Psychologist, 38,* 159–169.

McGrath, R. E., & Walters, G. D. (2010). *Taxometric analysis as a general strategy for detecting categorical latent structure.* Manuscript submitted for publication.

McGraw, R., Lubienski, S. T., & Strutchens, M. E. (2006). A closer look at gender in NAEP mathematics achievement and affect data: Intersections with achievement, race/ethnicity, and socioeconomic status. *Journal for Research in Mathematics Education, 37,* 129–150.

Meehl, P. E. (1978). Theoretical risks and tabular asterisks: Sir Karl, Sir Ronald, and the slow progress of soft psychology. *Journal of Consulting and Clinical Psychology, 46,* 806–834. doi:10.1037/0022-006X.46.4.806

Meehl, P. E. (1986). Causes and effects of my disturbing little book. *Journal of Personality Assessment, 50,* 370–375. doi:10.1207/s15327752 jpa5003_6

Meehl, P. E. (1990). Why summaries of research on psychological theories are often uninterpretable. *Psychological Reports, 66*(Monograph Suppl. 1), 195–244.

Meyer, G. J., Finn, S. E., Eyde, L. D., Kay, G. G., Moreland, K. L., Dies, R. R., & Reed, G. M. (2001). Psychological testing and psychological assessment: A review of evidence and issues. *American Psychologist, 56,* 128–165. doi:10.1037/0003-066X.56.2.128

Micceri, T. (1989). The unicorn, the normal curve, and other improbable creatures. *Psychological Bulletin, 105,* 156–166. doi:10.1037/0033-2909. 105.1.156

Michell, J. (2008). Is psychometrics pathological science? *Measurement: Interdisciplinary Research and Perspectives, 6,* 7–24.

Michell, J. (2009). Invalidity in validity. In R. W. Lissitz (Ed.), *The concept of validity: Revisions, new directions, and applications* (pp. 111–133). Charlotte, NC: Information Age.

Milligan, G. W., & Cooper, M. C. (1985). An examination of procedures for determining the number of clusters in a data set. *Psychometrika, 50,* 159–179. doi:10.1007/BF02294245

Moher, D., Liberati, A., Tetzlaff, J., & Altman, D. G., & The PRISMA Group. (2009). Preferred reporting items for systematic reviews and meta-analyses: The PRISMA statement. *PLoS Medicine, 6,* e1000097. doi:10.1371/journal.pmed.1000097

Morrison, D. E., & Henkel, R. E. (1970). *The significance testing controversy.* London, England: Butterworths.

Neyman, J. (1937). Outline of a theory of statistical estimation based on the classical theory of probability. *Philosophical Transactions of the Royal Society of London, 236A,* 333–380.

Neyman, J., & Pearson, E. S. (1933). On the problem of the most efficient tests of statistical hypotheses. *Philosophical Transactions of the Royal Society of London, 231A,* 289–337.

Nock, M. K., & Banaji, M. (2007). Prediction of suicide ideation and attempts among adolescents using a brief performance-based test. *Journal of Consulting and Clinical Psychology, 75,* 707–715. doi:10.1037/ 0022-006X.75.5.707

Nunnally, J. C., & Bernstein, I. H. (1994). *Psychometric theory* (3rd ed.). New York, NY: McGraw-Hill.

Oakes, M. L. (1986). *Statistical inference: A commentary for the social and behavioral sciences.* New York, NY: Wiley.

Parker, K. C. H., Hanson, R. K., & Hunsley, J. (1988). MMPI, Rorschach, and WAIS: A meta-analytic comparison of reliability, stability, and validity. *Psychological Bulletin, 103,* 367–373. doi:10.1037/0033-2909.103.3.367

Rasch, G. (1960). *Probabilistic models for some intelligence and attainment tests.* Chicago, IL: University of Chicago Press.

Reeve, B. B., Hays, R. D., Bjorner, J. B., Cook, K. F., Crane, P. K., Teresi, J. A., . . . Cella, D. (2007). Psychometric evaluation and calibration of health-related quality of life item banks: Plans for the Patient-Reported Outcomes Measurement Information System (PROMIS). *Medical Care, 45,* S22–S31.

Roberts, F. S. (1979). *Measurement with applications to decision-making, utility, and the social sciences.* Reading, MA: Addison-Wesley.

Rodgers, J. L. (2010). The epistemology of mathematical and statistical modeling: A quiet methodological revolution. *American Psychologist, 65,* 1–12. doi:10.1037/a0018326

Rogers, W. M., Schmitt, N., & Mullins, M. E. (2002). Correction for unreliability of multifactor measures: Comparison of alpha and parallel forms of approaches. *Organizational Research Methods, 5,* 184–199. doi:10.1177/1094428102005002004

Rosenthal, R. (1979). The file drawer problem and tolerance for null results. *Psychological Bulletin, 86,* 638–641. doi:10.1037/0033-2909.86.3.638

Rosenthal, R., Rosnow, R. L., & Rubin, D. R. (2000). *Contrasts and effect sizes in behavioral research: A correlational approach.* Cambridge, England: Cambridge University Press.

Rosnow, R. L., & Rosenthal, R. (1989). Statistical procedures and the justification of knowledge in psychological science. *American Psychologist, 44,* 1276–1284. doi:10.1037/0003-066X.44.10.1276

Rozeboom, W. W. (1960). The fallacy of the null hypothesis significance test. *Psychological Bulletin, 57,* 416–428. doi:10.1037/h0042040

Ruscio, J., Haslam, N., & Ruscio, A. (2006). *Introduction to the taxometric method: A practical guide.* Mahwah, NJ: Erlbaum.

Salvador, R., Suckling, J., Coleman, M. R., Pickard, J. D., Menon, D., & Bullmore, E. (2005). Neurophysiological architecture of functional magnetic resonance images of human brain. *Cerebral Cortex, 15,* 1332–1342. doi:10.1093/cercor/bhi016

Sawilowsky, S. S. (2002). A quick distribution-free test for trend that contributes evidence of construct validity. *Measurement and Evaluation in Counseling and Development, 35,* 78–88.

Sawilowsky, S. S., & Blair, R. C. (1992). A more realistic look at the robustness and Type II error properties of the t test to departures from population normality. *Psychological Bulletin, 111,* 352–360. doi:10.1037/0033-2909.111.2.352

Schenker, N., & Gentleman, J. F. (2001). On the significance of differences by examining the overlap between confidence intervals. *The American Statistician, 55,* 182–186. doi:10.1198/000313001317097960

Schmidt, F. L. (1996). Statistical significance testing and cumulative knowledge in psychology: Implications for training of researchers. *Psychological Methods, 1,* 115–129. doi:10.1037/1082-989X.1.2.115

Schmidt, F. L., Oh, I.-S., & Hayes, T. (2009). Fixed- versus random-effects models in meta-analysis: Model properties and an empirical comparison of differences in results. *British Journal of Mathematical and Statistical Psychology, 62,* 97–128. doi:10.1348/000711007X255327

Schulze, R. (2004). *Meta-analysis: A comparison of approaches.* Cambridge, MA: Hogrefe & Huber.

Schumacker, R., & Lomax, R. G. (2010). *A beginner's guide to structural equation modeling* (3rd ed.). New York, NY: Routledge.

Schwarz, N. (1999). Self-reports: How the questions shape the answers. *American Psychologist, 54,* 93–105. doi:10.1037/0003-066X.54.2.93

Sedlmeier, P., & Gigerenzer, G. (1989). Do studies of statistical power have an effect on the power of studies? *Psychological Bulletin, 105,* 309–316. doi:10.1037/0033-2909.105.2.309

Serlin, R. C., & Lapsley, D. K. (1985). Rationality in psychological research: The good-enough principle. *American Psychologist, 40,* 73–83. doi:10.1037/0003-066X.40.1.73

Shrout, P. E. (1998). Measurement reliability and agreement in psychiatry. *Statistical Methods in Medical Research, 7,* 301–317. doi:10.1191/096228098672090967

Shrout, P. E., & Fleiss, J. L. (1979). Intraclass correlations: Uses in assessing rater reliability. *Psychological Bulletin, 86,* 420–428. doi:10.1037/0033-2909.86.2.420

Shrout, P. E., Spitzer, R. L., & Fleiss, J. L. (1987). Quantification of agreement in psychiatric diagnosis revisited. *Archives of General Psychiatry, 44,* 172–177.

Siegel, S. (1956). *Nonparametric statistics for the behavioral sciences.* New York, NY: McGraw-Hill.

Smith, M. L., & Glass, G. V. (1977). Meta-analysis of psychotherapy outcome studies. *American Psychologist, 32,* 752–760. doi:10.1037/0003-066X.32.9.752

Smith, M. L., Glass, G. V., & Miller, T. I. (1980). *The benefits of psychotherapy.* Baltimore, MD: Johns Hopkins University Press.

Smith, P. C., Schmidt, S. M., Allensworth-Davies, D., & Saitz, R. (2009). Primary care validation of a single-question alcohol screening test. *Journal of General Internal Medicine, 24,* 783–788. doi:10.1007/s11606-009-0928-6

Sobel, D. (1995). *Longitude: The true story of a lone genius who solved the greatest scientific problem of his time.* New York, NY: Penguin.

Spearman, C. (1904). "General intelligence," objectively determined and measured. *The American Journal of Psychology, 15,* 201–293. doi:10.2307/1412107

Spelke, E. S. (2005). Sex differences in intrinsic aptitude for mathematics and science? A critical review. *American Psychologist, 60,* 950–958. doi:10.1037/0003-066X.60.9.950

Steinley, D. (2006). *K*-means clustering: A half-century synthesis. *British Journal of Mathematical and Statistical Psychology, 59,* 1–34. doi:10.1348/000711005X48266

Stevens, S. S. (1946, June 7). On the theory of scales of measurement. *Science, 103,* 677–680. doi:10.1126/science.103.2684.677

Stevens, S. S. (1959). Measurement, psychophysics and utility. In C. W. Churchman & P. Ratoosh (Eds.), *Measurement: Definitions and theories* (pp. 18–63). New York, NY: Wiley.

Strube, M. J. (2006). SNOOP: A program for demonstrating the consequences of premature and repeated null hypothesis testing. *Behavior Research Methods, 38,* 24–27.

Student. (1908). The probable error of a mean. *Biometrika, 6,* 1–25.

Taleb, N. N. (2007). *The black swan: The impact of the highly improbable.* New York, NY: Random House.

Thompson, B. (2002). "Statistical," "practical," and "clinical": How many kinds of significance do counselors need to consider? *Journal of Counseling and Development, 80,* 64–71.

Titchener, E. B., & Major, D. R. (1895). Minor studies from the psychological laboratory of Cornell University: On the affective tones of simple sense impressions. *The American Journal of Psychology, 7,* 57–77.

Tukey, J. W. (1977). *Exploratory data analysis.* Reading, MA: Addison-Wesley.

Turner, E. H., Matthews, A., Linardatos, E., Tell, R., & Rosenthal, R. (2008). Selective publication of antidepressant trials and its influence on apparent efficacy. *The New England Journal of Medicine, 358,* 252–260. doi:10.1056/NEJMsa065779

Vacha-Haase, T., Kogan, L. R., & Thompson, B. (2000). Sample compositions and variabilities in published studies versus those in test manuals: Validity of score reliability inductions. *Educational and Psychological Measurement, 60,* 509–522. doi:10.1177/00131640021970682

Vedula, S. S., Bero, L., Scherer, R. W., & Dickersin, K. (2009). Outcome reporting in industry-sponsored trials of gabapentin for off-label use. *The New England Journal of Medicine, 361,* 1963–1971. doi:10.1056/NEJMsa0906126

Velicer, W. F., Cumming, G., Fava, J. L., Rossi, J. S., Prochaska, J. O., & Johnson, J. (2008). Theory testing using quantitative predictions of effect size. *Applied Psychology, 57,* 589–608. doi:10.1111/j.1464-0597.2008.00348.x

Vul, E., Harris, C., Winkielman, P., & Pashler, H. (2009). Puzzlingly high correlations in fMRI studies of emotion, personality, and social cognition. *Perspectives on Psychological Science, 4,* 274–290. doi:10.1111/j.1745-6924.2009.01125.x

Ward, L. C. (2006). Comparison of factor structure models for the Beck Depression Inventory—II. *Psychological Assessment, 18,* 81–88. doi:10.1037/1040-3590.18.1.81

Webb, B. (2009). Animals versus animats: Or why not model the real iguana? *Adaptive Behavior, 17,* 269–286. doi:10.1177/1059712309339867

Westen, D., & Rosenthal, R. (2003). Quantifying construct validity: Two simple measures. *Journal of Personality and Social Psychology, 84,* 608–618. doi:10.1037/0022-3514.84.3.608

Whitlock, M. C. (2005). Combining probability from independent tests: The weighted Z-method is superior to Fisher's approach. *Journal of Evolutionary Biology, 18,* 1368–1373. doi:10.1111/j.1420-9101.2005.00917.x

Willard, J. E., Lange, R. A., & Hillis, L. D. (1992). The use of aspirin in ischemic heart disease. *The New England Journal of Medicine, 327,* 175–181. doi:10.1056/NEJM199207163270308

Woods, S. P., Rippeth, J. D., Conover, E., Carey, C. L., Parsons, T. D., & Tröster, A. I. (2006). Statistical power of studies examining the cognitive effects of subthalamic nucleus deep brain stimulation in Parkinson's disease. *The Clinical Neuropsychologist, 20,* 27–38. doi:10.1080/13854040500203290

Woolley, T. W. (1983). A comprehensive power-analytic investigation of research in medical education. *Journal of Medical Education, 58,* 710–715.

Zebrack, B. J., Ganz, P. A., Bernaards, C. A., Petersen, L., & Abraham, L. (2006). Assessing the impact of cancer: Development of a new instrument for long-term survivors. *Psycho-Oncology, 15,* 407–421. doi:10.1002/pon.963

Index

Research
conducting, 83–85
medical, 98
unpublished, 102, 104
used in meta-analysis, 100–102, 104
Richardson, M. W., 133
Risk ratio, 200
Robustness conditions
defined, 49
of parametric tests, 49–50
Robust statistics, 52–53
Rosenthal, R., 47, 71, 104
Rosnow, R. L., 71
Rubert, M. P., 195
Rulon method (internal reliability), 133

S
Salvador, R., 171
Sample demographics, 192
Sample distributions, 19
Sample mean, 23
Sample size
in significance testing,54, 68–69, 75–76, 78, 85, 89
Sampling distribution. *See also* specific families of
sampling distributions
defined, 16, 20
and directional null hypothesis, 65n3
and null hypothesis, 40, 41, 43
usefulness of, 22
Sampling distribution of the mean, 23–30
and biased/unbiased statistics, 23–24
conditions with, 24–28
defined, 23
and normal distribution, 26–28
t distribution vs., 30
Sampling error
defined, 15
estimation of, 23
and meta-analysis, 104
and multiple comparisons, 46
Sampling with replacement, 52–53
Sawilowsky, S. S., 49
Scatterplots, 201
Schmidt, F. L., 79, 80, 100, 144
Scree plot, 155
Sedlmeier, P., 74
Selection ratio, 116
SEM. *See* Structural equation modeling
Sensitivity, 116
Set correlation, 203
Shadish, W. R., 215
Shrout, P. E., 139
Signal detection analysis, 200
Significance, 85–88. *See also* Level of significance
Significance testing, 35–56, 69–71
and ANOVA, 188
benefits of using, 54–55
and confidence intervals, 95–97

defined, 56
Fisher's model, 36–39
for moderated regression, 213
multiple comparisons in, 46–48
nondirectional vs. directional null hypothesis,
39–46
Pearson and Neyman's model, 57–69
and test assumptions, 48–54
Sign test, 200
Simple regression, 201
Simplification, 6
Skew, 193
Smith, M. L., 101
Smith, P. C., 196
Sobel, D., 14
Sobel test, 208
Software
for computing ANOVA, 184
and confidence intervals, 98
factor analysis, 159, 163
for identifying problematic items, 137
for identifying sample size, 77, 78
for item response theory, 170
Spearman, C., 152, 164
Spearman–Brown prophecy formula, 138, 140
Spearman's rho, 201
Specificity, 116
Spencer, T., 76
Spitzer, R. L., 139
Split–half reliability, 133
Spurious relationships, 207–210
Squared Euclidean distance, 171, 172
Standard deviation (Σ_e), 193
and meta-analysis, 100
and sampling distribution of the mean, 28–29
and *t* distribution, 29, 30
Standard error
defined, 31
and significance, 38–39
Standardized mean difference
formula for, 67
and meta-analysis, 105
and population differences, 68
Standard error of measurement (Σ_e), 135, 139
STARD standard, 106n6
Statistic(s). *See also specific statistics*
choice of, 179, 181–182
criticisms of, 5
defined, 15
development of field, 14–15
use of, in quantitative modeling, 4
Statistical significance, 84–88
Stem-and-leaf plots, 193
Stevens, S. S., 180–182
Structural equation modeling (SEM), 163–164
additive relationships, 203
defined, 149

About the Author

Robert E. McGrath, PhD, is a professor of psychology at Fairleigh Dickinson University, where he currently directs both the doctoral program in clinical psychology and the master of science program in clinical psychopharmacology. He received his doctorate in clinical psychology in 1984 from Auburn University. He has since authored approximately 150 publications and presentations, primarily in the areas of assessment and measurement, statistical methodology, and professional issues in pharmacotherapy.

Dr. McGrath has been a candidate for president of the American Psychological Association (APA), served on the APA Division 12 (Society of Clinical Psychology) Committee on Science and Practice, and is a former president of APA Division 55 (American Society for the Advancement of Pharmacotherapy). He is the three-time winner of the Martin Mayman Award presented by the Society for Personality Assessment for contributions to the literature on personality assessment.